I Still Love Teaching Despite Having All The Reasons In The World To Quit

OBSERVATIONS OF THE EDUCATION SYSTEM

RENES LOPHANOR

I Still Love Teaching Despite Having All The Reasons In The World To Quit:
Observations Of The Education System
© Copyright 2024 Renes Lophanor

For more information, email info@reneslophanor.com
www.reneslophanor.com

ISBN: 979-8-89316-9-416 (paperback)
ISBN: 979-8-89316-9-423 (hardcover)
ISBN: 979-8-89316-9-409 (ebook)

DEDICATION

This book is dedicated to my students, past, present, and future. You guys are the real stars, always eager to learn and discover new things. This book is also for any student out there looking for a bit of happiness in school life. And, of course, to my amazing family: my parents, who gave me such a strong foundation in life; my brothers and sisters, the best teammates anyone could ask for; Jerry and Ryan, you are both a part of who I am. This book is for all of you.

CONTENTS

PROLOGUE

In a quiet neighbourhood in Port-au-Prince, there was a family that embodied both the struggles and dreams of this spirited city. This family, neither rich nor poor by local standards but certainly very modest by any global measure, lived in a humble home that also housed a small grocery shop. The shop, run by a resilient and hardworking woman, was to some extent the heart of their household, offering everything from everyday necessities to unexpected treasures.

The family was a tight-knit unit, bound together by love, mutual support, hope, and the unspoken understanding that their eldest child, a bright-eyed seven-year-old boy, carried their aspirations on his small shoulders. As the firstborn of six, with two of his siblings being twins, he was seen as the beacon of hope, the one who would lead the family name to new heights. His father, a dedicated electrician at Electricité d'Haïti, worked tirelessly to provide for the family. His hands were skilled in the art of taming electricity to light up their country, and he was often required to travel to other cities for several days.

One afternoon, under the warm Caribbean sun, the child and his father stood in front of their house, basking in the serenity of their shared silence. The father, his gaze filled with a blend of affection and earnestness, finally broke the stillness. He envisioned a future for his son, one where he could see him as an engineer or an architect, harnessing a power akin to electricity to bring creations to life and illuminate entire cities. He painted a picture of his son working with prestigious companies, igniting a sparkle in the child's eyes.

As the father's words continued to weave dreams, he shifted the imagery to the role of an architect. He described grand buildings reaching the clouds, structures born from simple drawings that would one day stand tall, admired by all. The child, his smile broadening, imagined himself at the helm of creating such towering edifices.

The father gently tempered these visions with reality, stressing the importance of hard work and education. He spoke of striving for excellence, studying abroad in renowned universities in Europe or the United States, and the prestigious jobs that would follow. These careers, he assured, would not only bring financial stability but also a home far grander than their current one. As he touched the boy's head, his gaze seemed to confirm the inevitability of these dreams, as if they were just a matter of time.

The child nodded, absorbing the gravity of dedication and learning.

The father concluded his thoughts with a vision of respect and admiration that the child would command in the future. He spoke of a world where people would look up to his son for his creations, problem-solving skills, and creativity, addressing him as "sir" out of profound respect. That child, that was me, and I decided to become a schoolteacher.

INTRODUCTION

B efore exploring the content of this book, let me provide you with a bit of personal background. As of the time of writing, I have been a qualified teacher for twenty-two years and have taught students from diverse social backgrounds across sixteen different schools. I have also worked as an examiner for one of the national exam boards in England. While my specialisation is in the teaching of modern foreign languages, including French, German, and Spanish, I have also taught geography, drama, art, English, and music. I ended up teaching all these subjects, particularly during my time as a long-term substitute teacher in various schools, where I had to utilise skills I had not previously needed, such as staging and playwriting.

What sparked my desire to become a teacher? I cannot say that any of my own teachers were the sole reason, not because they were not exemplary in that regard (in fact, some of them were, or later became, my sources of inspiration), but because I was initially on the path to becoming an engineer or an architect. I chose science and math as my main options, to the detriment of foreign languages, which I always loved. I only had one hour of English per week and was forced to drop German. The programme for English was too simplistic for me to fully enjoy the lessons, despite the teacher, Monsieur Lombard, being quite knowledgeable. However, he was incapable of controlling the class, for whom foreign languages were not a top priority.

In university, I reverted to learning foreign languages again and decided to study English and American literature and history, while adding German and linguistics as secondary options. Suddenly, I felt right at home.

During my time as a university student in Paris, I worked during lunch hours in primary schools for the Council of Paris to earn some extra money. It was during this experience that I made the decision to become a teacher. I enjoyed playing with the children in the playground, and they loved chasing me. Even when I started with just a couple of them, within minutes, the entire group of children on the playground stopped whatever they were doing to join forces and chase me. It was a magical moment for me. I wished that my teachers had played with us in primary school and even in secondary school.

When I decided to become a teacher, I wanted to be the kind of teacher that I had wished for and to teach the way I had wanted to be taught. I always kept in mind what my peers and I had liked and disliked in our own lessons.

My lessons have been observed by Ofsted on seven different occasions across three different schools, where I taught French, German, and music. Ofsted, which stands for the Office for Standards in Education, Children's Services and Skills, is a regulatory body in the United Kingdom. Its primary role is to ensure that these services provide a safe and effective learning environment. It achieves this by conducting regular inspections and publishing detailed reports on the performance of these institutions. These reports assess various aspects, including the quality of education, student welfare, and management effectiveness. The findings are made public, providing valuable insights into the functioning of educational services.

To date, the feedback I have received from Ofsted inspectors has been consistently excellent. It is noteworthy that these evaluations span three schools, each distinct in its catchment area, the social background of its pupils, and the available resources.

As an individual deeply immersed in the education sector, I have devoted considerable time to studying and working within various educational systems. This journey has included attending conferences and reading extensively about teaching methodologies and education systems in England, the US, Finland, France, Haiti, and China. Each of these systems offered intriguing insights, yet often, I found myself yearning for more. Certain topics were either overlooked or not delved into with the depth I had hoped. This, however, was not unexpected, given the myriad of perspectives and complexities in education, not all of which can be easily identified or encompassed in a single source. In the same vein, if you expect this book to be an all-encompassing resource that fully satiates your quest for knowledge, you might find yourself slightly disappointed. My approach, instead, will be to concentrate on a select few aspects I deem crucial, identifying and discussing how I have tackled them in my teaching practice.

Throughout my teaching career, I have informally interviewed numerous people from various social, cultural, and professional backgrounds, including students and parents. As a parent of two adult sons, I have also had discussions with other parents. At different stages in this book, I will clarify terminology that might be unfamiliar to those outside the education system. Additionally, I'll anticipate some questions you may have and offer answers in advance.

I want to clarify that the first part of this book, titled "Teaching," is not designed as a traditional teaching manual. Its primary goal is to share insights into the teaching profession, particularly for those who are new to it, aspiring to become teachers, or simply seeking to broaden their understanding of the field. In this section, I will share my personal teaching journey, including my methodologies, the reasoning behind them, and the benefits I have experienced. It's important to acknowledge that some aspects may not align with your current practices, and that's perfectly fine. My hope is that this book provides you with valuable insights or tips, even in a small way.

Given the diverse nature of perspectives and teaching styles, you may find that you already practise some or all the concepts I discuss, each in your unique way. Additionally, the views expressed in this book are solely my own and do not represent those of the schools with which I've been associated. An opinion is, after all, a reflection of an individual's perspective. Your viewpoints are shaped by your unique experiences, and it is entirely reasonable for them to differ from mine.

As we transition into the second section of this book, "The Education System," we delve into the intricate web that shapes the environments in which we teach and learn. This section aims to dissect the various components that constitute our education systems, exploring their strengths and limitations and their impact on educators, students, and society. Through my lens, I will examine the policies, structures, and societal expectations that frame our educational landscapes, drawing from both my experiences and broader observations.

When embarking on this exploration, it is crucial to recognise the diversity and complexity inherent in education systems worldwide. Each system's unique history, culture, and objectives offer valuable lessons on approaching learning and teaching. My reflections are intended to provoke thought, invite dialogue, and challenge prevailing norms. By understanding the broader context in which we operate, we can better navigate the challenges and opportunities presented by our profession. While the perspectives shared are deeply personal, I encourage you to engage with this section with an open mind, reflecting on how these insights resonate with your own experiences within the education system. The goal is not to prescribe a one-size-fits-all solution but to illuminate the diverse paths that education can take and inspire thoughtful reflection on our role in this system. My initial choice for the title of this book was "The Educational Box." I wanted to emphasise the sense of confinement, both physically and intellectually, that the current education system creates. Eventually, I chose a more positive focus on my love for teaching.

PART ONE

TEACHING

CONNECTION: RELATIONSHIP AND SHOWING OF INTEREST

When meeting someone for the first time, it's common for people to inquire about each other's interests. As common interests emerge, a bond between individuals can quickly develop as they share anecdotes about where they have lived, places they have visited, people they know, and things they have done. The more that is exchanged, the stronger the connection between the two becomes. From this connection, a friendship can develop, fostering a sense of mutual care, understanding, respect, and trust. Similarly, teaching students in a way that captures their interests requires establishing a relationship with them. The more significant the relationship, the more impactful the teaching.

The Canadian-born psychiatrist Eric Berne, creator of the theory of transactional analysis as a way of explaining human behaviour, recognised the importance of social relationships between human beings. He believed that insight could be gained by analysing patients' social transactions.[1] I believe this applies to teaching. I make it my objective to memorise my students' first names during the first lesson. In a class of thirty students, memorising

---

[1]   Eric Berne, *Games People Play* (New York: Grove Press, 1964).

everyone's names may seem challenging. However, I utilise various techniques to achieve this goal.

So, what do I gain as a teacher by calling my students by their names in the classroom, especially during the first lesson? The truth is it immediately elevates their appreciation of my role as their teacher. I become the teacher who knew their names on the first day, evoking a positive response from them. Knowing that I remember their names encourages their active participation in the lesson, deters misbehaviour (because I "know" their names), and helps create empathy on both sides. Empathy is a complex psychological process that allows us to form bonds and establish rapport with another person, making them feel heard. This is particularly important because many students believe that their teachers do not genuinely care about them, do not listen to what they have to say, and do not allow them to voice their ideas or concerns.

Freud argued in his theories that the human personality is multifaceted.[2] The job of a teacher is extremely complex. We are dealing with the most intellectually advanced species on this planet. When we must individually manage five or six classes of thirty human beings per day and deal with everything happening in their inner world while trying to deliver our lessons effectively, it is a feat that even Superman would find challenging. Therefore, a good teacher is a Superman with no superpowers.

For simplicity, I will categorise teachers into three distinct types: a developing teacher, a standard teacher, and a teacher-educator.

1. **A developing teacher:** This type of teacher is at the beginning of their educational journey. They might still be finding their footing as far as connecting effectively with students. In this preliminary stage, they are honing their skills in classroom management, lesson planning, and understanding the diverse needs of students. Although they might face challenges in facilitating optimal learning experiences,

---

[2] Sigmund Freud, *The Ego and the Id* (1923; repr., London: Hogarth Press and the Institute of Psycho-Analysis, 1949).

their growth potential is significant. They are characterised by the fact that they still lack the ability to *connect* with their students. If this preliminary stage is not fulfilled, both teaching and learning will be unlikely to occur in the classroom.

2. **A standard teacher:** Representing the majority, a standard teacher has successfully surpassed the initial stage of establishing a connection with students. They are competent in delivering lessons that engage and educate, ensuring students learn and grow. These teachers are often viewed as the benchmark in education. They balance subject expertise with pedagogical skills, and their classrooms are usually environments of consistent learning.

3. **A teacher-educator:** This category represents a good teacher who transcends traditional teaching roles. They possess the unique ability to teach across disciplines, including areas outside their specialisation, and excel in fostering critical thinking. They adeptly utilise and integrate diverse knowledge and skills into their teaching, sparking curiosity and deep learning. These educators guide students in applying their existing knowledge to novel situations, encouraging them to think creatively and solve problems innovatively. The teacher-educator embodies the true essence of "education" in its etymological sense, aspiring to cultivate wisdom and adaptability in their students.

Ultimately, this framework demonstrates a continuum of professional development in teaching, with each category representing a crucial stage in the journey towards educational excellence. The overarching goal for all teachers should be progression towards becoming a teacher-educator, someone who not only imparts knowledge but also inspires, challenges, and equips students to be lifelong learners and problem-solvers.

Establishing a connection is paramount to becoming an effective teacher or a teacher-educator. As mentioned earlier, achieving a connection with my students involves using various techniques that have proven effective for me. The first impression is particularly significant, especially in the eyes of adolescents. I utilise the first lesson to learn about each student in the class. Once the legally required class roll call has been completed, I ask each pupil for their name:

Teacher: *"Comment tu t'appelles? Moi, je m'appelle Monsieur Lophanor. Et toi?"*
Student : *"Je m'appelle Jasmine."*

This translates as: Teacher: *"What is your name? My name is Mr Lophanor. And you?"*
Student: *"My name is Jasmine."*

I will continue in the same manner until I have heard from everyone. After that, I allow them to ask me a total of ten questions to get to know me better. The first question is usually "How old are you?" I see large smiles on their faces while waiting for my reaction or response. I answer the question without any fuss, and from that moment onwards, a bond is created. I have disclosed to them what most teachers tend to keep secret, and they start seeing me as a normal person. Let's be clear about this: for a teenage student, a teacher is *not* a normal person. Besides teaching our subject, there is nothing else they think we are good for. They believe our only friends are other teachers who work in the school. They believe that when we leave school, we go home and stay there until the next school day. Every aspect of a teacher's life outside of school is a mystery to the students. That is why when one of them sees you in town, in a shop, or in the park, they are shocked and panicked to the point that they don't want you to see them. The news goes around that a teacher was sighted in some place. *Oh my god, what were they wearing? Was s/he alone (no friend)? Was s/he accompanied by someone? Who was that? The boyfriend? The girlfriend? The children?*

Once I answer the first question without reservation or shame, they gain confidence in asking broader questions such as "Do you have children?"

"How long have you worked in this school?" "How many languages do you speak?" and so on. Following this, I engage the class in activities where I strive to involve everyone, and when a student wants to contribute orally, they must say their name first. I then make a mental note of it, using clues, mnemonics, and anything else to assist my memory, including glimpsing at their logbook cover while walking past them. My seating plan is a valuable aid, allowing me to check a student's name just by looking at where they sit in the classroom. At the end of the lesson, I dismiss the class by naming each student as they walk past me towards the door. They leave the classroom happy. The fact that I know their names makes them feel valued and acknowledged. Subsequent lessons see happy returns.

Once established, the connection must be sustained inside and, where possible, outside of our classroom throughout the students' time in the school. Creating the connection is relatively easy, but maintaining or fostering its growth presents a bigger challenge, especially when dealing with teenagers subject to mood swings at this stage of their lives. They are emotionally driven, and even the slightest reprimand may be perceived by them as the end of the world.

Research indicates that students who have a good relationship with their teacher work hard for that teacher. They strive to avoid disappointing the teacher and exhibit heightened empathy, especially when the teacher is feeling unwell. In a noisy class, others may help manage the behaviour by urging the class to be quiet. They willingly assist with tasks such as carrying our laptops or bags and even help take the register by calling out the names for us if we have a sore throat or have lost our voices. I have experienced this before, and I am immensely thankful for their support.

Lesson Observation Anecdote

Once, a colleague of mine observed one of my lessons with a notoriously challenging Year 9 class, focusing on assessing my behaviour management skills. Despite the class's reputation for disruptive behaviour, the lesson went remarkably well – there were no major incidents or disruptions, and the students appeared engaged and enjoyed the lesson.

However, when my colleague graded my lesson, she could only award me a "good" rating. When I inquired why she couldn't rate it higher, she explained that the students worked for me because they liked me, and she couldn't consider that as effective behaviour management.

I was confused. Wasn't building a positive relationship with my students the essence of effective behaviour management? Children are more likely to learn from someone they like and respect. As the saying goes, kids don't care how much you know until they know how much you care.

While I understood my colleague's perspective, I couldn't help but disagree. She was merely ticking boxes on an official observation sheet, and regrettably, there was no box for a lesson where the students behaved well because they genuinely liked their teacher. I strongly believe that if you love teaching your students, and they can see that you genuinely do, they will love your lessons and you as a human being.

RESPECT

Respect is a crucial aspect of any relationship between human beings, laying a strong foundation for collaborative efforts towards a common goal. Imagine living or working with someone who does not respect you or to whom you do not show respect – they likely treat you unkindly in front of others, act without considering your feelings, and diminish your efforts. Failing to demonstrate respect sabotages relationships with others. Building trust and respect is crucial, as it helps with communication – a key element in every human interaction.

Respect can be defined as a profound admiration for someone or something elicited by their abilities, qualities, age, social status, or achievements. A child's respect for their parents, for instance, encompasses these qualities, along with the biological link that places the parents permanently above the child in some way. Similarly, a football enthusiast may have tremendous respect for Lionel Messi, Maradona, and Pelé, while a tennis player may respect Venus and Serena Williams, Rafael Nadal, and Novak Djokovic for their achievements. While respect is often based on a person's role or achievements, it's equally important to show respect to those who may not have power or social status.

For some people, the importance of respect is evident, while others may need to witness it in action to be able to emulate it. It's crucial to show respect to our students in a way that they understand and acknowledge, starting by recognising their opinions, ideas, wants, and feelings – even if they go against pre-established rules or codes of conduct. Simply acknowledging them is often enough to build trust and respect. We must respect the child as a human being, with both positive and negative moments, honouring their values and interests, such as charity work, sports, or hobbies. If we damage the connection at the start by not giving the children opportunities to express themselves, all our efforts to teach them will be in vain.

Giving respect to others makes us better human beings. The teacher's primary role, in my opinion, is to help students become good human beings, cultivating a set of core qualities that will serve them well in all aspects of life. These qualities include kindness, compassion, empathy, honesty, integrity, patience, tolerance, respect, generosity, self-awareness, humility, courage, commitment, and strength. By developing these traits, students will be better equipped to navigate the challenges of the world and create positive change in their communities. These qualities are not only important for personal growth but also for building healthy relationships, achieving professional success, and contributing to society. Getting to know the personalities of our students is essential, as the more we know them, the easier it will be to show and earn respect. When a student suggests something for the class, we should avoid dismissing their idea without explanation, regardless of how impractical or utopian it may seem, as children see more possibilities where adults see impossibilities. We must respect them as intelligent beings and treat them accordingly.

I remember one day when I asked my class a question that led me to ponder the concept of intelligence. I asked, "Including me, who is the most intelligent person in the classroom?" The responses favoured me unanimously, but when asked for reasons, most cited my status as a teacher or my age. Something was missing from their responses, prompting me to illustrate my point differently.

I pulled out my smartphone and posed another question to the class: "Does this phone, connected to the internet, know more things than I could ever hope to know in my lifetime? Does that make it more intelligent than Albert Einstein or Elon Musk?" The classroom fell silent as students contemplated my question. Some looked surprised, while others appeared confused. But then, smiles began spreading across their faces as they understood the point I was making. The class engaged in thoughtful discussion about the true meaning of intelligence and what it means to be considered intelligent.

Before tackling classroom management, behaviour, or learning strategies, we must establish mutual respect with our students. Respect is a two-way street; we cannot expect it simply because of our status as teachers. We must show our students respect and treat them as intelligent beings worthy of our consideration.

Children are not always aware of how to behave appropriately in a different context, such as our classroom. It is our responsibility as teachers to create an environment fostering mutual respect and encouraging students to value the opinions and contributions of others.

When we show respect to our students, we pave the way for them to emulate that behaviour. Respect is the hallmark that efficiently brings humans together, applying to both children and adults alike. Leading by example and demonstrating through actions that we value our students and their contributions is essential. Only then can we expect them to value our words and heed our advice.

The Story of Ryan

Allow me to share a story about a student named Ryan, who was in my Year 9 French class. Ryan, I must say, was quite a handful. Possessing a boisterous and strong-minded personality, he often came across as rude and disrespectful to almost every staff member in the school. He would use profanity with any teacher who put him in a bad mood, resulting in frequent temporary exclusions or days spent in "isolation."

During my lessons, Ryan occupied the second row by the wall, with the table between him and the next student intentionally kept empty. One day, he turned to me and said, loud enough for everyone to hear, "Sir, I hate French. I don't get it." Without missing a beat, I replied, "Well, that's fine, Ryan. French loves you. That makes up for you hating it." The class erupted in laughter.

On another occasion, while the class was engrossed in written activities, I approached Ryan, who was on report that week for swearing at the deputy headteacher, to ask him a question. "Tell me, Ryan, there's something I would like to understand."

He replied with a simple "Wha'?"

I continued, "You're always in trouble in the school and almost constantly on report. Yet, I have never had any problem with you, even though I know you hate French. Why is that?"

Ryan hesitated and then said, "Well, you're not like them."

I asked, "What do you mean I am not like them?"

Ryan repeated, "You . . . You're not like them."

I pointed out, "I am a teacher, and they are teachers."

During our conversation, Ryan avoided making eye contact with me, focusing on the French worksheet in front of him, as if he were more interested in getting on with his work than talking to me. The rest of the class was quietly working too, but it was evident they were all tuned in to our exchange. Suddenly, Ryan looked up at me and said, "You talk to us. You don't act like you're superior to us, like bossy and stuff. You're more like us. You say hi to us, and you even come and chat with us on the playground. Not like those . . . " He didn't finish the sentence, but we all knew what he meant. He was referring to the other teachers, for whom he clearly didn't have the same respect.

Until that conversation with Ryan, I had been unsure why he treated me differently from the other teachers. I hadn't done anything special to earn his respect or sympathy. I was simply being myself in the classroom. While I had to remove him from my lesson a couple of times to send him to the head of department's class, it never escalated to the point of breaking up our relationship in the classroom. Ryan understood my boundaries and knew that misbehaving in my lesson wouldn't be tolerated, but it wouldn't ruin our relationship. I treated every lesson as a new beginning, and Ryan understood that I wasn't going to hold his previous misbehaviour against him. In fact, his misbehaviour wasn't even directed towards me but towards other students.

Looking back, I'm grateful for Ryan's trust and respect towards me. I hope he's doing well wherever he is now.

Respect versus Fear

Respect and fear are often misconstrued, but the difference between them is profound. Fear is a response to consequences and doesn't necessarily entail respect for the person involved. This can result in discomfort, a lack of empathy, and an unwillingness to interact with the individual. True respect, on the other hand, entails feeling at ease and even actively seeking out the person's company. When we respect someone, we're more inclined to heed their advice, assist them when needed, and express gratitude for their efforts.

Reflecting on my past as a student, I never thanked my teachers for their lessons, even when I was grateful for them. It wasn't until I became a teacher myself that I recognised the profound impact they had on me, and I am now grateful for the opportunity to thank them. As a teacher, I frequently receive gratitude from my students for my lessons, and I take that responsibility seriously. This is why I'm writing this book, to convey my appreciation to all the students I've taught over the years and to those I will teach in the future.

One of the ways that I demonstrate respect to my students is by maintaining a calm and composed demeanour at all times. I firmly believe in avoiding yelling, except in the context of a fun sing-along where we compete to see who can sing louder. Even then, I usually end up losing because my students collaborate to out-sing me. I consistently emphasise that receiving a poor score in a test does not change the value I place on them. I convey my trust in them, and I make a point to express it whenever the opportunity arises. This trust extends to their behaviour, honesty, and willingness to give their best effort in class activities.

When students feel that their teacher trusts them, they feel more comfortable approaching and asking questions. They're more likely to follow the teacher's advice and learn from them. This mutual respect proves beneficial for both the teacher and the students.

In terms of apologising to my students, I don't hesitate. If I recognise that I have done something wrong or made a mistake that could have been avoided, I apologise without a second thought. Whether it's in front of the whole class or in private, I take ownership of my mistakes and assume responsibility for them.

In one instance, a student who hadn't been putting much effort into her classwork and homework received a low grade on a test. Recognising her lack of preparation, I seized the opportunity to turn the moment into a valuable lesson. During the next class session, as students eagerly inquired about their test results, I highlighted this student's poor performance, attributing it to her lack of preparation, and emphasised that the test served as a wake-up call before the real exam. While I praised the positives and expressed satisfaction with addressing weaknesses collaboratively, I unintentionally embarrassed her.

As the lesson progressed, I noticed a shift in her demeanour, but it wasn't until the end of the class, when I asked her to stay behind to discuss what was bothering her, that I understood the impact of my words. Accompanied by another classmate, she candidly expressed her discomfort with my public acknowledgement of her poor performance.

In that moment, I offered an unreserved apology, prioritising the acknowledgement of her feelings and ensuring she left the classroom without any resentment. My sincerity was met with understanding, and I promised to be more mindful in the future. Her classmate, witnessing this exchange, seemed surprised by my straightforward apology, noting that it was rare to see teachers admit their mistakes so openly.

This incident was a powerful reminder that as educators, our words and actions have a profound impact on our students. Apologising when necessary shows our human side and teaches a valuable lesson in humility and respect.

It's crucial to recognise that as teachers, we often expect our students to apologise for a laundry list of things: forgetting their books, being late, not finishing their work, and so on. So, if we want our students to take responsibility for their actions, it's only fair that we model this behaviour ourselves. By apologising to our students when we make mistakes, we show them that apologising is a simple act of respect towards another person, encapsulated in the five-letter word "sorry."

Allow me to conclude by outlining the sequence in which I lay the foundations with my classes at the beginning of each school year, unless it is a class that I taught the year before and they are already familiar with my classroom rules.

Firstly, I introduce myself to the class and ask them to reciprocate by introducing themselves to me. This not only helps me learn their names but it also fosters an environment where students get to know each other.

Secondly, I outline the classroom rules, emphasising specific behaviours that I do not tolerate in my classroom. I take time to explain why I have these rules and engage in a discussion with the class. I firmly believe that rules should be sensible and reasonable. When students understand the rationale behind a rule, they are less likely to break it. Furthermore, I stress my flexibility, acknowledging that unforeseen circumstances beyond their control, such as transportation issues or unexpected events, should not result in punishment.

To illustrate the importance of flexibility and understanding, I recount a moving video I watched on YouTube. The video depicted a young boy consistently arriving late to class and being physically reprimanded by the teacher with a ruler each time. Eventually, the teacher discovered the boy was late because he was helping a physically disabled person in a wheelchair. This experience underscored the importance of showing compassion and refraining from punishing students for reasons beyond their control.

I make a concerted effort to familiarise myself with my students, and one effective method is by seeking their feedback on what they would like to see in the classroom. For new classes, I ask them to write on a small piece of paper something they would like us to do in the lesson and something they don't enjoy. I try to accommodate their requests in my lesson planning, taking their suggestions seriously even if certain requests, such as not giving homework or tests, may not be feasible. After collecting the notes, I allow the class to ask me a few questions about myself, fostering a better understanding of me as a person. Building a personal connection with my students is key to establishing a positive learning environment, and once we've had the chance to know each other a little better, we proceed with the day's plan.

Finding My Authority

Today, I feel completely in my element, like a fish in the ocean, when I am in the classroom facing thirty unique individuals, each with their distinct perspective and understanding of the world. However, it wasn't always this way. When you read this book, you might get the impression that teaching has always been easy for me. I chose to focus on the positive aspects of my teaching journey because we often hear about the hardships, pain, frustration, and verbal and physical violence that come with the profession, especially in countries like England, the United States, and France. But make no mistake, I've had my share of difficult times, and the challenges continue today, although at a much lower level. The struggles persist unless one retires or leaves the profession, as many have done.

My first daunting experience was during a placement in my teacher training year. Everything seemed manageable when observing the class teacher, but the dynamic shifted dramatically when it was my turn to lead a Year 10 class (fourteen to fifteen years old). Attempting to replicate the methods of an experienced teacher, I quickly realised I was off the mark. Reflecting on it now, I better understand the feedback received from observers during that training period and in subsequent years. The students didn't see me as an authority figure, making it difficult to maintain silence in the class. A couple of years later, I faced challenges with four particularly difficult Year 9 classes. The classes would have been manageable if not for four or five pupils who, once agitated, disrupted the entire lesson. The dread of upcoming classes with them was palpable, often leaving me yearning for an unforeseen event like a school trip, an assembly, a snow day, or even a drill to avoid the class.

Handling students who were abusive to each other in the classroom was another hurdle. My attempts to intervene often got lost in the chaos, and a sense of helplessness prevailed, knowing that assistance, when called, could take ages to arrive. The students recognise this vulnerability and exploit it, just as we did in our school days. With experience, I honed my skills in managing these situations, and so will you. But beyond experience, cultivating the right mindset for this profession is crucial to safeguarding your personal well-being and ongoing development.

INSPIRATION

Inspiration

I n today's digital age, an abundance of inspirational videos on platforms like YouTube, Instagram, and Facebook makes motivation easily accessible. The term "inspiration" comes from the Latin word *inspirare*, which means "breathe into."[3] It's that moment when a spontaneous urge to do something creative or important overwhelms you. You know, that moment when things become clear in your mind, and you say to yourself, "Yes, I've got it!" or "Eureka!" This kind of inspiration often lies dormant in our brains until sparked by someone or something.

Teachers play a pivotal role in inspiring their students, both as role models and creators of an environment that nurtures creativity and personal growth. Feeling inspired in our daily lives plays a major role in what we are able to achieve each day. So, let's find inspiration wherever possible and use it to become the best versions of ourselves.

Additionally, patience is key in building a strong rapport with students. It allows us to listen, understand their struggles, and create a safe environment to ask questions, make mistakes, and learn from these mistakes. When

---

[3] "Inspiration," *Merriam-Webster*, accessed April 19, 2024, https://www.merriam-webster.com/dictionary/inspiration.

students struggle with a concept, it is important to take time to explain it in a way that they can understand and provide the resources they need to succeed.

Patience is a crucial skill for a teacher that can be developed and improved upon over time, requiring practice and self-reflection. Identifying situations that may test our patience and finding ways to remain calm and composed are integral aspects of honing this skill.

As educators, it's beneficial to remind our students that we, too, are on a continuous learning journey. Often, students perceive us as repositories of all knowledge, as they don't see our own process of learning and growth. To bridge this gap, I enrolled in an evening Arabic course at the university, driven by a desire to grasp the fundamentals of the Arabic alphabet and basic greetings. This experience offered me a unique opportunity to reverse roles in the classroom. Seeking assistance from students fluent in Arabic, I sought to hone my pronunciation skills. They eagerly stepped into the role of teacher, enthusiastically embracing the chance to share their knowledge. This exchange not only enhanced my language skills but also demonstrated to my students the value of humility and perpetual learning, reinforcing the idea that education is a shared, lifelong journey for both teachers and students.

Madame Paolini was a rather strict teacher, but her methods were effective. Her passion for the French language, culture, and literature was contagious. She made sure that we all knew the grammar and vocabulary inside out. Every week she spent time talking about French books, their authors, and historical contexts. She brought piles of books and asked us to choose one, read it at home, and write a book report. I was in 4ème (Year 9 in the UK). This was pre-internet, so research was done in the library, which was a place I visited to read comics and short story books or to draw. Madame Paolini opened a window in my mind, revealing a whole world waiting to be discovered within the pages of a good book. Another teacher, Madame Villanueva, reinforced that joy for reading during my college years (sixteen years old) while teaching geography. The library was one of my favourite playgrounds.

Recently, I reached out to Madame Paolini via my German teacher. Madame Paolini was pleased to hear how she impacted my life, even though she did not remember me.

I learned from another teacher that Madame Paolini had been a teacher for more than thirty-eight years and never received a message of gratitude from a former student, making her wonder if she had made a difference in the lives of any students. I can rightfully say that my message, via my German teacher, came at the right time and reminded her why she initially became a teacher.

This story demonstrates the uncertainty teachers face regarding their impact on students. We may never know if we have changed somebody's life. What matters is doing our job to the best of our ability, with passion, dedication, and an unwavering commitment to our students. We may be the only positive influence in their lives, and that is a responsibility that we cannot take lightly.

Building Bridges: The Teacher as a Relatable Guide

As a teacher, I firmly believe in the power of relatability. It is crucial in breaking down the invisible barrier between educators and students, showing them our similarities. This philosophy guides my approach in the classroom, where I often share personal stories, especially those connected to the subject matter. Whether recalling childhood anecdotes, revealing personal challenges, or sharing hobbies, these snippets offer more than just a glimpse into who I am – they serve as a bridge, connecting me to my students on a more human level.

I share details about my musical tastes, my favourite sports, my dance preferences, the football team I support, my travel experiences, my favourite anime, and insights into my birth country. Students often assume their teachers were born in the same country where they teach, even if they speak the language with a foreign accent.

Sharing your personal experiences and struggles creates connection, making you a relatable figure rather than just a teacher. It communicates that even successful adults face challenges and obstacles, but through hard work and perseverance, they can overcome them. This inspires and motivates students to keep pushing through difficult times and striving towards their goals.

It is important to note, however, that there is a fine line between sharing personal experiences and oversharing. Teachers must always maintain appropriate boundaries and avoid discussing sensitive or inappropriate topics while maintaining a professional demeanour that remains relatable and approachable.

Beyond teaching, I have a diverse range of skills and interests, which I often incorporate into my lessons. I believe it's important for teachers to have hobbies and passions outside of work, as they help alleviate the stress and demands of the job. Sharing these interests with students breaks down the barriers between teachers and students.

Personally, I enjoy sharing my hobbies and interests. I am also passionate about sports, particularly athletics, parkour, table tennis, and volleyball. Sometimes, I even join an after-school club to play some volleyball and ping-pong.

As I've noticed many of my students enjoy drawing, I allow it during my lesson if it doesn't hinder their attention. I used to draw a lot in class and could focus on class material while doing so. In fact, most of my own drawings were done during lessons I enjoyed and excelled in. The exception was maths in Year 7 and 8 (eleven and twelve years old); I was average at maths but drew a lot because my best friends were constantly drawing in that lesson. I learned how to draw dragons, muscular characters, and horse heads from them.

I often draw during staff meetings to maintain concentration and alertness, especially after a demanding teaching day. I have a folder with over one hundred of my drawings, spanning from eleven years old to my early twenties. Many of these drawings are anime, a shared interest among my students. We share our drawings and techniques for shading and drawing eyes.

I believe shared interests are a great way to connect with students. Some of my students are interested in video editing, and so am I. Others enjoy playing video games like *Apex Legends, Roblox, Overwatch,* and *The Sims,* which I do as well.

The teacher-student relationship resembles a transactional interaction where both parties stand to benefit. The teacher is like a seller who has a product to offer (educational content), while the students are potential customers, though they are not necessarily willing buyers. They are often compelled by parents and the education system to attend lessons and learn. Therefore, to engage students, the teacher must ensure the learning experience is appealing, which can be achieved by incorporating fun activities aligning with the students' interests.

Just like any profession, teaching requires training, and the best place to learn is in the classroom itself. To inspire and motivate students, the teacher must be present and actively engaged with them. By demonstrating intelligence and problem-solving skills and encouraging peer-to-peer learning, teachers can encourage students to develop their own ideas and skills. The ultimate goal is to create an enjoyable learning environment where students are motivated to participate and learn.

Inspiration is key to motivation. Without it, students may struggle to find the drive to do something, especially when graded. Making subject material appealing, according to students' definition of fun, is crucial. If students are not inspired to learn, they are less likely to apply themselves to the task at hand and more likely to fail. While failure is a natural part of the learning process, it can be demotivating for students. Children are still in the process of discovering the world, while adults may believe they already know everything. It is important for teachers to remain humbly confident, admitting when they do not know something. There is no shame in not knowing everything, and students will appreciate the honesty. Honesty about limitations teaches students the value of honesty in their relationships with others.

I enjoy learning from my students as well. If I am asked a question to which I do not know the answer and it is something quickly searchable, we look it up together, learning in the moment. For more complex matters, I commit to researching and sharing in the following lesson or assign it as homework for the next lesson. Although our time spent with students is brief, the memory of an inspiring teacher is everlasting.

MOTIVATION

Understanding Motivation: Listening to the Voices of Our Students

Motivation, in the realm of education, is akin to the flame that ignites the candle of learning. It's what keeps students eager, engaged, and excited about their educational journey. As a teacher, I've always maintained that understanding students' motivation isn't a monologue; it's a dialogue. Actively involving students in this conversation requires listening to their concerns, apprehensions, and suggestions.

Delving deep into the psyche of my students, I sought to decipher their reasons for disengagement by posing the question "Why don't you like school?" Their responses were candid, providing invaluable insights into the challenges they face daily. The recurring theme of "boring lessons" suggests that traditional pedagogical methods might not resonate with today's tech-savvy and dynamic generation. Instead of dismissing their concerns, I probed further, challenging students to envision solutions by asking them to step into the shoes of a teacher and reimagine a more engaging classroom experience. The responses were insightful, from suggesting more real-world application of concepts to integrating technology and multimedia elements. Some even highlighted the value of interactive group discussions over traditional lectures.

The pressure of incessant testing emerged as another significant demotivating factor. While assessments are pivotal for tracking progress, maintaining a balance is crucial to ensure that the joy of learning isn't overshadowed by anxiety over performance metrics. Peer interactions also play a vital role in shaping a student's academic experience. Disallowing students to sit with friends or interact freely might inadvertently suppress their social growth and collaborative learning experiences.

Simple yet often overlooked factors also came to light: early school hours, the rigidity of uniforms, and strict regulations. While structure is essential for discipline, exploring a middle ground that respects individuality could be beneficial. The sedentary nature of traditional classrooms was another concern. Introducing short breaks and stand-up discussions or integrating physical activities into lessons could be transformative.

One noteworthy concern is the perception that "it's always the teacher who decides what we are doing." This emphasises the need for a more collaborative approach. Pupils want to have a say in what and how they learn. Offering them choices, even if minor, can instil a sense of ownership and drive.

Surprising, yet vital, feedback highlighted the quality of canteen food. Nutrition plays an integral role in cognitive development, and if students aren't receiving wholesome meals, their concentration, their energy, their mood, and ultimately their motivation can wane.

In conclusion, understanding and addressing these concerns goes beyond boosting motivation; it's about respecting our students, recognising their individual needs, and striving to make education a collaborative effort. By valuing and acting upon their feedback, we create an environment where they feel heard, respected, and, most importantly, motivated to learn.

How I Try to Address Some of These Issues

Boredom: I try to incorporate interactive activities, discussions, and hands-on projects to keep the students engaged. I also encourage them to share their own ideas and interests and incorporate those into the lesson plans whenever possible.

Tests: I don't control the number of tests students must take, as this is always embedded in the department's scheme of work, in line with the school's development plan. However, I make an effort to space them out and provide ample preparation time for the students.

Sitting with friends: I am flexible with seating arrangements and grant students the privilege to sit with someone they feel comfortable with, as long as it fits my teaching plan and doesn't disrupt learning in the class.

Combatting the early wake-up time: I focus on creating a classroom environment that's both comfortable and inviting. Occasionally, I kick off my lessons with a fun activity to help students shake off sleepiness and get excited about what we're about to learn. For instance, I might challenge the class to spot a deliberate mistake on the board, fostering participation and enthusiasm. This could involve intentionally introducing errors like writing the wrong day or month in French, placing "th" after the number in the date (which only occurs in English), or misspelling a word like "practise" (the verb) with a "c" to capture their interest and encourage them to earn a reward stamp.

Addressing strict rules: I explain the reasons behind the rules and how they help to create a safe and productive learning environment.

The Delicate Balance of Setting Appropriate Goals for the Classroom

The art of setting goals in a classroom environment is akin to walking a tightrope. On one side lies the abyss of unattainable, overly ambitious objectives, and on the other, the pitfall of underachievement stemming from goals set too low. Striking the right balance is crucial for the students' academic advancement and their overall development and well-being, as it can also have lasting psychological and motivational impacts on students.

Appropriate goal setting dictates the pace, challenges, and milestones that learners will encounter. It is imperative that educators strike the right balance when setting these objectives.

Goals that are too lofty can inadvertently sow seeds of self-doubt and frustration among students. Targets consistently out of reach may cause students to internalise perceived failures, leading them to question their capabilities, erode their self-esteem, and diminish their passion for learning. It's akin to constantly trying to reach a tantalising piece of fruit that's just beyond one's grasp – eventually, one may give up from sheer exhaustion. Moreover, overly high goals can induce undue stress, leading to burnout, anxiety, and even physical health concerns. This pressure can eclipse the joy and curiosity of learning, making education a chore rather than an enriching experience.

Conversely, setting goals that are too modest can be equally detrimental. Goals that are easily attainable might offer momentary satisfaction but can lead to complacency and stagnation. Without being adequately challenged, students are missing the opportunity to explore the boundaries of their potential. The danger here is twofold: Firstly, students might not develop the resilience and grit required to tackle more complex challenges in the future. Secondly, they might harbour a false sense of accomplishment, which can be jarring when faced with real-world scenarios or higher educational pursuits where the bar is set much higher.

Furthermore, goals that are not stimulating can lead to disengagement and boredom, depriving students of the zest for discovery, the thrill of overcoming a challenge, and the satisfaction of acquiring new skills. These essential elements of the learning journey are lost when goals are not aligned with a student's capabilities and potential.

Therefore, as an educator, I take on the responsibility of assessing the abilities, aspirations, and needs of students, setting goals that are both challenging and achievable. This means establishing objectives that stretch the students, encouraging them to reach just beyond their grasp, without overwhelming them. This approach fosters an environment where learning is a rewarding journey marked by challenges overcome, skills honed, and knowledge gained. This delicate balance ensures students remain engaged, motivated, and primed for success, both in the classroom and beyond.

The Limitations of Using SATs as Universal Benchmarks for Subject Target Setting

Using the results of SATs as the primary determinant for setting targets in all subjects presents a limited view of a student's multifaceted capabilities, focusing narrowly on three specific subjects (English, mathematics, and science). This approach, while administratively practical, fails to recognise the rich scope of diverse skills and talents students possess.

A particularly glaring oversight of this method emerges when considering students for whom English is not their first language. Relying on SAT scores in English may inadvertently place these students in lower sets across all subjects, masking their exceptional proficiency in subjects like music, modern foreign languages, cooking, art, and others. English proficiency, in this context, acts as an unrepresentative filter, potentially obscuring a student's true potential in other areas.

My personal experience in secondary school in Paris reflects the consequences of such teaching methods. Before that, I was studying in Haiti, where my proficiency in French was average at best since it wasn't my mother tongue. I mainly read and wrote French in class, as even our teachers rarely used it to address us. I moved to France after the first term of my Year 7 in Haiti. Skipping Year 6 in primary school, I had already covered the same curriculum as the Year 6 pupils in Haiti during my Year 5. However, in France, I was placed in a low-ability group because of my limited proficiency in the French language, despite excelling in mathematics, geography, physical education, and English.

Lacking a sense of challenge in my classes, my motivation stagnated, and I spent a lot of time drawing with a couple of other talented students during lessons. This lack of motivation had significant consequences, leading to my placement in the Year 9 branch that focused on less academic subjects. It quickly became clear that I was not where I was supposed to be academically. Recognising the disparity, my parents and my godmother's boss, who believed in my potential, secured an agreement with the headmaster: If I could increase my average level in each individual subject to at least 12 out of 20 marks (France uses marks rather than grades) by the end of the first term, I would be moved to one of the top sets. I accomplished this goal and was transferred to the top set in Year 9, enabling me to begin learning a second language, German. This move rekindled my motivation and determination to learn.

Why Do Schools Keep Using SATs for Target Setting?

Using SATs as universal benchmarks for subject target setting is a contentious issue in the education system. When I look closely at the matter, I find the following advantages and disadvantages of this approach.

Advantages:

Standardisation:
    SATs provide a standardised measure, ensuring that all students are evaluated based on the same criteria. This helps schools maintain consistency in their target setting across diverse cohorts.

Ease of Administration:

Using a single benchmark streamlines the administrative process for schools. It simplifies the process, eliminating the need for multiple tests or assessments to set targets for various subjects.

Predictive Value:

Studies have shown that SAT scores can be predictive of future academic achievement, implying their potential value as a reasonable gauge for setting targets in other subjects.

Accountability:

Schools are often under pressure to demonstrate academic achievement. Using SATs as benchmarks helps schools set clear, measurable targets and facilitates accountability for student progress.

Objective Measure:

SAT scores are seen as an objective measure, which can minimise biases in target setting.

While these advantages underscore the rationale behind using SATs for target setting, it's crucial to recognise the associated disadvantages to foster a comprehensive understanding of the practice.

Disadvantages:

One Size Doesn't Fit All:

Using SATs as a universal benchmark can oversimplify the complexities of individual student abilities. Students have varied skills, and a single test might not accurately reflect their potential across different subjects.

Potential for Misplacement:

As mentioned earlier, for students with English as a second or third language, their English SAT score might lead to placement in lower sets in subjects where they could otherwise excel. This misplacement denies them access to advanced resources, coursework, and extracurricular opportunities available to students in higher sets.

Overemphasis on Test Results:

Relying heavily on SATs can create an environment of "teaching to the test," limiting broader educational experiences and creative teaching approaches.

Stress on Students:

The significant weight placed on a single test can increase stress and anxiety levels among students. This not only affects their SAT performance but also their overall well-being.

Limited Scope:

SATs cover specific areas of English, mathematics, and science. Using these results to set targets for subjects like art, music, physical education, and modern foreign languages might not be appropriate or accurate.

Potential for Neglecting Other Skills:

Relying solely on SATs might lead schools to neglect other essential skills like critical thinking, creativity, and social skills, which are not directly tested in SATs but are crucial for holistic student development.

Potential Social Implications:

Being placed in a lower set can have social repercussions, as peers might perceive these students as less capable, creating a skewed social dynamic and potential stigmatisation.

Motivation serves as the heartbeat of the learning process, driving students to actively engage, participate, and internalise the essence of what they learn. Throughout this chapter, we delved into various facets of motivation, exploring how educators can inspire students to crave knowledge and take ownership of their educational journey.

From listening to student feedback to setting appropriate goals, this chapter underscores the importance of understanding students' individual needs and perspectives. As we've seen, a one-size-fits-all approach rarely works. Students are unique, with diverse backgrounds, interests, and challenges. What motivates one student might not have the same impact on another.

Using tools like SATs as universal benchmarks, while beneficial in some respects, can have unintended consequences if applied too rigidly. In the realm of motivation, it's essential that educators strike a balance, ensuring targets are both challenging and achievable.

Central to all is the teacher-student relationship. Building trust, showing faith in a student's abilities, and fostering a positive learning environment can transform even the most disengaged student into an enthusiastic learner. As educators, our ultimate goal isn't just to transfer knowledge but to ignite a passion for learning that lasts a lifetime. In the pursuit of this mission, understanding and nurturing motivation is our most potent tool.

PASSION

P assion is a driving force, compelling us to pursue activities that bring joy and satisfaction. This intense emotion is not easily swayed by external factors and inspires us to achieve great things. Passionate individuals demonstrate heightened motivation, creativity, and persistence, often surpassing expectations. While Confucius,[4] China's most famous teacher, philosopher, and political theorist, may have been overly optimistic about the relationship between passion and work, it is true that having a passion for your job can make the experience more fulfilling and enjoyable. Passion infuses meaning and purpose into our work and encourages us to constantly strive for excellence. As a teacher, being passionate about education and inspiring others can help you create a more engaging and effective learning environment for your students.

Let me share an anecdote from my early teaching days. It was my first job interview after completing my teacher training, and I was scheduled to teach German to a Year 8 class. The class consisted of about thirty students, grouped based on their academic abilities, with the brightest students in the top set, the average ones in the middle, and the less able ones in the bottom set. Despite my nervousness, the class went well, and I remember feeling

---

[4] Annping Chin, "Confucius, Chinese Philosopher," *Britannica*, last updated February 16, 2024, https://www.britannica.com/biography/Confucius.

relieved once it was over. To my surprise, the headteacher and department head sought feedback from the class on my teaching as part of the interview process. I had never heard of such a custom before, and I didn't know what to expect.

Thankfully, the students' feedback was positive, securing me the job. This experience got me thinking about the role of students' voices in shaping the education system. Their input and feedback can give valuable insight into the effectiveness of teaching methods. It also made me reflect on the issue of target setting and whether it is an effective way of grouping students based on their abilities.

Finally, the headteacher praised my passion for teaching, which was evident in my interaction with the class. To my surprise, the class had one unanimous desire: they wanted to call me "Mr Smiley." Despite this quirky feedback, I was thrilled to have secured the position.

Passion is vital in any profession, including teaching. It provides the drive and energy to face the challenges that come with the job. However, it's important to note that passion alone is not enough. It needs to be coupled with dedication, perseverance, and a commitment to continuously learn and improve. Even if you love your job, like I do, there are inevitably tough moments, requiring hard work, where dedication and perseverance come into play. Moreover, passion for teaching can develop over time as you witness the positive impact you have on your students' lives. So, while it's ideal to have a passion for teaching, it's not the only factor that determines success in the profession.

How I Sustain My Passion

Throughout my experience, I have encountered teachers with decades of experience who maintain the same level of passion as when they began. These individuals strike the perfect balance between personal and professional life, constantly seek to improve their teaching skills, embrace feedback, and seek new and innovative ways to engage their students. These teachers inspire and motivate their students to reach their full potential.

One of the keys to maintaining passion in teaching is always remembering your initial motivation for becoming a teacher. Personally, it was the desire to make a positive impact on young people's lives, helping them develop their full potential and instilling in them a love for learning. When facing challenging moments, I recall this purpose, and it provides me the strength to persevere.

Having a supportive team is instrumental in nurturing and sustaining passion for teaching. When teachers feel valued, appreciated, and supported, they exhibit greater resilience and motivation to navigate job challenges. This support can come in various forms, such as regular opportunities for professional development, constructive feedback, recognition for hard work, and a positive work culture that fosters collaboration and teamwork. The importance of having a supportive team cannot be overstated, as it plays a significant role in retaining teachers and enabling them to thrive. A happy and motivated teaching staff positively impacts the students' learning experience.

Passion generates inspiration, leading to motivation. Any teacher entering the profession devoid of a genuine passion for working with children or young adults risks disappointment and frustration. It's impossible to fake passion, as students are perceptive and can discern insincerity. Unfortunately, adults often underestimate the intelligence of children.

As a teacher, I prioritise helping my students discover their passions and encourage them to devote time to pursuing those activities. Identifying their passions enables them to actively cultivate these interests in their daily lives, fostering a recurring and powerful sense of fulfilment. Some students find that passion in the friends they surround themselves with (as I have with some of my own friends, including my siblings), while others discover it in the books they read (I have certain authors whose works always leave me feeling inspired), games they play (such as volleyball, ping-pong, athletics, and even board games like Monopoly), or engaging discussions or debates (such as those about philosophy, science, or human nature), which can leave them feeling excited and motivated to learn more.

Pursuing your passion can lead to a happier, healthier, and more fulfilling life. If you are passionate about teaching, it's likely your enthusiasm will be contagious to your students. Once they have contracted the passion virus, they can spread it throughout the classroom. Peer influence is powerful, and children often learn more readily from their peers. Observing the passion that has been transmitted to others in the class can convince even the most resistant students to embrace that passion for learning.

In conclusion, passion is a crucial element in teaching. It is the fuel that drives us to continue, even in the face of challenges. By maintaining our passion and constantly seeking to improve our skills and engage our students, we can inspire and motivate them to reach their full potential.

Laughter as an Instant Vacation

The quote "Laughter is an instant vacation," often attributed to Milton Berle, resonates deeply with me. When laughter fills the classroom, any perception students may harbour of being unwillingly confined to school vanishes, even if just momentarily. In those moments, teaching feels like a vacation, surrounded by individuals genuinely engaged and receptive to the lessons I provide.

Children have a knack for observing details that adults might overlook. Their keen observations often transport me back to my own school days, reminding me of the instances when my peers and I speculated about our teachers' lives. While most of our assumptions were mere childish conjectures and often off the mark, occasionally, they rang true. I distinctly recall one class where students noticed a deviation from my usual cheerful demeanour. They pointed out that I wasn't "Mr Smiley" that day and inquired about my uncharacteristic sternness. With a smile, I explained that while physically well, I was mentally preoccupied with pressing matters, leading to my serious expression. Their observation caught me off guard; I hadn't realised my internal struggles were manifesting externally. This experience highlighted not only the students' perceptiveness but also their genuine concern for my well-being. It was evident that their concern transcended mere curiosity; they truly cared for their teacher.

An example that is worth repeating, and that will resonate with many colleagues, is that when you're feeling under the weather, some classes – often those labelled as challenging – tend to exhibit better behaviour when informed of your condition. Members of the class might even take it upon themselves to reprimand peers who misbehave or are overly loud. I experienced this in one of my lessons. Despite the day being long and tiring, that moment of empathy made it much more pleasant.

Laughter as a Straight Line

Archimedes claimed that the shortest path between two points is a straight line. Similarly, Danish-American comedian Victor Borge once remarked, "Laughter is the shortest distance between two people."[5] Drawing from these insights, I posit that laughter serves as a direct connection, a straight line, between individuals. Even a simple, sincere smile can bridge this gap. Naturally, people aren't drawn to those with stern expressions, which often evoke feelings of fear, severity, or danger. In contrast, a warm smile symbolises security, trust, and empathy.

Power Source:

I have developed a passion for playing chess. Although I only recently learned to play, within a few months, I found myself engaged in matches against students during school lunch breaks. They eagerly challenge me,

---

[5] Roger Abrantes, "Laughter is the Shortest Distance Between Two People," *Ethology Institute*, last updated April 23, 2014, https://ethology.eu/laughter-is-the-shortest-distance-between-two-people/#:~:text=%E2%80%9CLaughter%20is%20the%20shortest%20distance,from%20other%20forms%20of%20life.

relishing the opportunity to compete against a teacher, driven by the immense joy derived from a potential victory over me. Fortunately, many of them were at or near my skill level, allowing me to outwit them on occasion and secure more wins than losses. Yet, the enthusiasm to play – and I want to emphasise the word "play" – remains strong for both me and the students.

Given all the tasks teachers juggle, even during our lunch breaks, finding time to play chess with students feels like a luxury. I would gladly forgo my lunch if it meant squeezing in a game or two. While some draw energy from the food they consume, I find that same vitality in my interactions with the students, much like when I'm on stage performing with my band.

The classroom is where the magic happens. When I'm standing at the front, board pen in hand, and see those eager eyes following every word and movement, there's an electricity in the air. Every question they ask, every concept they grasp, propels me forwards. During particularly long days, when fatigue might start to creep in, a single moment of realisation in a student's eyes can rejuvenate me more than any cup of coffee ever could, even though I do not drink coffee.

There is something about the laughter, the camaraderie, and the sheer fun of playing games with the students. Whether it's a simple sing-along in the classroom, a sport event during Sports day, a volleyball or ping-pong match during an after-school club, or even just a game of chess during lunch break, these moments become my personal wellspring of energy. Each cheer, each high-five, feeds my spirit in ways that words often can't capture.

School trips have always been more than just a change in scenery. The joy of discovery, witnessing students experience new environments, cultures, or historical sites, is unparalleled. Observing their reactions, from the awestruck (when they saw the Eiffel Tower lighting up at night during a trip to Paris) to the curiously pensive, is a balm to any weariness I might feel. These trips aren't just about leaving the school premises; they're about entering a realm of endless possibilities, where every moment becomes a teaching and learning opportunity.

I occasionally attend various clubs run in the school, purely out of curiosity. Watching students come together, driven by a shared passion, whether it's for literature, science, sport, music, or art, is truly special. Their dedication, the way they organise, brainstorm, and execute projects, brings to light their potential, and in doing so, reinforces my purpose. In these club sessions, I'm reminded that teaching goes beyond textbooks; it's about nurturing passions.

By nature, I am a beacon of positivity. My Haitian heritage, a testament to resilience and hope, has shaped this outlook. In Haiti, despite the daily challenges, the people carry an indomitable spirit and an unwavering positive perspective. It's this cultural foundation that's amplified when I interact with my students. They don't just inspire me; they energise my very being. Through each lesson, game, club activity, and trip, I find my strength renewed, my spirit uplifted. It's clear to me now: when it comes to education, my true source of energy has always been, and will always be, the students themselves.

TESTS/EXAMS/EVALUATION

You can attempt to soften the impact by using terms like "informal assessment," "check-up," "mid-module assessment," or "monitoring," but to kids, it all boils down to the same thing: a test. And that test, in the eyes of their peers, their parents, society, and, most importantly, their own mind, determines whether they are perceived as smart or labelled as a complete failure – good-for-nothing, useless, worthless, or stupid. I'm not exaggerating by using negative terms; this is exactly how kids perceive it.

I strongly believe that we should reduce the importance placed on grades and take the time to explain to our students what they truly represent. In reality, grades merely measure how well a student is performing in a specific subject at a particular time during the school year. They don't reflect their inherent intelligence or their worth as a person. Understanding this allows students to shift their focus from the relentless pursuit of high grades to a more holistic development of their skills and knowledge.

Origin of Examinations

Examinations, tests, and assessments have been integral components of the education system since its inception. In fact, the origins of examinations can be traced back to ancient civilisations such as China, India, and Greece, where individuals underwent assessments of their knowledge in subjects like mathematics, foreign languages, and philosophy. Initially designed to select individuals for high-ranking government positions, over time, examinations have become an essential tool for evaluating student performance and gauging their academic progress. However, the impact of examinations extends far beyond academic performance, affecting students' intellectual, social, and physical well-being.

In his book *The Case Against Standardized Testing: Raising the Scores, Ruining the Schools*,[6] author Alfie Kohn, who is an educator and fervent critic of education's obsession with standardised testing, argues that examinations have become "a distorting force in education," undermining students' intrinsic motivation to learn and creating a culture of competition that values test scores over genuine understanding. Moreover, studies have shown that excessive testing can lead to increased stress levels, anxiety, and even physical illness in students. Thus, it is imperative we approach examinations with caution and explore alternative methods of evaluating student performance that prioritise true learning and overall well-being.

Author and educator Yong Zhao, an American educator and, at the time of writing, the newest Foundation Distinguished Professor at the University of Kansas, writes in *What Works May Hurt: Side Effects in Education*[7] that we must shift our focus from test scores to "developing the whole person, promoting well-being, and nurturing creativity and entrepreneurship." Embracing this perspective encourages a holistic approach to education that values the individual growth and flourishing of each student beyond the constraints of standardised testing.

---

[6] Alfie Kohn, *The Case Against Standardized Testing: Raising the Scores, Ruining the Schools* (Portsmouth, NH: Heinemann, 2000).

[7] Yong Zhao, *What Works May Hurt: Side Effects in Education* (New York: Teachers College Press, 2018).

The Mandatory Use of Examinations

The mandatory use of examinations in schools globally varies depending on the country and region. Some countries integrated examinations into their education system in the nineteenth century, while others adopted them much later. For example, standardised testing became mandatory in the United States with the passage of the No Child Left Behind Act in 2001. In contrast, countries like China and Japan have a centuries-old tradition of using examinations to evaluate student performance. The widespread use of examinations across the globe can be attributed to the rise of industrialisation and the need for a standardised method of evaluating individuals' knowledge and skills. As education historian Diane Ravitch notes in *The Troubled Crusade: American Education, 1945–1980*,[8] the rise of standardised testing and examinations was a direct response to the need to prepare individuals for the demands of the modern workforce. Despite its widespread use, the impact of examinations on student well-being and genuine learning remains a topic of debate among educators, policymakers, and scholars.

While examinations have been employed to evaluate student performance for centuries, recent decades have seen a significant increase in their use and importance. Standardised testing, in particular, has become a ubiquitous element of many education systems worldwide, with many countries relying on test scores to assess student progress and school quality. However, the emphasis on testing and examinations has also sparked controversy and criticism. Many educators and scholars argue that it has led to a narrow focus on test preparation at the expense of authentic learning and student well-being. It's important for students to have time for social interaction and personal development, as these skills are crucial for their overall well-being and success in life. A singular emphasis on testing and exams can leave students feeling stressed, anxious, and burnt out, potentially

---

[8] Diane Ravitch, *The Troubled Crusade: American Education, 1945–1980* (New York: Basic Books, 1983).

leading to long-term negative effects on their mental health and academic performance.

As educators, it's crucial to find a balance between testing and true learning while prioritising the holistic development of our students. In *The Testing Charade: Pretending to Make Schools Better*, education researcher Daniel Koretz claims that the focus on test scores has resulted in a "troubled system" that fails to deliver on its promise of improving education outcomes.[9] Similarly, in *The Tyranny of Metrics*, author Jerry Z. Muller,[10] professor emeritus of history at the Catholic University of America and the author of several other books, argues that the overemphasis on metrics and testing has resulted in a "perverse incentive system" that rewards gaming the system over genuine improvement. Consequently, there is a growing acknowledgement among educators and policymakers that we must reassess the role and impact of examinations in our education systems and explore alternative approaches to evaluating student performance, ones that promote well-being, creativity, and genuine learning.

In recent years, mounting concerns among educators, policymakers, and parents have surfaced regarding the potential negative impact of examinations on student well-being. Research suggests that high-stakes examinations, such as standardised tests, can create a culture of competition and stress, undermining student motivation and learning. Moreover, high-stakes examinations can lead to anxiety, depression, and physical health problems, such as headaches, sleep disorders, and digestive issues.[11] The article "Fighting Back Against Achievement Culture: Cheating as an Act of Rebellion in a High-Pressure Secondary School," by Harvard educator Dr Alexis Redding, explores the complex dynamics of cheating among

---

[9] Daniel Koretz, *The Testing Charade: Pretending to Make Schools Better* (Chicago: University of Chicago Press, 2017).

[10] Jerry Z. Muller, *The Tyranny of Metrics* (Princeton, NJ: Princeton University Press, 2018).

[11] Joseph J. Fraas, "School counselors' perspective on high-stakes testing: Exploring the impact of high-stakes testing on students and counsellors," University of Pittsburgh ProQuest Dissertations Publishing, 2014. 3648012.

high-achieving students at Stuyvesant High School. It reveals that students resort to cheating not solely for personal gain but as a communal act of rebellion against an overly competitive and unjust academic system. The study emphasises the need for a more nuanced understanding of academic dishonesty, suggesting that systemic pressures and the school's achievement culture significantly influence student behaviour.[12] Furthermore, research suggests that high-stakes testing may contribute to the achievement gap, as students from marginalised backgrounds are often at a disadvantage in terms of test preparation and performance.[13]

A study by Superintendent of Oswego City School District Raymond W. Kilmer III, titled "High School Stress and Cheating: Developing an Understanding of the Factors that Influence Stress and Cheating in High School Students," presents key findings on the relationship between stress, academic dishonesty, and various demographic variables in high school students. The research identifies course load, social stress, and the acceptability of cheating behaviours as significant predictors of stress and attitudes towards academic integrity. It advocates for schools to review homework, grading, and assessment practices to mitigate student stress and suggests implementing honour codes and academic integrity education to foster a culture of honesty.[14]

The complex issue of high school stress and cheating necessitates a multifaceted approach that addresses both institutional policies and the cultural environment surrounding education. Schools should implement comprehensive academic integrity policies, including honour codes, to

[12] Alexis Brooke Redding, "Fighting Back Against Achievement Culture: Cheating as an Act of Rebellion in a High-Pressure Secondary School," *Ethics & Behavior* 27, no. 2 (2017): 155-172, DOI: 10.1080/10508422.2016.1145058.

[13] Laura-Lee Kearns, "High-stakes Standardized Testing and Marginalized Youth: An Examination of the Impact on Those Who Fail," *Canadian Journal of Education* 34, no. 2 (2011): 112-130.

[14] Raymond W. Kilmer III, "High School Stress and Cheating: Developing an Understanding of the Factors that Influence Stress and Cheating in High School Students" (2017). *Education Doctoral*. Paper 339. https://fisherpub.sjf.edu/education_etd/339

clearly define expectations around honesty and consequences for dishonesty. Coupled with rigorous education about academic integrity, such policies can foster a culture of honesty and transparency.

Educational institutions need to re-evaluate the importance given to grades and test scores as the main indicators of academic achievement. A more holistic approach to student evaluation, which includes assessments of creativity, critical thinking, and collaboration skills, can reduce the pressure to achieve high marks through any means possible. This shift in focus can promote a healthier learning environment and alleviate student stress.

Thirdly, reducing student workload is essential. Schools should critically evaluate the amount and difficulty of homework and assignments, ensuring they contribute to learning without overwhelming students. Utilising flexible scheduling, providing periods of rest, and encouraging extracurricular activities not tied to academic performance can help students manage stress more effectively.

Creating a supportive school environment that prioritises mental health and well-being is vital. This might include offering readily available counselling services, as well as workshops on managing stress, and establishing secure areas where students can discuss their worries and obstacles.

Lastly, engaging parents and the broader community in conversations about the expectations placed on students can help mitigate external pressures. Encouraging a shift in perspective from valuing academic achievements to valuing learning and personal growth can reduce the incentive to engage in academically dishonest behaviours.

In summary, addressing high school stress and cheating necessitates a comprehensive strategy that involves revising educational policies, fostering a culture of integrity, supporting mental health, and re-evaluating societal expectations surrounding academic success. Through these measures, schools can create an environment that supports ethical behaviour and the well-being of all students.

In response to these concerns, educators and policymakers are exploring alternative methods of evaluating student performance that prioritise well-being and promote a more holistic approach to education. Project-based assessments, portfolios, and performance tasks are examples of alternative assessment forms focusing on students' ability to apply their learning authentically. These methods offer a more accurate and comprehensive picture of student learning and development, encouraging deeper learning and critical thinking. Additionally, educators are working to create supportive and inclusive learning environments that prioritise student well-being and promote a growth mindset, treating mistakes and failure as opportunities for learning and growth. By prioritising student well-being and embracing a more holistic approach to education, educators and policymakers can create a more meaningful and effective learning experience for all students.

In *The Tyranny of Metrics*, author Jerry Z. Muller argues that the overemphasis on metrics and data in education systems and other sectors has resulted in an unbalanced approach to evaluating performance that neglects non-quantifiable skills and qualities. He notes that while metrics and data can be useful tools for assessing performance and driving improvement, an overemphasis on them can lead to unintended consequences, such as the "gaming" of metrics, the prioritisation of short-term goals over long-term objectives, and the overlooking of non-quantifiable skills essential for success in life and work.[15]

Muller contends that the education sector's overemphasis on metrics and data has led to a narrow focus on test preparation and performance, sidelining the development of non-quantifiable skills like creativity, critical thinking, and problem-solving. Test scores, while informative about student performance, do not provide a complete picture of student learning or potential. Moreover, this overemphasis can foster a culture of competition and stress, undermining student well-being and motivation.

---

[15] Jerry Z. Muller, *The Tyranny of Metrics* (Princeton: Princeton University Press, 2018), chap.I

To address these concerns, Muller calls for a more balanced approach to evaluation that recognises the value of non-quantifiable skills and qualities, advocating for a broader, more holistic view of education. He suggests that teachers and legislators should focus on creating learning environments that foster creativity, critical thinking, and problem-solving, rather than solely preparing students for tests. Additionally, he advocates for the development of new metrics and evaluation tools that recognise the value of non-quantifiable skills and qualities, promoting a more balanced approach to performance evaluation.[16]

Rethinking Examination Standards: The Controversial Practice of Grade Normalisation

The practice of adjusting grade boundaries after examination marking by national exam boards is a contentious issue that raises significant questions about fairness and the accurate measurement of student achievement. This method, widely accepted as the norm, ensures that exam results are distributed along a predetermined curve to maintain standards and consistency across years. However, this approach has profound implications for both students and the perception of educational achievement.

To elucidate for those unfamiliar with the intricacies of this system, consider a scenario in which 100 students undertake an examination scored out of 50 marks. Intuitively, one might expect a clear, consistent threshold for passing and grading distinctions: for instance, 25 marks for a C grade (a pass), 40 marks for an A grade, and 47 for an A*. In an ideally fair system, such straightforward benchmarks could indeed result in years when 100 percent of students pass or even when a large majority secure top grades based on their actual performance.

---

[16] Jerry Z. Muller, *The Tyranny of Metrics* (Princeton: Princeton University Press, 2018), chap.III

However, the reality diverges sharply from this ideal because of the practice of adjusting grade boundaries after exams are marked. This adjustment means that the value of a student's mark is fluid, dependent not solely on their knowledge or performance but on how their peers perform and on the board's determination of what constitutes an A, B, or C grade in any given year. Such variability introduces an element of unpredictability and, some argue, unfairness into the examination process. The rationale often cited for this practice is the need to maintain a consistent standard yearly and prevent grade inflation. Nevertheless, this raises the critical question: Are we prioritising the maintenance of statistical distributions over recognising actual student learning and achievement?

Critics argue that this system can demotivate students who find that their considerable efforts translate into something other than the grades they anticipated or deserved based on a consistent, transparent standard. Moreover, it can distort the accurate measure of a cohort's capabilities and progress, potentially masking improvements in teaching effectiveness and student learning. The variability in grade boundaries may also contribute to stress and anxiety among students acutely aware of these exams' high stakes and potential impact on their futures.

Furthermore, in an era when education systems worldwide are being scrutinised for their ability to prepare students for a rapidly changing global landscape, the fixation on maintaining a bell curve of results seems increasingly anachronistic. It underscores the need for a broader conversation about educational assessment, what we value as student success, and school effectiveness indicators.

In conclusion, while standardisation and maintaining rigorous academic standards are undoubtedly important, the methodology employed to achieve these ends warrants re-evaluation. The practice of adjusting grade boundaries to fit a preconceived distribution curve rather than reflecting the actual achievements of students seems at odds with the principles of fairness and transparency. As educators, policymakers, and stakeholders in the educational system, it is crucial to advocate for practices that genuinely reflect student learning and achievement, fostering an environment where every student's effort and knowledge are accurately recognised.

What Is Formative Assessment Exactly, and Why Do I Prefer It Over Summative Assessment?

Formative assessment serves as an ongoing feedback mechanism during the learning process, aiming to improve students' understanding and performance. Unlike summative assessments, which assess learning at the end of a unit or course, formative assessments are used throughout the learning process, providing timely feedback that can guide instruction and help students improve their understanding. Personally, I prefer incorporating formative assessments in my lessons, as they provide a more accurate and real-time gauge of students' learning, rather than relying solely on a formal final test. The other positive aspect of formative assessment is its minimal impact on students, allowing me to make subtle changes in the learning process as appropriate.

Teacher observations stand out as a specific form of formative assessment involving a teacher actively observing a student's performance or behaviour in the classroom. During a teacher observation, the teacher attentively watches a student as they work on a task or participate in a class activity, making detailed notes on their performance, behaviour, and level of engagement.

Teacher observations offer valuable insights into a student's understanding and learning requirements. For example, a teacher might observe a student struggling to complete a task, prompting timely intervention to provide additional support or guidance.

I use various forms of formative assessments, including quizzes, polls, exit tickets, and teacher observations. An exit ticket is used to quickly and informally assess student understanding at the end of a lesson or class period. Typically, these tickets consist of brief prompts or questions that ask students to summarise what they learned or reflect on their understanding of a concept. These prompts may ask students to identify the main idea of a lesson, explain a key concept, or describe how they can apply their knowledge to a real-world scenario.

Teacher observations provide insights into students' performance and behaviour in the classroom. During teacher observations, I closely watch and take notes on students' engagement, behaviour, and performance as they participate in class activities or work on tasks.

Teacher observations offer a deeper understanding of students' learning needs and comprehension. If I observe a student struggling to complete a task, I can intervene by providing additional support or guidance. Alternatively, if I observe a student actively engaged or demonstrating a high level of understanding, I use the observation to reinforce positive behaviour.

I conduct teacher observations using various techniques based on the task or activity being observed. This may include observing a student during a class discussion, an individual task, or a group project. The observation can focus on specific skills or behaviours, such as collaboration, critical thinking, and communication.

One significant advantage of teacher observations is their ability to provide a comprehensive view of a student's learning and behaviour, offering insights into their approach to tasks, interaction with peers, and responses to challenges. This information enables me to provide targeted support and feedback to the student and identify areas where the student may need additional support.

The key feature of formative assessment lies in its focus on providing feedback that can be used for guiding future instruction and enhancing student learning. For example, I utilise quizzes to identify areas where students are struggling and adjust my instruction to provide additional support. Similarly, an exit ticket helps assess student understanding at the end of a lesson, allowing me to tailor my instruction for the next day based on the feedback received.

One analogy often used to describe formative assessment is that of a GPS system. Similar to how a GPS system provides continual feedback to a driver about their location and direction, formative assessment provides ongoing feedback to students about their understanding and progress. This feedback serves as a guide, enabling students to make adjustments and course-correct, much like a driver might alter their route based on feedback from their GPS system.

Research conducted by education scholars like Dylan Wiliam and Paul Black has shown the significant impact of formative assessment on student learning and achievement. In their seminal work, *Inside the Black Box: Raising Standards Through Classroom Assessment*, Black and Wiliam found that formative assessment can improve student achievement by up to 50 percent by helping students identify areas of struggle and providing them with the necessary feedback to enhance their understanding. They based their findings on a selection of 20 studies and over 500 articles made on the topic.[17]

Formative assessment, encompassing various forms like quizzes, polls, and teacher observations, is a dynamic tool designed to offer ongoing feedback to students during the learning process. Analogies like the GPS system can help to illustrate its key features. Research by scholars like Black and Wiliam substantiate the significant impact of formative assessment on student learning and achievement.

The landscape of school subjects has undergone limited changes over the past century. One hundred years ago, education focused primarily on reading, writing, and arithmetic, heavily emphasising rote learning and memorisation. Basic skills such as sewing, cooking, and woodworking, as well as history, geography, and literature, were also included. Science and technology held minor positions, and the arts were often considered secondary, yet present.

One noteworthy change is the increased focus on technology in education. Contemporary schools provide students with access to computers

---

[17] Paul Black and Dylan Wiliam, *Inside the Black Box: Raising Standards Through Classroom Assessment* (London: King's College London, School of Education, 1998), pp2-3

and digital devices, integrating technology into lessons across a range of subjects. For instance, virtual reality simulations may be used for history lessons, and data analysis tools for scientific studies.

However, critics argue that the technology focus has marginalised other vital areas, including the arts and humanities (languages, philosophy, physical education, law, media studies, psychology, economics, history, geography, and more). There are ongoing debates about the most effective ways to teach and assess twenty-first-century skills, such as critical thinking, collaboration, and problem-solving.

While the core subjects remain relatively stable, there are significant changes in elective courses offered and an increasing emphasis on technology and STEM subjects. These changes reflect broader societal and economic shifts, aiming to equip students for the challenges and opportunities of the twenty-first century.

Assessment Today and in the Future

First and foremost, I want to express my agreement with the fact that some form of assessment is vital to measure progress and pinpoint areas for improvement. However, maintaining a balance between the amount of assessment and the learning process is crucial. Excessive testing can induce stress and anxiety for students, hampering their ability to learn effectively. Additionally, tests and exams should not be the only method of assessment, as they do not capture the full range of a student's skills and knowledge. Therefore, it is imperative to employ a variety of assessment methods, including formative assessments, peer evaluations, and project-based assessments, for a comprehensive and accurate understanding of a student's progress and capabilities.

While assessment plays a pivotal role in education by supporting teaching, motivating students, and focusing their efforts, there is a tendency to disproportionately reward achievements over effort. In my view, both achievement and effort should be rewarded. The prevailing culture of excessive testing has raised concerns in recent years, as it contributes to stress and anxiety among students and negatively impacts their mental health and well-being.

It is crucial for schools and education systems to re-evaluate their approach, viewing assessment as a tool to support learning rather than an end in itself. Teachers and educators are increasingly encouraged to embrace a variety of assessment methods, which can provide immediate feedback to students, facilitating their improved learning.

I advocate shifting from high-stakes summative assessments, such as standardised tests, to more authentic assessments that better reflect the real-world skills and competencies essential for students to succeed in life. This includes performance-based assessments, in which students are tasked with demonstrating their understanding and skills through real-world tasks and projects.

Curriculum

When it comes to education, a curriculum that emphasises problem-solving and brings joy to children is more aligned with the realities of life. As adults, we continually encounter challenges requiring immediate solutions, and the solution that worked yesterday may not be applicable to similar problems in different contexts tomorrow. We must constantly adapt and devise our strategies and solutions, whether we confront challenges over days, weeks, months, or even our entire lives. Life is anything but static or predictable, and while some aspects are foreseeable, most events unfold randomly.

Regrettably, the education system often falls short in preparing students for life's unpredictable and ever-changing nature. Overemphasis on standardised testing and rote memorisation can leave students ill-equipped to handle real-world challenges. It is crucial to develop problem-solving skills early on and cultivate a sense of curiosity and joy in learning.

By advocating for a curriculum that encourages problem-solving and makes learning enjoyable, we can better equip students for the future challenges they will encounter. Life is unpredictable, and our education system should reflect that reality. With the right approach, we can empower students with the skills and mindset needed to navigate life's uncertainties with confidence and resilience.

As a teacher, I believe in guiding my students towards answers instead of simply providing them. When a student is struggling, rather than providing solutions, I show them one of the many paths leading to the answer. Understanding each student's individual needs, I guide them along a tailored path, fostering a better understanding of the material. While this approach may require more time, it benefits both my teaching effectiveness and the student's long-term self-confidence.

Witnessing the joy of a student's smile after they discover the answer independently is one of the most rewarding parts of my job. By promoting independent problem-solving skills and encouraging students to find solutions, I actively help build their confidence and prepare them for future challenges.

The curriculum design should foster creativity and avoid repetitive activities within a short timeframe, preventing monotony for students. While some may argue that children need a more traditional, directive approach, dismissing the demands of contemporary students, it's crucial to reflect on whether past students truly enjoyed their educational experiences. If students are not engaged or enjoying their education, they are less likely to retain the knowledge and skills they are taught. As educators, it's our responsibility to make learning both enjoyable and engaging, requiring a creative and adaptable teaching approach. By doing so, we aim to instil a love of learning that will serve students throughout their lives.

In my lessons, I consistently strive to maintain student engagement and interest in the subject matter. Using the technique of sharing interesting and relevant facts, I capture their attention and spark their curiosity, resulting in a lot of questions from the students. By responding to these inquiries, I aim to nurture critical and creative thinking. By fostering inquisitiveness and innovative thought, I believe I contribute to equipping my students with the essential skills for success. In a time when thinking outside the box and generating original ideas is paramount, keeping students engaged and encouraging creative thinking becomes instrumental. Thus, my goal is to empower them with the tools needed to succeed in both academic studies and future careers.

Implications of Examinations on Children's Mental Health

The Pervasiveness of Exam-Induced Stress

Examinations have become synonymous with stress for many students, a reality underscored by mental health statistics. The burgeoning number of young people seeking counselling for exam-related stress and anxiety emphasises the toll academic pressure is taking on their mental health. The role of educational institutions is crucial; they must not only acknowledge the gravity of the issue but also actively provide supportive measures.

Childline's report highlights a distressing surge in the demand for mental health support due to exam-related stress. A stark comparison reveals a near doubling of counselling sessions from September 2021 to March 2022, reflecting the crescendo of anxiety as exams drew nearer. During the 2021–22 academic year, Childline administered 1,734 counselling sessions specifically targeting concerns over exams and revision, a staggering 62 percent increase from the previous year. This surge is more than a mere statistic; it is a clear signal that the current examination system may be contributing to a mental health crisis among young learners.[18]

---

[18] Catherine Lough, "Childline Increases Counselling Sessions Over Exam Anxiety," *Independent*, May 14, 2022, https://www.independent.co.uk/news/uk/childline-children-gcses-alevels-nspcc-b2078866.html.

The timing of these spikes in counselling sessions is particularly telling. The notable rise in March 2022 sessions signals an acute escalation of stress levels as the exam period approached. This heightened anxiety period merits special attention from schools and educational policymakers. It is crucial for these institutions to implement a proactive strategy addressing students' well-being during these critical periods.

Schools, in collaboration with educational policymakers, must prioritise the mental well-being of students with the same vigour applied to academic achievements. Resources must be allocated not only for academic support but also for mental health care, ensuring students have access to the necessary tools to navigate their stress and anxiety effectively.

The urgency of the situation has been articulated by Alex Gray, service head at Childline, who in May 2022 underscored the gravity of the issue. He highlighted the "mounting concern felt by children and young people"[19] as they faced their exams. Gray's statement not only amplifies the voices of distressed students but also serves as a clarion call for a systemic change in how educational success is measured and supported.

The data presented by Childline goes beyond reflecting increasing awareness and a willingness to seek help; it is a symptom of a deeper systemic issue within our educational frameworks. It emphasises the need for a holistic approach to education – one that balances academic rigour with emotional support, helping students to thrive without being overwhelmed by the weight of examinations. The evidence at hand presents a compelling case for re-evaluating the role and impact of exams on children's mental health. It is incumbent upon educators, parents, and policymakers to chart a path forwards that values the mental health of students as much as their academic success, thereby fostering a more supportive and less stressful educational environment.

---

[19] Catherine Lough, "Childline Increases Counselling Sessions Over Exam Anxiety," *Independent,* May 14, 2022, https://www.independent.co.uk/news/uk/childline-children-gcses-alevels-nspcc-b2078866.html.

Examinations Amidst the Pandemic

Unprecedented Stress on Students

The year 2020 marked a global crisis unlike any other. The COVID-19 pandemic triggered widespread lockdowns, sending shockwaves through every facet of society, including the education system. As a witness to the unfolding events, I observed the pervasive narrative of fear deeply affecting our most vulnerable population: children and young adults. While the importance of physical health was evident, the crucial psychological impact, particularly on students, warranted equal attention.

During this tumultuous time, one potential strategy to mitigate stress among students could have been the cancellation of exams. Teachers' assessments could have served as an alternate measure of academic performance. Unfortunately, rather than adapting to the circumstances, the system clung to standardised tests. The insistence on traditional examination methods, even if conducted within the relative safety of schools, became a source of intense pressure for many.

The situation was particularly exacerbated for students from less privileged backgrounds, and the system faced stark disparities in accessing online education. The image of a single computer shared among multiple siblings symbolised this inequality. The notion that exams could have been suspended during the pandemic seemed like a logical solution to me, a gesture prioritising mental well-being over academic rigidity in a time of crisis.

In hindsight, it appears that the well-being of students may not have been at the forefront of policymakers' and exam board leaders' decisions. The failure to acknowledge the added stress imposed by examinations during an already distressing period revealed a significant oversight. This was especially disheartening considering the clear socioeconomic divisions and uneven access to educational resources that became more pronounced because of the pandemic.

In January 2022, the World Economic Forum brought attention to the tangible learning setbacks resulting from the pandemic-induced school closures. Data from countries like Brazil, rural Pakistan, India, South Africa, and Mexico unveiled profound declines in mathematics and reading skills. The impact was particularly severe in low- and middle-income countries, correlated with the duration of school shutdowns. The extent of educational deficits varied greatly, influenced by factors such as socioeconomic status, gender, and grade level.[20]

These insights demand reflection on how we approach education during crisis. The pandemic presented an opportunity to re-evaluate the necessity of traditional examinations, considering the severe mental health repercussions and learning losses. We should question whether the insistence on holding exams during such times is justified or if we should instead embrace alternative, more empathetic methods of assessment. The lessons learned throughout the pandemic have the potential to guide the development of more resilient and compassionate educational practices for future generations. This is my hope. If we encourage our students to be resilient and learn from past mistakes, it is only fitting that we model that behaviour ourselves.

The Economic and Educational Ripple Effects of COVID-19 on Global Learning

Correlation Between School Closures and Learning Losses

The learning loss linked to school closures, as confirmed by global simulations, underscores the profound impact of the COVID-19 pandemic on education. Particularly in low- and middle-income countries, the duration

---

[20] Centre for the New Economy and Society, "The Global Education Crisis is Even Worse Than We Thought. Here's What Needs to Happen," *World Economic Forum,* January 16, 2022, https://www.weforum.org/agenda/2022/01/global-education-crisis-children-students-covid19/.

of school closures exhibits a directly proportional effect on the extent of learning deficits. This correlation strongly argues for the necessity of maintaining uninterrupted learning, even in the face of crises.

Educational repercussions of the pandemic have not been uniform. Younger students, those hailing from economically disadvantaged backgrounds, and girls have borne a greater burden of the crisis. The variability of learning loss, highlighted by large standard deviations, indicates that these impacts are uneven both within and across nations. Such findings point to the need for customised educational recovery strategies that can effectively address the unique challenges faced by diverse student demographics.

The alarming report from December 2021 by leading global organisations, like the World Bank, UNESCO, and UNICEF, paints a grim picture of the future, projecting a staggering loss of $17 trillion in potential lifetime earnings for the current generation of students, a figure approximating 14 percent of today's global GDP. This projected loss surpasses prior estimations and portrays a more drastic scenario than initially apprehended.[21]

In a particularly concerning development, the concept of "learning poverty" has been introduced to describe the potential plight of up to 70 percent of children in low- and middle-income countries. These children face the dual threats of prolonged school closures and ineffective remote learning strategies. Without decisive intervention, the accumulation of learning deficits may compromise not only current educational outcomes but also future learning potential.[22]

It is indeed striking to observe that the crisis is often evaluated in monetary terms. The trend of quantifying human experiences and potential in terms of financial loss is both disheartening and potentially myopic. While

---

[21] UNESCO, UNICEF, and World Bank, "The State of the Global Education Crisis: A Path to Recovery," *World Economic Forum*, 2021, https://unesdoc.unesco.org/ark:/48223/pf0000380128, https://doi.org/10.54675/JLUG7649.

[22] UNESCO, UNICEF, and World Bank, "The State of the Global Education Crisis: A Path to Recovery," *World Economic Forum*, 2021, https://unesdoc.unesco.org/ark:/48223/pf0000380128, https://doi.org/10.54675/JLUG7649.

it is necessary to understand the economic implications, such an approach risks overshadowing the intrinsic value of education and the human cost of these losses. There's a concern that an overemphasis on economic valuation could lead to neglect of the more profound human and societal consequences.

The projected loss of $17 trillion in student lifetime earnings underscores an urgent need for action to counter the effects of the educational crisis. The disproportionate impact on countries with fewer resources necessitates not only increased educational investment in these areas but also innovative solutions to bridge the widening learning gap. The warning is clear: without immediate and effective measures, the learning losses are poised to compound, threatening the educational and economic futures of entire generations.

Mentally Healthy Schools: Addressing Academic and Exam Stress in the UK Education System

Scope of Student Stress in Educational Settings

Mentally Healthy Schools stands as a crucial online resource in the United Kingdom, dedicated to assisting schools and further education settings in managing mental health issues. The platform sheds light on the widespread nature of academic and exam stress among students, detailing how such pressures can significantly affect mental well-being. They cite high academic expectations, a perceived lack of support from teachers and peers, and an overwhelming workload as primary school-based risk factors that heighten this stress.

The Dual Dynamics of Risk and Protection

In the landscape of academic pressure, several risk factors play a critical role in escalating stress levels among students. These include the intense pressure to perform academically, feelings of isolation due to inadequate support systems, and the strain of managing a heavy workload that can often lead to burnout.

However, there are protective factors that serve to mitigate the adverse effects of academic and exam stress. These encompass nurturing positive relationships between teachers and students, cultivating robust coping strategies, and fostering a school environment that prioritises support and encouragement.

Strategies for Intervention and Support

The organisation outlines several strategies and interventions to combat academic stress. Stress management programmes can provide students with the tools and techniques to navigate academic challenges effectively. Within the school context, the incorporation of relaxation techniques stands out as an immediate resource, offering students tangible methods to alleviate anxiety. Moreover, revisiting and adjusting academic expectations and workloads can create a healthier educational setting where students can thrive without the constant burden of stress.

The Vital Role of an Empowering School Environment

The necessity of a supportive and empathetic school environment is a recurring theme. Mentally Healthy Schools stresses the important roles educators, parents, and the students themselves play in nurturing mental health within the educational sphere. Engaging all parties involved in education helps ensure a collective and effective approach to mental health challenges.

As a resource, Mentally Healthy Schools provides an invaluable wealth of information for anyone invested in the mental health of students.[23] With comprehensive insight into the effects of academic and exam stress and various strategies for intervention, it serves as a guide for creating a more conducive atmosphere for student mental health.

The call to action is clear: embracing the guidance provided by Mentally Healthy Schools can lead to the establishment of educational environments where mental health is prioritised, thereby ensuring that students can pursue academic excellence without compromising their well-being. This balanced approach is essential to cultivate resilient learners who are equipped to face the pressures of their educational journeys and subsequent professional lives.

The Fast and the Studious: Ramadan's Academic Impact

In a country like England, where the Muslim community holds significant presence, a noteworthy aspect comes into focus – the intersection of academic pressures during Ramadan. This period, deeply revered in the Islamic faith, imposes a strict fast from dawn until sunset. For Muslim students, this adds an extra layer of challenge to an already demanding time.

Visualise a typical day in the life of Amina, a Muslim student, during Ramadan. She rises before dawn to partake in the pre-dawn meal, Suhoor, knowing it will be her last nourishment until sunset. As the sun rises, so does her stress level, not just from impending exams but from the physical demands of fasting. Her day at school becomes a marathon of concentration and self-discipline, navigating through lessons and revision sessions while her body quietly yearns for sustenance.

The physical effects of fasting, including gnawing hunger and creeping fatigue, are just the tip of the iceberg. A deeper, more nuanced psychological battle unfolds. Amina finds her focus wavering during the most crucial

---

[23] Anna Freud Mentally Healthy Schools, "About," *Mentally Healthy Schools,* April 2020, https://mentallyhealthyschools.org.uk/about/.

parts of her revision. Concepts that would be easily grasped under normal circumstances seem just out of reach. Meanwhile, her classmates indulge on snacks and sip water, everyday luxuries she has temporarily forsaken. It's not just the absence of food and water; it's the constant awareness of this absence that disrupts her concentration.

Yet, amidst these challenges, a profound sense of community and shared experience emerges. Amina is not alone in the observing of Ramadan; many of her peers are also fasting. They exchange understanding glances and words of encouragement, drawing comfort from their collective sacrifice. This sense of togetherness may not completely alleviate the physical and mental demands, but it certainly provides a layer of emotional support. Out of compassion, I make a conscious effort to minimise eating in front of students observing Ramadan, recognising the significance of this gesture in fostering a supportive environment.

As the sun sets and Amina breaks her fast, there's a moment of relief – a brief period to nourish her body and mind. But this respite is fleeting. The night is spent juggling between Tarawih prayers and the relentless pressure of upcoming exams. Sleep becomes a luxury, often sacrificed on the altar of academic achievement.

To alleviate stress for students like Amina, who observe Ramadan fasting, several suggestions could be implemented. While some are easier to implement than others, they provide a starting point:

1. *Flexible scheduling*: Schools and universities could offer more flexible scheduling during Ramadan. This could include options for later start times, allowing students who had a late night for Tarawih prayers and studying to get adequate rest. Additionally, institutions could provide the option to reschedule exams or major assignments outside the fasting period.

2. *Quiet spaces for rest and reflection*: Designate quiet areas where fasting students can rest during breaks, especially since they

cannot engage in typical lunchtime activities. These spaces can also be used for meditation or quiet reflection, helping students rejuvenate mentally.

3. *Awareness and sensitivity training*: Conduct awareness sessions for teachers and fellow students about Ramadan and its implications. This fosters a more supportive and understanding environment where teachers might be more mindful of the energy levels of fasting students and peers are more considerate.

4. *Nutritional guidance*: Provide guidance on nutrition and effective meal planning to help students maintain their energy levels throughout the day. These can be workshops or leaflets on preparing a balanced Suhoor (pre-dawn meal) and Iftar (meal to break the fast).

5. *Counselling and support services*: Offer counselling and support services for students who may struggle more significantly with the combined stresses of fasting and academic demands. Having a space to talk about their challenges and learn coping strategies could be highly beneficial.

6. *Study and revision support:* Organise special study and revision sessions tailored to fasting students' needs. Schedule these sessions at more convenient times, such as later in the evening after Iftar, and focus on efficient study techniques to maximise learning while minimising fatigue.

7. *Community Iftar events*: Hosting community Iftar events at school can provide a sense of belonging and collective support. This allows non-fasting students and staff to participate and show solidarity with their fasting peers.

8. *Modified physical education classes:* Adjust the intensity of physical education classes for fasting students. Offer lighter, less strenuous activities to accommodate lower energy levels, ensuring students do not overexert themselves while fasting.

9. ***Extended library hours:*** Extend library hours to accommodate students who prefer studying late at night after breaking their fast. This provides a quiet and resourceful environment for students to catch up on their studies without disrupting their fasting schedule.

10. ***Peer support groups:*** Facilitate the creation of peer support groups or study circles specifically for fasting students. These groups can offer moral support, share study tips, and create a community where students can discuss and manage their challenges together.

11. ***Online learning resources:*** Increase the availability of online learning resources and recorded lectures, allowing fasting students to learn at their own pace and during the most suitable times, such as late nights or early mornings.

12. ***Relaxation and stress-management workshops:*** Provide specially designed sessions that concentrate on relaxation and stress reduction methods aimed at fasting students. Practices like mindfulness, meditation, and efficient time management are especially beneficial.

13. ***Special accommodations for exams:*** Provide special accommodations during exams, such as allowing extra time and breaks to pray or providing a quiet and comfortable environment. This can help alleviate exam pressure during fasting.

14. ***Engaging with parents and community:*** Schools can engage with parents and the local community to better understand fasting students' needs and seek support in implementing effective strategies.

15. ***Nutritional snacks for breaking the fast:*** Provide healthy snacks and water at school for students to break their fast immediately at sunset, especially if they have after-school activities or study sessions.

16. ***Mindfulness and reflection sessions:*** Organise short mindfulness or reflection sessions during the day. These sessions can offer spiritual and mental nourishment, which can be as crucial as physical nourishment.

17. ***Encouraging empathy among non-fasting students:*** Foster an environment of empathy and understanding among non-fasting students, teaching them the significance of Ramadan and how to support their fasting peers.

The Stress Spectrum: From Academia to Well-Being Concerns

British Parents and the High-Stakes Exam Culture

Within the UK, parental concerns about the psychological impact of pivotal exams like GCSEs and A-levels have gained attention. Reports from media outlets like *The Guardian* reveal that some children are grappling with severe anxiety symptoms, sleep disruption, and panic attacks, suggesting that the pressure to succeed academically has reached critical levels.[24]

Mental Health Struggles in the UK's Higher Education System

The article from *The Guardian* titled "'The way universities are run is making us ill': inside the student mental health crisis" delves into the escalating mental health crisis among university students in the UK. It highlights a significant shift in the nature of challenges faced by students over the years, moving from issues related to physical safety and security to an increasing number of mental health incidents. Terry Vass, head of security at Brunel University London, notes a marked increase in calls related to mental health emergencies, including situations where students are suicidal.

The piece outlines a surge in student anxiety, mental breakdowns, and depression, alongside a sharp rise in dropout rates and an alarming number

---

[24] Sarah Ayoub, "When Young Children Battle Anxiety, Parents Don't Need to Feel Like Helpless Bystanders," *The Guardian*, June 15, 2021, https://www.theguardian.com/commentisfree/2021/jun/16/when-young-children-battle-anxiety-parents-dont-need-to-feel-like-helpless-bystanders.

of suicides. It points to a broader crisis in young people's mental health, exacerbated by budget cuts to essential services over the last decade. The article discusses the pressures of modern university life, including the impact of high fees, the competitive job market, and the expectation for students to excel academically while managing financial and social pressures.

The narrative includes personal stories from students and insights from university staff, highlighting the struggle to balance academic demands with mental health needs. It criticises the commercialisation of higher education and the insufficient support structures for students facing mental health challenges. The article calls for a re-evaluation of the role of universities in supporting student well-being and questions whether the current educational model is sustainable or fair to students.[25]

Global Parental Pressure: A Comparative Look

When examining the international context, the Pew Research Center's Global Attitudes Project conducted a survey in 2011, revealing stark contrasts in perceptions of parental pressure on students between Americans and the Chinese. In the United States, a significant majority (64 percent) believe parents do not exert enough pressure on their children for academic success, a sentiment that has grown by eight percentage points since 2006. This view is now more uniformly shared across genders, age groups, educational backgrounds, and political affiliations, with notable increases among women, individuals aged thirty to forty-nine, those with some college education, and Democrats.

Conversely, in China, where the economy is booming, about two-thirds (68 percent) of the public believe parents place too much pressure on their children to succeed academically. This makes China the only country

---

[25] Samira Shackle, "'The Way Universities Are Run Is Making Us Ill': Inside the Student Mental Health Crisis," *The Guardian*, September 27, 2019, https://www.theguardian.com/society/2019/sep/27/anxiety-mental-breakdowns-depression-uk-students.

surveyed where a majority feels excessive parental pressure. Other countries, including Lithuania and Spain, share the American perspective somewhat. At the same time, India, Kenya, and Pakistan see significant portions of their populations believing in undue pressure by parents on students.

This survey highlights a cultural divide in attitudes towards educational pressure from parents, suggesting a complex interplay between societal expectations, educational aspirations, and perceptions of academic success across different countries.[26]

North America stands out for having a segment of parents refraining from exerting any academic pressure. Meanwhile, in regions like Latin America and the Middle East, there's an almost universal tendency among parents to place some expectation of academic performance on their children.

Exploring Regional Variations in Academic Pressure

Disparities in academic pressure across different regions can be attributed to a confluence of factors, ranging from economic to cultural influences. Understanding these variations uncovers multiple dimensions shaping the educational experiences of students globally.

Economic Factors Influencing Academic Pressure

Regions with more advanced economic development, industrialisation, and urbanisation often intensify competition for resources and opportunities, resulting in greater pressure. This is evident in areas like Asia, Latin America, and the Middle East, where the fast-paced life and the need to excel in a competitive environment may lead to heightened stress among students.

---

[26] "Americans Want More Pressure on Students, the Chinese Want Less," *Pew Research Center*, August 23, 2011, https://www.pewresearch.org/global/2011/08/23/americans-want-more-pressure-on-students-the-chinese-want-less/.

The Role of Population Density

Population density plays a crucial role, particularly in densely populated regions like Asia. The sheer number of individuals vying for limited resources, jobs, and educational opportunities naturally breeds a competitive atmosphere, escalating stress and pressure, particularly in academic settings.

Cultural Expectations and Academic Pressure

Cultural norms and values significantly influence perceptions and attitudes towards work, success, and education. In certain cultures, especially in some Asian contexts, there is a pronounced emphasis on hard work and academic excellence, amplifying pressures on students. Conversely, regions like Europe might cultivate a culture that values a balanced approach to work and life, contributing to an environment of relatively lower academic pressure. While this is a positive finding, there is room for further improvement.

The Role of Political and Social Stability

Political and social stability creates an atmosphere in which life pressures, including academic demands, are mitigated by a sense of security and opportunity. Social support structures, such as family and community networks, also serve as buffers against the pressures of life. However, in regions marred by instability or unrest, resulting uncertainty can translate into increased academic pressure, as education is often viewed as a pathway to stability and security.

The Study of Peer and Parental Influence in Pakistan

The document "The Effect of Peer and Parent Pressure on the Academic Achievement of University Students," authored by educators Dr Zarina Akhtar and Shamsa Aziz, delves into the nuanced impacts of social pressures on student academic outcomes. Conducted across various departments of a university, this research gathered data from 156 students, examining the differential effects of peer and parent pressures. The study reveals a complex landscape in which parental pressure, in contrast to peer pressure, tends to enhance student academic performance. This positive correlation between parental pressure and academic success is particularly pronounced among female students, suggesting a gendered dimension to how students respond to external pressures. Furthermore, the study uncovers department-specific variations in the impact of these pressures, hinting at the role of disciplinary cultures in shaping academic experiences. The research underscores the multifaceted nature of social influences on education, highlighting the need for a nuanced understanding of how different types of pressure can foster or hinder academic achievement. It points to the potential benefits of parental involvement in students' academic lives while also cautioning against the detrimental effects of negative peer influences, thereby offering valuable insights for educators, parents, and policymakers aiming to support student success.[27]

---

[27] Zarina Akhtar and Shamsa Aziz, "The Effect of Peer and Parent Pressure on the Academic Achievement of University Students," *Language in India* 11, no. 6 (June 2011).

CREATIVITY

The Intersection of Creativity and Education

The discussion surrounding the relationship between creativity and education has been a long-standing subject of debate. Many argue that the structure of traditional educational systems, intended for knowledge dissemination, can inadvertently stifle a student's creative development. Instead of nurturing innovation and original thought, these systems may create a confined space where students learn to produce work within a narrow set of acceptable standards.

Creativity as a Form of Liberation

A clear definition is essential to understanding creativity as a form of liberation. Creativity is often regarded as the ability to transcend traditional ideas, rules, patterns, relationships, and the like, to create meaningful new concepts, forms, methods, interpretations, and more. Sir Ken Robinson, a prominent thinker in educational innovation, eloquently defined creativity as "the process of having original ideas that have value."[28] This perspective places creativity at the core of personal growth and societal development.

The Early Promise of Creativity

In the 1960s, the quest to understand creativity took a scientific turn when general systems scientist Dr George Land and Beth Jarman developed a test for NASA to identify potential engineers and scientists with innovative thinking abilities. They extended this test to examine how children's creativity evolves with age. Their longitudinal study, spanning from testing children at five, ten, and fifteen years of age to adulthood, revealed startling statistics. While an impressive 98 percent of five-year-olds displayed creativity at a level deemed "genius," this percentage plummeted as these individuals grew older. Only a fraction of the original cohort maintained this level of imaginative prowess into adolescence and adulthood.[29]

The decline in creative thinking, as illustrated by Land and Jarman's research, was dramatic: from nearly all of five-year-olds to just a fraction in adulthood. These findings prompt a crucial discussion on the potential impact of traditional education methods on creativity. As students progress through the educational system, they often encounter an increasingly narrow framework for success – one that prioritises standardisation and conformity rather than fostering exploration and innovation.

The implication is clear: without adaptation, traditional educational environments may inadvertently stifle the innate creativity displayed by children. Instead of cultivating spaces where creativity and critical thinking can flourish, these models might unintentionally suppress these valuable traits. In response, there is a growing call for educational systems to embrace

---

[28] Sir Ken Robinson, "Ken Robinson - What is Creativity?" YouTube video, 10:47, September 18, 2017, https://www.youtube.com/watch?v=X1c3M6upOXA.

[29] Tedx Talks, "TEDxTucson George Land The Failure Of Success," YouTube video, 16:33, February 16, 2011, https://www.youtube.com/watch?v=ZfKMq-rYtnc.

a more expansive definition of learning success, one that actively includes and encourages creativity and innovation.

Fostering a Creative Educational Environment

Creating an educational system that values and nurtures creativity involves providing students the freedom to explore their interests passionately and without undue restriction. Encouraging students to think differently, challenge norms, and engage with their education in personally meaningful ways can lead to a more motivated and engaged student body. By reshaping education into a platform for exploration rather than merely a path to standardised achievements, we can aspire to preserve and enhance the creative capabilities that are abundant in early childhood.

Understanding creativity not as an optional extra but as an essential component of development is vital. If the goal of education is to prepare students not just for the world of today but for the challenges and opportunities of the future, then nurturing creativity becomes not just beneficial but necessary.

This Is Not Proper Art

Creativity Constrained: An Artistic Anecdote From Year 7

My initial foray into the formal study of art is a memory etched with both anticipation and disappointment. As a fervent enthusiast of drawing, my excitement for the first art lesson in Year 7 was palpable. Eager to master the strokes that could bring the dynamic scenes from comic books and cartoons to life on paper, I envisioned a canvas of limitless possibilities. However, the reality of the lesson fell short of my expectations.

The setup was simple: fruits placed on a table, an exercise in still life. This was not the artistic journey I had imagined, but I approached it with the optimism of a beginner, considering it a preliminary step towards more exhilarating projects. As the lessons progressed, there was no evolution from the initial exercise; the subject remained unvaryingly the same. Additionally, my preference for pencil work, with its rich gradations and textures, clashed with an expectation to infuse colour into our creations – an element I found little joy in incorporating.

Driven by a blend of frustration and a yearning for self-expression, I decided to diverge from the prescribed path. Once the obligatory fruits were sketched, I let my pencil dance to a different rhythm, illustrating a character from *Saint Seiya: Knights of the Zodiac*, a cherished Japanese cartoon that sparked my imagination.

Proudly, I presented this piece of personal artistry to my teacher, anticipating encouragement, or at least a nod to creative initiative. The response I received was a stark contrast to my expectations: "This is not the proper art that we do here." The rebuke was a jarring note, echoing the sentiment that only certain forms of expression were worthy of recognition within those classroom walls.

This encounter could have been a deterrent, yet it proved to be a defining moment. It imparted a vital lesson on the significance of self-expression and the perils of stifling artistic potential under the guise of educational norms. Undeterred by my teacher's narrow definition of "proper" art, I continued to sketch fervently outside the confines of the classroom. My expression found a sanctuary in a folder, a personal gallery of my progression as an artist.

Now, looking back at that collection of drawings, a sense of pride swells within me. The illustrations trace a journey of growth and resilience, proof of the undiminished joy I derive from drawing even today. My artistic pursuits, which endured despite the classroom's constrictions, continue to be a source of personal satisfaction and creative liberation.

This anecdote serves as a poignant reminder that the flame of creativity, once ignited, can withstand moments of disregard. It affirms that true artistry is not about conforming to a narrow set of standards but rather about honouring one's unique perspective and passions. The fulfilment that comes from such authenticity in self-expression is, in its own right, a masterpiece.

Grouchy Smurf

Tailoring Drama to Unlock Creative Potential

Venturing into the realm of drama education with a cohort of students known for their behavioural challenges was a role I approached with some reservations. Yet, this assignment, nestled within my broader teaching career, came with a unique liberty granted by the school's leadership: the freedom to tailor the curriculum to meet the distinct needs of my class.

In our initial gathering, I initiated a candid discussion, aiming to tap into the students' real-life preferences and dislikes. This exercise was not merely about breaking the ice; it was an effort to genuinely understand the individuals I was about to guide through the world of drama. Given my existing rapport with most of the students, this process of connection unfolded with relative ease.

Armed with these insights, I embarked on a creative enterprise: drafting an original script that mirrored the distinctive traits of each student. My goal was to infuse the play with elements that resonated personally with the cast, weaving in their individual quirks and personalities. To enrich the experience further, I incorporated music, dancing, and singing, adding layers of dynamism to the narrative. The strumming of my acoustic guitar was more than a background melody; it was a thread that tied the story to the reality of our shared space. The plot was intentionally hyperbolic and humorous, aiming to capture their attention and sustain their engagement.

The script, which consumed many nights to perfect, was finally brought to the classroom, ready to be inhabited by its inspirations. Together, we fine-tuned the dialogue and action, a collaborative refinement that deepened the students' investment in the play. I took on a role myself, the continually unhappy counterpart, akin to Grouchy Smurf, deliberately positioning myself against the grain of my inherent optimism.

As we moved through rehearsals and into the spotlight of the school's Easter concert, the students embraced their roles with a zeal that perhaps even they hadn't anticipated. Witnessing their transformation from hesitant participants to confident performers was an indication of the power of personalised education.

Reflecting on that singular year of teaching drama, I am reminded of the profound impact that a student-centred approach can have. Shaping the learning experience around the students' identities and interests inadvertently created a medium for their creativity and self-assurance to flourish. This attempt in drama, though a lone episode in my teaching career, reinforced an invaluable pedagogical truth: education at its best is not just about imparting knowledge but about igniting the spark of self-discovery and expression in every learner.

The Importance of Creative Freedom in Teaching

In the realm of education, creativity transcends mere artistic expression; it serves as a catalyst for overall growth, igniting curiosity and fostering deeper understanding. Central to this concept is the freedom afforded teachers to be imaginative and innovative in their approach, transforming conventional classrooms into vibrant hubs of exploration and discovery.

Granting teachers the latitude to craft lessons beyond the confines of a standard curriculum becomes a game-changer. It caters to diverse learning styles, recognising that not all students thrive in a traditional lecture-driven environment. Some may grasp concepts better through visual stimuli, while others may benefit from kinaesthetic or auditory activities. A creative approach allows educators to design lessons that resonate with everyone, ensuring inclusivity. It also sparks interest and engagement by introducing unconventional methods or materials, such as multimedia elements, field trips, hands-on experiments, and collaborative projects.

Moreover, a creative approach plays a crucial role in nurturing critical thinking and problem-solving skills. Instead of relying on rote memorisation, students are encouraged to question, analyse, and connect the dots. Such an environment cultivates independent thinkers, equipping them to tackle real-world challenges with a fresh perspective.

However, despite the undeniable advantages, there are reasons why teachers might hesitate to embrace this freedom. Institutional constraints, for instance, can be a significant barrier. Schools often adhere to set curriculums with tight schedules, leaving little room for deviation. The looming pressure of standardised testing adds another layer of complexity. When performance metrics hinge on specific exam results, educators might feel compelled to "teach to the test," prioritising test-taking techniques over holistic understanding. In France, many teachers have criticised the limited flexibility they are afforded by school administrators, who receive directives from the academy. This, I believe, is detrimental to student learning. I personally know many teachers in France and in England who have suffered from this, and some have already left the profession.

Additionally, there's the challenge of resources. Creative teaching often demands materials or technologies that might not be readily available or might strain the school's budget. There's also the fear of failure. Stepping away from tried-and-tested methods is a risk, and not every innovative approach will resonate with every class.

While the benefits of creative freedom in teaching are profound, from encouraging inclusive environments to honing real-world skills, there are genuine challenges to its implementation. The key is finding a balance, ensuring that while creativity flourishes, the core objectives of education aren't overshadowed.

Finding a school that encourages creative teaching can not only enhance your lessons but also positively impact the entire school community.

Meeting the Inspectors for the First Time

My first Ofsted inspection as a young, qualified teacher was a defining moment in my career, one that reinforced the value of authenticity in the classroom. The report from the inspection highlighted a moment during a Year 7 German lesson when I used my guitar and sang a composition about animals, prompting students to identify key words. This creative engagement was my usual approach, but it felt particularly validating to have it recognised by the inspectors. Here is the exact wording of the report:

"A magical moment and an excellent feature of a Year 7 lesson occurred as the teacher played the guitar and sang his own composition featuring favourite animals, from which students had to recognise key words."

The school atmosphere was tense when Ofsted first announced their visit. Everyone was on edge, knowing inspectors would be evaluating us. In the midst of this, I could have succumbed to the pressure and changed my teaching methods to something more conventional in an attempt to "impress." However, I stuck to my usual style, fearing any deviation might unsettle my students or come across as disingenuous if I were to suddenly transform in the face of an inspection.

Reflecting on this experience, it's clear that retaining a genuine teaching persona is crucial, especially under scrutiny. Any drastic deviations in style or content could unsettle students, leading to a cascade of confusion and anxiety. Their response, after all, is a direct reflection of the learning environment we cultivate. The assurance of continuity, that a lesson will proceed as usual even in the presence of visitors, communicates confidence and stability to the students.

Incorporating games into the classroom has been another area where authenticity and innovation converge. Games serve as a conduit for formative assessment, delivering immediate and actionable feedback. By embedding quizzes and interactive challenges into gameplay, students engage with the material in a dynamic and enjoyable manner, alleviating the stress that conventional testing methods can induce.

The project-based learning approach, in which students design their own educational games, has proven to be an effective method of assessment. This strategy not only gauges students' comprehension of the content but also encourages the development of a host of other skills, including collaboration, creativity, and critical thinking. The presentation of their games, both the design process and the end product, provides insights into their understanding and application of the subject matter.

Moreover, game analytics serve as a powerful tool to track and assess student progress. With educational games like Quizlet, Kahoot!, Français Facile, and Merriam-Webster, I can analyse data to fine-tune my teaching strategies and provide more focused feedback to my students. The immediacy of this feedback is invaluable, guiding instructional adjustments and pinpointing specific areas that require additional support or enrichment.

Looking back on that Ofsted inspection, I am reminded that staying true to my teaching philosophy, even under the microscope of external evaluation, is crucial.

Some of the Games That We Enjoy Using in Class

Below are a few examples of games I use in my lessons to promote learning and engagement:

Word Jumble. Word Jumble, a classic word game, finds valuable application in language learning. In this game, the teacher provides a list of jumbled words related to the target language. Students, either individually or in pairs, unscramble the words and write them correctly. This game is instrumental in promoting vocabulary acquisition and spelling skills.

Language Jeopardy. Language Jeopardy serves as an effective tool for reviewing vocabulary or grammar concepts. In this game, the teacher creates a Jeopardy board with categories related to the target language, such as "verbs," "adjectives," and "food vocabulary." Students take turns selecting a category and answering questions related to that category. This game promotes recall and retention of language concepts.

Boggle. Boggle is a word game that can be adapted for language learning. The teacher provides a grid of letters related to the target language. Students, individually or in pairs, identify as many words as possible using the letters in the grid. This game contributes to vocabulary acquisition and spelling skills. It's known as *Baccalauréat* in French.

Charades. Charades, a game for practising language skills like verbs, adjectives, or prepositions, encourages interactive learning. The teacher provides a list of target words or phrases, and students act them out without speaking while others guess the word or phrase. This game promotes communication and critical thinking skills, with the flexibility for students to use words alongside miming.

Two-Word Tango. Two-Word Tango is a fun game frequently played with my French and Spanish language students. A few students stand in a line at the front of the classroom, taking turns saying a French or Spanish word with music playing in the background. Some choose to say a short phrase, but that's not in their advantage. The music provides a gap of one bar for each student to say their word. The music continues for two and a half minutes and gradually speeds up. Students are not allowed to repeat any words that have already been spoken. If they hesitate or fail to say a word during their turn, they are eliminated. Eliminated students silently return to their seats. The game continues until the music stops or only one student remains, with multiple winners possible if more than one student remains after the music stops.

Taboo. Taboo is a word game using descriptive language and circumlocution in an engaging language activity. In this game, the teacher provides a list of target words or phrases, and students take turns describing them to a partner without using certain "taboo" words. This game encourages the development of communication and critical thinking skills.

I hold a particular fondness for the Taboo game, and my students seem to share the enjoyment. To expand on the description, Taboo is a word-guessing game in which I divide the class into two teams. The objective is to describe a word or short phrase on the board to your team without using a list of related words considered "taboo" or off-limits. During their turn, each team can have as many members at the front of the classroom as they want, as long as there is at least one person left to present the word or phrase that needs to be guessed. The keyword or phrase appears on the top of the whiteboard, and on one side are the "taboo" words that the player cannot use in their description. For instance, if the keyword is "apple," the taboo words might be "fruit," "red," "pie," and "tree."

During their turn, the team attempts to describe as many keywords or phrases to their teammates as possible under a time limit, typically around ninety seconds. The challenge lies in avoiding the use of any taboo words while providing hints. The team earns a point for each correctly guessed word or phrase, but the turn ends if a taboo word is used.

The game continues with each team taking turns and concludes after the bell rings or when I run out of keywords. To win, a team must accumulate the most points by the end of the game. Taboo is popular because it encourages creative thinking and effective communication, making it both challenging and entertaining.

Although Taboo was originally a card game, I have adapted it to suit my purposes. Adding a personal touch, such as using funny words or even incorporating some of the students' names in the phrases they need to guess, enhances the fun – for example, *Shrek et Tanya sont intelligents* ("Shrek and Tanya are intelligent"), with Tanya being one of the students' names. Personalising the game for each class always brings excitement and laughter, even from the more reserved students in the class.

REFLECTING ON SCHOOL EXPERIENCES: A PERSONAL AND GLOBAL PERSPECTIVE

Reflecting on one's school days often evokes a mixed bag of emotions and memories, significantly influenced by the educational climate and culture of the country. Personal experiences can vary greatly based on the specific environment of the school and the teaching approaches used. As an educator with roots in Haiti, my own retrospection of primary school is tinged with the austerity of their prevailing teaching methods.

In my experience, teachers wielded a strictness that bordered on severity, employing teaching methods that, through the lens of my current professional understanding, I recognise as ill-suited to fostering a nurturing learning environment. Such rigidity can dampen the joy of learning, casting a long shadow over the formative years of education that should ideally be filled with curiosity and discovery.

Now, let's engage in a simple reflective exercise to underscore the lasting impact of educational experiences. If I ask you to quickly think of two positive school memories, you might find this challenging. The difficulty of this task suggests that, for many, school experiences lean more heavily towards the challenging or negative. On the flip side, if asked to recall two negative memories, these might come to mind with disconcerting ease, which speaks volumes about the human tendency to retain and recall negative experiences more readily than positive ones.

This propensity isn't just a reflection of personal bias; it's rooted in what psychologists may refer to as the negativity bias, the idea that things of a more negative nature have a greater effect on one's psychological state and processes than neutral or positive things. This could be a factor in why many individuals might find it easier to recollect adverse school experiences over favourable ones.

It's important to consider this phenomenon when discussing school memories because it highlights the critical role that educational systems play in a child's life. The environment we create in our schools can provide students with either a reservoir of positive memories that buoy them through life or a well of less pleasant recollections that may colour their perception of learning and education for years to come.

The Story of Jerry

Jerry's experience in our French class is an anecdote that encapsulates the delicate balance between learning and the teaching methods used. This story, etched in my memory from my primary school years, is a complex incident that blurs the lines between a positive and a negative experience.

Mr Maxo, our teacher, held unquestionable authority in the classroom, a common setup in our primary school. The situation unfolded on what was a routine day until Mr Maxo presented us with a seemingly straightforward task: to write a dictated phrase on the board. Jerry, a classmate, was called upon to transcribe a phrase onto the blackboard. The phrase in question, *J'en veux* ("I want some"), seemed simple enough, but the lack of context turned it into a linguistic trap. Jerry, with the innocence of a primary school student, wrote *Jean veut* ("Jean [a person's name] wants"). This was an understandable error given the aural similarity of the phrases in the absence of context.

Observing Jerry's mistake and the consequent harsh discipline he received set a daunting stage for my turn. With the benefit of insight gained from his error, I wrote the phrase *J'en veux*, which Mr Maxo accepted as correct. While my decision spared me from the same fate as Jerry, the fairness of the outcome was questionable.

In the aftermath, the incident lingered in my thoughts, stirring a sense of injustice. It was clear that Mr Maxo's approach, which lacked the provision of adequate context, inadvertently positioned Jerry for failure. This error was compounded by the lack of explanation following the reprimand, leaving both Jerry and myself in a state of confusion. The realisation dawned on me that without context and clarity, education could become a minefield in which students might be unfairly penalised for misunderstandings rather than guided towards understanding.

The lesson I derived from this event transcended the immediate relief of having avoided punishment. It instilled in me an appreciation for the critical role of context in education. It underscored how imperative it is for me to provide clear guidance and explanations to foster understanding, rather than simply policing right or wrong answers. The memory serves as a reminder of the delicate balance teachers hold in shaping a student's learning experience, in which the absence of clarity can lead to unnecessary mistakes and, more importantly, to a student's loss of confidence and enthusiasm for learning.

What Are Your Best Memories of Being in School?

Here are some examples of what people have shared with me regarding their most cherished experiences in school:

Positive social interactions: Many individuals recall positive experiences with their friends and classmates in school. These social interactions fostered a sense of belonging, support, and opportunities for personal growth and development.

Field trips: Numerous people highlight positive experiences with field trips that gave them the chance to explore new places and learn in a hands-on manner. Field trips provide a refreshing change from traditional classroom learning, allowing students to see real-world applications of the concepts they study.

Team projects: Positive experiences often involve collaborative team projects, fostering communication, problem-solving, and leadership skills. Such projects can instil a sense of accomplishment and pride in the final product.

Learning new skills: Many individuals cherish the moments of learning a new skill or hobby in school, be it playing a musical instrument, mastering a foreign language, or engaging in a new sport. Learning new skills contributes to personal growth, a sense of accomplishment, and avenues for self-expression and creativity.

Graduation: Positive experiences frequently revolve around final celebration assemblies, proms, graduation ceremonies, and other milestones marking the end of a significant period of students' lives. Graduation ceremonies provide a sense of accomplishment, closure, and opportunities to celebrate with friends and family.

Positive relationships with teachers: Fond memories often include positive experiences with teachers who were supportive, inspiring, or instrumental in helping them discover a love for learning. Almost everyone can recall a teacher who made them feel valued and encouraged pursuit of their interests.

Extracurricular activities: Positive experiences extend to extracurricular activities such as sports, music, or drama. These activities foster a sense of belonging and identity and provide opportunities for personal growth and skill development.

Cultural events and festivals: Cultural events or festivals that allowed individuals to learn about and celebrate different cultures and traditions were shared positive experiences. These events promote cultural awareness, empathy, and understanding, and provide opportunities for personal growth and self-expression.

For instance, a study by the National Federation of State High School Associations revealed that students participating in high school sports reported higher levels of self-esteem, leadership skills, and academic achievement.

As I reflect on that experience now, it becomes increasingly evident to me how important it is for teachers to cultivate creativity and permit students to express themselves in their unique ways. Each child possesses distinct interests and talents, and it's imperative to encourage and nurture those talents. Granting children the freedom to explore their creativity allows them to realise their full potential and produce their best possible work.

Now, I invite you to reminisce about your favourite memories from your school days, whether in primary or secondary school. Do any of the points I've highlighted resonate with your experiences? What about your worst memory? Is it something that still affects you or can be observed in today's educational landscape (if you are currently a student)?

SURPRISE AND FLEXIBILITY

Offer Choices as Often as Possible

The integration of surprise and flexibility into the framework of teaching has the potential to transform the classroom environment and enrich the educational experience. Drawing inspiration from Jean de La Fontaine's fable, in which the reed stands resilient because it bends with the wind rather than breaking,[30] I have woven the principle of adaptability into my educational practice.

Surprise, when coupled with flexibility, becomes a potent element in teaching, leaving an indelible mark on a student's memory and setting a teacher apart. It keeps the learning environment dynamic, making a lasting impression on students. The power of surprise lies in its capacity to disrupt patterns and expectations. When students anticipate a punitive response to misbehaviour, choosing instead to respond with understanding can have a profound impact. I experienced this when I opted to offer help to a disruptive student, not only defusing the situation but also establishing a channel of trust and communication. This unexpected act of kindness allowed the student to share their struggles and work towards improvement.

---

[30] Jean de La Fontaine, "The Oak and the Reed," in *Fables of La Fontaine*, trans. Walter Thornbury (London: Cassell, Petter, and Galpin, 1868).

For lasting impact of these surprise moments, they must be part of a consistent teaching philosophy. It requires a deliberate effort to embody this approach, making it ingrained in one's teaching style. As this approach became habitual for me, the classroom underwent a significant transformation. It went beyond improved engagement or learning outcomes; it became a space for cultivating relationships. The classroom became a place of shared understanding, where the rigidity of traditional punishment gave way to the fluidity of human connection.

In essence, the readiness to adapt and the ability to bring delight through the unexpected are not mere tactics; they are fundamental to a teaching philosophy that views education as a dynamic, relational, and responsive journey. Through this lens, I have observed that when students perceive me as an ally rather than an enforcer, their educational journey becomes more engaging, impactful, and harmonious.

A Guitar and a Cake

The utilisation of music in the classroom exemplifies the impact of unconventional teaching methods on student engagement. My decision to replace the monotonous tone of a textbook recording with the strumming and singing of a guitar validated this approach. The formal and unvarying voice of the textbook often failed to capture the students' attention, but with music, the atmosphere transformed. The once listless room suddenly became vibrant with curiosity and surprise. Initially, I sang without expecting them to answer the exercises; it was about letting them experience the moment. This initial encounter with the material through song was crucial – it prioritised engagement before education.

By the second time, the novelty had evolved into a learning tool. As I sang, I encouraged the students to focus on the lyrics and uncover the answers to the questions before them. With my guitar in hand, I had the flexibility to slow down or repeat crucial parts of the script, guiding those who seemed adrift in this new sea of learning. The dreariness associated with standard audio recordings dissipated and was replaced by a room full of engaged learners. This experience solidified my belief that sometimes the simplest changes can reignite a child's interest in learning.

The decision to replace the textbook recording with my own singing was driven by instinct. Observing my students' faces and body language, I could tell they were becoming bored, anxious, and disengaged. Each time I mentioned a listening activity, the classroom atmosphere noticeably dimmed. I recall my own experiences in German lessons, when I often struggled with the listening activities and dreaded them, mainly because the teacher expected everyone to participate. These memories, coupled with my students' reactions, prompted me to trust my instincts. So, I picked up my guitar and approached the task in a more creative and engaging way.

This philosophy isn't new to me; it resonates from my own days as a student. At seventeen, in the austere setting of Madame Rogué's history class, none of us would have considered crossing the invisible line of her strictness. Yet, one day, she delivered a jolt that remains vivid in my memory. With a dramatic pause and a slap on the desk, she commanded the room's attention with an announcement of *"cessons les hostilités"* ("let's cease hostilities"). The tension that phrase conjured was instantly undercut by the most unexpected of sights: Madame Rogué revealing a cake from within a plastic bag, a homemade offering to her students.

That singular act of kindness, so out of character from the Madame Rogué we thought we knew, endeared her to us. It broke down barriers, showing us the complex nature of someone we had pegged as strict and uncompromising. Such moments become keystones of our educational journey, serving as reminders of the humanity that underlies education. It is these instances that stay with us, shaping not just our academic lives but also our perceptions of people and the world.

Madame Rogué's surprise demonstrated that the role of a teacher is also to build a rapport and create a nurturing environment for learning. That day, she didn't just share a cake; she shared a part of herself, fostering a connection that would resonate with us for years to come. In my case, it was a lesson in pedagogy as much as a fond memory; her action highlighted that sometimes, stepping out of the box can be the most effective educational strategy.

Now, you might wonder how you could achieve a similar outcome with your class, especially if you cannot play a musical instrument, sing, or bake. I am aware of these potential limitations and have compiled a list of other suggestions that may be worth trying. Feel free to personalise and combine these ideas as you see fit to suit your unique teaching style and classroom environment:

1. *Interactive Technology:* Infuse lessons with interactive technology. This could be as simple as using educational apps or games that align with the lesson's objectives. Virtual reality (VR) or augmented reality (AR) experiences can also provide immersive learning experiences.

2. *Guest Speakers:* Invite guest speakers from diverse fields to share real-world experiences related to the subject matter. This could be anyone from local community leaders to experts in the field, offering students a fresh perspective.

3. *Outdoor Classes:* Break the routine by occasionally holding classes outdoors or in unconventional locations. A change of scenery can invigorate students and make the learning experience more memorable and engaging.

4. *Hands-on Projects:* Implement hands-on, project-based learning that allows students to create something tangible. This could be anything from science experiments and art projects to building a small model or prototype.

5. *Role-Playing and Simulations:* Use role-playing or simulations to bring subjects to life. This method is particularly effective in history and literature classes, where students can act out historical events or scenes from a book.

6. ***Themed Days:*** Organise themed days around a subject, making the day's activities cohesive around a particular theme or topic. This can also include dress-up days to make the experience more immersive.

7. ***Creative Writing and Storytelling:*** Encourage creative expression through storytelling or creative writing exercises. This allows students to use their imagination and could be related to the lesson topic.

8. ***Interactive Quizzes and Competitions:*** Use quizzes and competitions to make learning more dynamic. Tools like Kahoot! or Quizizz can turn quizzes into interactive and competitive games.

9. ***Classroom Transformation:*** Temporarily transform the classroom to align with a specific theme or subject being studied, such as turning the classroom into a mock archaeological site for a history lesson.

10. ***Collaborative Art Projects:*** Engage the class in a collaborative art project in which each student contributes to a more significant piece. This could be a mural, a large canvas, or a digital project.

11. ***Mystery Solving or Treasure Hunts:*** Design a mystery-solving activity or a treasure hunt that incorporates lesson objectives, encouraging students to work together to solve puzzles or find clues.

12. ***Cultural Celebrations:*** Introduce students to different cultures through celebrations, music, and food. This could be aligned with language classes or social studies.

13. ***Personal Story Sharing:*** Share personal stories or experiences related to the subject. Teachers sharing their own journey can inspire and connect with students on a personal level.

14. ***Science Demonstrations:*** Conduct exciting science demonstrations or experiments that captivate attention. Engaging activities like chemical reactions, physics demonstrations, and biology dissections bring abstract concepts to life, promoting understanding.

15. ***Mindfulness and Yoga Sessions:*** Introduce short mindfulness or yoga sessions to help students relax and refocus, which is especially beneficial during stressful periods like exams.

ACKNOWLEDGING THE STUDENTS' OTHER SKILLS

Showing Understanding

One of the main reasons I chose to stay in England after leaving Paris was the abundance of opportunities for personal growth and development. While some who have lived in France could see things differently, I speak from my personal experience and that of acquaintances, be it relatives, friends, or connections. In England, I could explore and develop a diverse set of skills, including music, radio broadcasting, translation, interpretation, and salsa teaching, as well as various other subjects. The freedom to pursue many interests has allowed me to flourish both personally and professionally. Why is this relevant to our discussion?

Understanding and acknowledging a student's potential beyond the classroom is essential for instilling confidence and fostering success in their academic pursuits. Like I found opportunities for development in England, students also possess diverse talents and interests that can enhance their learning experiences.

Teachers can create a more engaging and supportive learning environment by investing time in understanding their students and their varied interests. For instance, a student excelling in music but struggling in mathematics might find clarity by integrating musical concepts with math lessons. Personally, I took the opposite approach, leveraging my mathematical knowledge to enhance my music reading skills.

Likewise, a student with artistic talents might encounter difficulties in writing. By introducing creative writing assignments or visual storytelling exercises, their skills could improve significantly. I recall a student in my Spanish class who hesitated to speak aloud because of concerns about her pronunciation, feeling like a "failure" compared to her peers. During a parent-teacher meeting, I discovered her active involvement in a theatre club outside of school and her deep passion for acting.

In response, I adapted my teaching approach by incorporating class activities involving acting and creating dialogues aligned with the curriculum. This adjustment bolstered her confidence, leading her to excel in acting compared to her peers and transforming her self-perception. No longer viewing herself as a failure, she became more willing to read aloud in Spanish.

Recognising a student's potential beyond the confines of the classroom can significantly enhance their confidence and self-esteem, leading to greater success across all areas of their lives. Encouraging students to explore their diverse skills and interests not only nurtures a growth mindset but instils a lifelong love of learning.

In the schools where I have worked, many of my students are bilingual, often speaking languages other than English. Leveraging this knowledge, I've employed creative ways to help them grasp concepts in French or Spanish while maintaining a focus on English. Initially, coaxing them to converse in their mother tongue within the classroom proved to be a challenge. The surprising reluctance and embarrassment they exhibited when it came to speaking their native language underscored the societal stigma associated with multilingualism.

To bridge this gap, I shared anecdotes from my own childhood, recounting my initial reluctance to speak Creole in front of my school friends. Most of my classmates who were bilingual felt similar shame when it came to conversing in their mother tongue in front of their French friends. In my late secondary school years, I transitioned from embarrassment to a profound sense of pride.

My perspective shifted when I observed my peers confidently conversing in Arabic with their parents and classmates on the playground. Despite not finding anyone at my school who spoke my native language, this experience fuelled a sense of pride in my own heritage. It inspired me to incorporate Creole dialogues into the comics I created during school. These comics became popular, partly because my friends and I shared a similar taste in cartoons and comics. This experience enabled me to connect with my students, successfully fostering a sense of pride in their multilingual abilities.

With this battle won, I could seamlessly integrate their language's grammar points with those of French, Spanish, and, in the earlier stages of my teaching career, German. This holistic approach allows me to draw parallels, facilitating their understanding of English language rules as well.

Learning from and with My Students

Learning from and alongside my students has always been a cornerstone of my teaching philosophy. As an example, within the realm of language development, the memorisation of vocabulary lists emerges as a task that can be both tedious and challenging, depending on the complexity of the words, given that many of my students are polyglots. I encountered an opportunity to assist two polyglots in Year 8, a boy and a girl, who were grappling with memorising a French vocabulary list.

In an effort to provide more effective support, I proposed a challenge. I encouraged them to translate the same French vocabulary list assigned as homework into their mother tongue – either Urdu or Punjabi (though regrettably, I cannot recall which). What added excitement to this initiative was my lack of knowledge in either Punjabi or Urdu.

I made a commitment to my students that I would put forth my best effort to perform well on the test. My objective wasn't to outperform them but to demonstrate what could be achieved with dedicated learning. This announcement sparked genuine surprise and excitement among both students and the entire class. I had never seen a class await a vocabulary test so eagerly.

The challenge was set with a nine-day timeframe for learning the vocabulary list, with just one lesson scheduled within that period. Remarkably, almost half of the class requested I move the test to the very next lesson. Their enthusiasm was not solely driven by a desire to take the test sooner; rather, it was fuelled by curiosity about how well (or poorly) their teacher would fare.

I made an additional promise to the entire class: I would award bonus points equivalent to the difference in marks they had over me. For instance, if I scored eight out of fifteen, and a student earned nine out of fifteen, they would receive an extra point, bringing their final score to ten. I coined this *le bonus d'amour-propre*, or the "pride bonus." My intention was to instil pride in them as they surpassed their teacher. For me, finding immense pride in being surpassed by those I aimed to elevate beyond my own achievements became a testament to the impact of collaborative learning.

The Multilingual Classroom Advantage

Throughout my teaching journey, I have found myself in classrooms echoing with the sounds of languages from across the globe. Imagine, amidst just twenty-nine students, being surrounded by eighteen different languages! This is not just a fun fact; it's a genuine advantage when teaching.

This linguistic diversity becomes a gold mine for me, especially when navigating complex grammar concepts. Let's consider the different ways languages might address someone to convey "you," depending on the relationship:

- In **French**, it's *Tu* for a friend and *Vous* in a more formal setting.
- **Spanish** speakers use *Tú* for a casual chat and *Usted* for formal or official interactions.
- Over in **Croatian**, it's *Ti* for the informal and *Voče* for the formal occasions.
- And in **German**, they would use *Du* with friends and *Sie* in more formal interactions.

When explaining the French *Tu* and *Vous* to a Spanish speaker, I might point out the parallels with *Tú* and *Usted*. It's akin to providing a familiar stepping stone, easing the understanding of something new.

Employing these linguistic connections goes beyond simplifying the lesson. It's a deliberate effort to recognise and value the diverse backgrounds of each student. Each time a student identifies a fragment of their own language reflected in the lesson, it's a gentle reminder that despite our diverse sounds, we're all part of this global conversation. This approach acknowledges and celebrates the various backgrounds of my students, creating a more inclusive and relatable learning environment.

Witnessing students discover facets of their cultural identity within their lessons is a beautiful experience. It reinforces the idea that, while languages may vary in words and syntax, the essence of communication remains universal.

Vision for the Future: Innovative Proposals for Transforming Education

It's safe to say that we all recognise the need for change in the school system. Change is a daunting prospect for the human mind, whether it leads to improvement or decline. Our differences lie in the methods we propose for making these changes and improving the system. Here are some constructive suggestions we can explore:

Flexible Curriculum: Develop a curriculum that adapts to the changing needs of students and society, allowing more personalised learning paths.

Incorporate Life Skills: Integrate practical life skills such as financial literacy, emotional intelligence, and problem-solving into the core curriculum.

Diverse Teaching Methods: Encourage educators to employ a variety of teaching techniques, catering to different learning styles and abilities.

Modernise Facilities: Upgrade school infrastructure to create a conducive learning environment, incorporating modern technology and comfortable spaces.

Focus on Well-Being: Prioritise the mental and physical well-being of both students and staff by offering counselling services and stress-relief programmes.

Community Engagement: Foster stronger connections between schools and their communities, including parents, to enhance local support and resources.

Teacher Training: Invest in continuous professional development for educators, ensuring they stay abreast of the latest teaching methods. Most importantly, create an environment where trying new approaches is encouraged without fear of disqualification by the school senior leadership team or the academy inspectors (Ofsted).

Assessment Reform: Rethink assessment methods to de-emphasise standardised testing and promote holistic evaluation. Align school policies with the acknowledgement that each student is an individual, avoiding a one-size-fits-all approach.

Cultural Awareness: Equip students to become well-rounded global citizens. In today's interconnected world, it's essential that students are well versed in their local histories and cultures and possess a broader understanding of global dynamics.

Student-Centred Learning: Shift the educational focus from content delivery to actively engaging students in critical thinking, problem-solving, and project-based learning.

By embracing these suggestions, we can pave the way for a more adaptable, supportive, and effective educational system that prepares students for the challenges of the future.

My personal goal is to establish a school, anywhere in the world, where I can instil in students the freedom to evolve into innovative thinkers, real-world problem-solvers, and fearless individuals unafraid of failure.

Considering all I have shared so far, you might be wondering whether I perceive myself as a developing teacher, a standard teacher, or a teacher-educator. Yes, I do categorise myself as a teacher-educator. Not solely because colleagues or inspectors have affirmed the positive impact I have had on my students academically – as one can always prepare for their visits and present lessons in the best light possible. Instead, I deem myself a teacher-educator because the majority of my students have explicitly conveyed this sentiment, either in person or in writing, through their interactions in my lessons. Who better to assess the effectiveness of what you claim to teach than the students themselves? Therefore, based on the criteria outlined in this book, the answer is affirmative – I am a teacher-educator. However, I remain mindful that these standards are continually challenged by the ever-changing nature of life.

FEEDBACK

Marks Versus Meaningful Feedback

At its core, feedback is a response or reaction that informs someone about their performance or output, aimed at guiding improvement and facilitating learning. Yet merely providing feedback is not sufficient; it needs to resonate with the recipient. For students, meaningful feedback acts as a mirror, reflecting not only what they've done but illuminating how they can progress further. It transcends simply pointing out the right or wrong, delving deeper into the "why" and "how" of their performance. The significance of feedback in the educational landscape cannot be overstated. When done right, it bridges the gap between current understanding and potential growth. It transforms mistakes into valuable lessons and successes into stepping stones for further achievements. Most importantly, it positions students as active participants in their learning journey, propelling them beyond just absorbing information to actively refining their skills and understanding.

The dichotomy between marks and meaningful feedback remains a pressing issue in education. It's a scenario well known to educators: a student receives a graded assessment, and immediately, their attention fixates on that singular number or letter indicating their score. That singular mark, in many cases, holds outsized influence, often overshadowing the rich, detailed feedback provided alongside. For many students, that score becomes a label, a summation of their efforts that obscures the constructive insights capable of fostering genuine growth. And why wouldn't it? This fixation on grades is not unfounded; it is a byproduct of an educational culture that consistently prioritises quantifiable achievements.

The issue with this grade-centric view is that it condenses the complexity of learning into a simplistic measure, frequently ignoring the richness inherent in learning itself. The true value of educational assessments lies in the feedback – those tailored comments that furnish students with clear guidance on improving and developing their skills. Changing this ingrained perspective is one of the many challenges educators confront. We need to elevate the status of feedback, positioning it as a pivotal element of the educational dialogue, rather than a footnote to a grade.

To propel this shift, feedback must transcend generic platitudes; it must be specific, actionable, and connected to the individual's learning objectives. It's about igniting a conversation that focuses on the learning process, understanding mistakes, celebrating strengths, and charting a path for future progress.

However, the ideal of personalised feedback runs into the stark reality of classroom logistics. With teachers often handling vast numbers of students across multiple classes, providing in-depth, individualised feedback is a Herculean task. Addressing this necessitates structural changes in the education system. Reducing class sizes to around twenty students and alleviating teachers of excessive administrative burdens by employing support staff are pivotal steps that could furnish educators with the necessary bandwidth to engage in meaningful feedback practices.

Elevating Feedback Beyond Clichés

Elevating feedback in education requires a departure from habitual phrases that, while affirming, lack the specificity needed for concrete student improvement. Comments like "well done" or "try harder," while convenient, do not address students' core need for precise and actionable guidance in their learning journey. Vague or overly generic feedback not only proves unhelpful but also risks inadvertently conveying a lack of genuine engagement with the student's efforts.

To truly elevate the learning experience, feedback must be as individualised and specific as the diverse array of students we teach. It should dissect and commend particular strengths, such as recognising a student's acute understanding of a literary character's motivations or acknowledging the sophistication of their argument structure. Similarly, when improvement is needed, feedback should illuminate specific paths students can tread to elevate their understanding – whether through a review of foundational concepts or by applying theoretical knowledge to practical situations.

Crafting feedback that is clear, detailed, and directly related to the elements of students' work transforms the feedback loop from a one-way communication into a meaningful conversation. This approach resonates with students, demonstrating thoughtful evaluation and investment in their individual progress. It shifts the narrative from mere grades to active participation in the process of learning and development.

Nuanced feedback reinforces students' strengths and clearly addresses areas for growth, making the learning process transparent and goals attainable. Understanding precisely what they did well empowers students to build on those successes, while clarity on areas of improvement equips them with the tools to enhance their skills. This specificity and guidance not only bolsters students' confidence but also equips them with the knowledge and skills to become self-regulated learners capable of critically assessing their own work.

Thus, departing from feedback clichés and adopting a detailed, constructive, and personalised approach can significantly impact students' academic progress and overall motivation. It reinforces the educator's role not merely as an evaluator but as a mentor and guide in their students' journeys towards academic excellence and self-improvement.

The critical importance of timeliness in providing feedback cannot be overstated in educational settings. Feedback's value is intrinsically tied to its delivery time. After submitting assignments, students enter a period of expectancy, a psychological state in which the anticipation of results can significantly impact their engagement and emotional well-being. With each passing day, the potential efficacy of feedback starts to diminish; the immediacy and context that give feedback its power to resonate begin to fade.

Delayed feedback poses multiple issues. Firstly, there's the issue of waning interest. What starts as eager anticipation can slowly turn into indifference as students mentally shift to other projects and priorities. When the feedback finally arrives, the educational moment, ripe for constructive reflection, may have already passed. Moreover, prolonged waiting can give rise to anxiety – an emotion that not only clouds judgement but can also hinder the ability to absorb and act on the feedback received.

Conversely, promptly provided feedback capitalises on the students' heightened state of receptiveness. When feedback is given while the details of their efforts are still vivid in their memories, students can directly correlate their work with the feedback, fostering a deeper understanding of the material and a clearer sense of how to improve. This immediacy enhances the learning experience by making it active and dynamic, rather than a passive reflection on past work.

Providing swift feedback communicates to students that their work is a priority and that their learning journey is actively supported. It underscores an educator's commitment to their students' progress and conveys respect for the time and effort they have invested. Additionally, prompt feedback cycles encourage a culture of continuous progress and adaptability, in which gained insights can be immediately integrated into current and future academic pursuits.

In essence, timely feedback is a foundation of effective teaching and learning. It sustains the momentum of learning and ensures that the educational dialogue between teacher and student remains open, relevant, and impactful.

The Power of Personalised Verbal Feedback

The essence of effective feedback lies in both the content and its delivery – a craft I've honed and refined throughout my teaching career. I have grown to appreciate the distinctive potency of personalised verbal feedback. While written notes hold merit, providing a tangible record students can refer back to, the dynamic nature of verbal feedback brings its own set of powerful advantages.

Verbal feedback possesses an immediacy and urgency that written words on a page might not convey. When I speak directly to a student, I am not just transferring information; I am engaging with them. The nuances of my tone, the pitch of enthusiasm or concern, even pauses for emphasis, make the feedback feel more significant. There's a certain magic in the way spoken feedback demands attention, perhaps because it is fleeting, or perhaps because it speaks to the human need for direct interaction.

Moreover, speaking directly to a student is a form of recognition; it's a tacit acknowledgement of their individual efforts and the distinct value of their contribution. In contrast to the static nature of written comments, a verbal exchange is inherently personal. It's a dialogue, not a monologue, providing space for immediate clarification and deeper understanding. Students can respond, question, and engage in a way that written feedback does not typically allow.

This is not to diminish the value of written feedback. On the contrary, combining both written and verbal feedback can offer the best of both worlds – the durability and detail of notes with the warmth and immediacy of conversation. Unfortunately, because of time constraints, I have primarily applied this dual approach with senior classes. Yet, I harbour the ambition to extend this practice to younger students, firmly believing that they, too, would reap the benefits of this rich feedback culture.

I recall watching a colleague who mastered the art of integrating written feedback with verbal discourse. With her Year 12 students, she not only provided detailed annotations but also dedicated class time specifically for discussing these comments. This approach facilitated a holistic feedback cycle; students could digest the written advice and then engage in clarifying discussions, further solidifying their understanding and learning. It was clear that the students deeply appreciated this method, engaging with the material and their teacher with a heightened level of inquiry and interest.

Moving forwards, my ambition is to incorporate this balanced feedback model more consistently across all levels of teaching. The challenge is, and always has been, finding time within the packed curricular demands and the busy rhythm of the academic year. Yet, the endeavour to do so is worthwhile, for the payoff is a richer, more engaged learning experience for every student.

Samples of Feedback

This image features a sample of a student's work that I have evaluated. The feedback below was printed and given to the student, along with instructions to affix it in her French book. The image presented here is a photograph taken from her book, which I had collected for grading purposes. It's important to note that I did not make any marks directly in her book. The goal of this exercise was for students to leverage my feedback to enhance their tasks during subsequent lessons. During this time, I was available to answer questions and provide further clarifications as needed.

Sample Work

Line 1: «*je pense*» ("I think") is ALWAYS FOLLOWED BY *QUE* ("that").

Line 2: «*ne eu pas milieu des champs*» does not make sense. I cannot guess what you were trying to say. Come and talk to me so I can help you rephrase it.

Line 3: «*il y a beaucoup de nature*» ("there is a lot of nature") – change it to «*il y a beaucoup de paysage vert*» ("there are a lot of green landscapes") for better clarity.

Content: 6/15

Range/complex: 5/12

Accuracy: 4/5

Total: 15/32 (You would have gotten up to 15 for CONTENT if you had mentioned two sentences which contain an opinion AND a justification EACH – e.g., «*je pense QUE ma maison est super, parce qu'il y a un grand jardin*»

Also, you could have received more than 6 for RANGE if you had more than just one tense.

Note that you received 4/5 for accuracy, meaning that your piece of writing is great for what the task requires: a description of a house that you want to sell. So, just remember that the exam board will need you to include the things I mentioned above to be eligible for a higher mark. Thank you very much for doing this one, Tyler.

Below is a survey I conducted with my Year 11 class to assess the helpfulness of my written feedback to them. I have changed the students' names to protect their privacy.

NAMES	TARGET GRADE FRENCH	Pre-Public Exam Result	11 Predicted French 2	what my students say about the written feedback comments, specifically
Janet	7	8	8	graded work is helpful/add suggestions of good vocab/highlighting the good bits in her work
Vicky	5	4	5	graded work is helpful/correct the mistakes rather than letting her work it out on her own/highlighting the good bits in her work
Anna	8	5	6	graded work is helpful/correct the mistakes rather than letting her work it out on her own/highlighting the good bits in her work
Jack	7	6	7	highlighting the good bits in his work/graded work is helpful
Tyler	6	4	6	graded work is helpful/oral feedback/highlighting the good bits in his work/correct the mistakes rather than letting him work it out on his own
Sabrina	6	3	4	graded work is helpful
Tom	8	5	6	highlighting the good bits in his work/graded work is helpful/give examples of alternative vocab
Leila	8	9	9	graded work is helpful
Paul	8	5	6	highlighting the good bits in his work/graded work is helpful/tell him when to redraft
Simon	8	4	5	highlighting the good bits in his work/graded work is helpful/correct the mistakes rather than letting him work it out on his own
Carlton	6	4	5	highlighting the good bits in his work/graded work is helpful/correct the mistakes rather than letting him work it out on his own
Tiana	8	7	7	graded work is helpful/give good alternative vocab

Year 11 Survey

The comments clearly indicate that nearly half of the class preferred having their mistakes fully corrected, while the rest were content to work through errors using my notes and advice. A unanimous request from all students was to have their work graded according to the exam board's grading system, providing them a clearer understanding of their progress. This survey provided me with the opportunity to tailor my teaching to better meet each individual's needs.

I conducted the survey to gain insight into the students' perspectives on the effectiveness of my feedback approach. People have specific preferences for receiving feedback, often because certain methods are more effective for them in making improvements.

The survey comprised only two questions:

1) What do you like about the way I give you feedback?

   I intentionally chose not to ask students what they *didn't* like about my way of giving feedback. Instead, the second question of the survey was framed positively:

2) What would you like me to do differently?

   I chose to solicit constructive suggestions rather than criticisms, which aligns with a positive approach to feedback and improvement.

Peer Feedback

Fostering Constructive Critique and Accountability

There's a unique power in feedback coming from peers. It shifts the dynamic of the learning environment, moving away from the traditional top-down teacher-student feedback approach to a more collaborative, lateral one. In group work, a method I have found particularly effective involves students performing conversations they have crafted in the target language, while their classmates actively engage in providing feedback. I distribute a guide sheet

(Sheet 1 for lower ability classes and Sheet 2 for the others) segmented into "What I liked" and "What can be improved," turning students into active evaluators who listen intently and critically.

This method offers multiple advantages. Firstly, it requires students to be present and attentive, recognising their role and responsibility to their peers. Their level of focus noticeably intensifies when entrusted with the task of constructive critique. Furthermore, peers can often be more candid than a teacher. They share a unique vantage point, having faced similar struggles and triumphs in their learning journeys. They can sometimes pinpoint areas of improvement or excellence that might go unnoticed in a more formal evaluative setting. While they might be more critical at times, this isn't necessarily a drawback. Sometimes, a little peer-driven push can motivate students to dig deeper and refine their skills, striving not just for teacher approval but for the respect and acknowledgment of their peers – a drive that can be incredibly potent in fostering academic growth.

FEEDBACK SHEET			
What I liked		What can be	
Group 1 ***		improved	
Group 2 *		***	
* *		* *	

Feedback Sheet

Sheet 1

FEUILLE D'ÉVALUATION		
Groupe	Ce que j'ai aimé	Conseil pour s'améliorer

Feuille d'évaluation

Streamlined Feedback: The Power of Criteria Sheets in Language Learning

Teaching languages, whether it's English or modern foreign languages like French, Spanish, or German, poses unique challenges. One significant hurdle is the extensive time often needed to provide thorough feedback on student writing. It goes beyond identifying spelling or grammar errors; it involves grasping the nuances, structures, and cultural contexts embedded within each sentence.

To tackle this challenge, my colleagues and I introduced a tool commonly used in primary schools and especially by English teachers in secondary schools: the criteria sheet. While it may appear as a simple checklist at first glance, it serves a more profound purpose. This tool was designed with the dual purpose of streamlining the feedback process for educators and enhancing comprehension for students. Instead of penning lengthy comments, we can now efficiently tick boxes aligned with predefined criteria. This not only reduces the time spent per assignment but also ensures consistency in feedback across all students.

The criteria sheet covers various aspects of language learning, from fundamental grammar rules like tense usage to higher order skills like opinion justification. It provides students with a clear overview of their strengths and areas needing improvement. But it's not a one-size-fits-all tool; it's fully customisable, allowing educators to tailor it to their specific curriculum or the unique needs of their student cohort.

However, introducing the criteria sheet is only half the journey. It's imperative to teach students how to interpret and act upon this feedback. Just as educators undergo training to use it effectively, students also need guidance. They should understand not just what each box signifies but also the implications of a ticked (or unticked) box. With this understanding, they can take actionable steps towards improving their language proficiency.

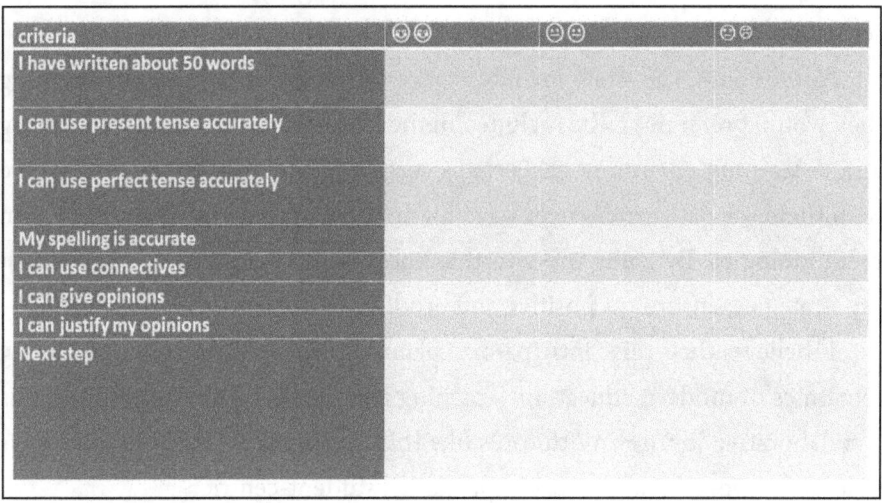

criteria	☺☺	☺☺	☺☺
I have written about 50 words			
I can use present tense accurately			
I can use perfect tense accurately			
My spelling is accurate			
I can use connectives			
I can give opinions			
I can justify my opinions			
Next step			

Criteria

Anticipatory Planning: Empowering Student Feedback for Effective Lesson Design

In the realm of education, understanding the needs and preferences of our students is paramount. This not only ensures that our lessons resonate with the learners but also fosters an environment of trust, respect, and open communication. With this in mind, I've developed a unique anticipatory planning tool designed to bridge the gap between educator intentions and student expectations.

The sheet, presented below, is straightforward yet powerful. It clearly outlines the upcoming lesson topic – discussing holidays using past and future tenses. However, what sets this tool apart are the next segments.

Firstly, it provides students with the opportunity to express any specific methodologies or tools they would like to see incorporated into the lesson. This could range from interactive activities and multimedia presentations to collaborative group tasks. By giving students a say in how they would like to learn, I am not only catering to diverse learning styles but also instilling a sense of ownership and responsibility in the learning process.

Additionally, the sheet includes space for students to mention anything they would prefer not to be included in the lesson. This is crucial for creating a safer learning environment. Perhaps certain teaching styles don't resonate with them, or past experiences have made them apprehensive about certain methodologies. By being privy to this information beforehand, I can adjust my strategies, ensuring a positive and productive classroom experience.

I believe that this anticipatory planning sheet reflects the evolving dynamics of modern education. Teaching is no longer a one-way street; it is a collaborative journey. With tools like this, I can ensure that the journey is tailored, responsive, and, most importantly, student-centric.

THE NEXT TOPIC WE ARE GOING TO LEARN IS: WRITE AND TALK ABOUT HOLIDAYS IN THE PAST AND FUTURE TENSE.

IS THERE ANYTHING IN PARTICULAR YOU WOULD LIKE ME TO USE IN THE LESSONS THAT YOU THINK WILL HELP YOU TACKLE THIS TOPIC BETTER? OF COURSE, I WILL REVISE THE PAST TENSE AND FUTURE WITH THE CLASS.

ANYTHING YOU WOULD RATHER I DON'T DO (IF ANYTHING):

The Next Topic

FORGING INDEPENDENCE

The cultivation of independence is a fundamental aspect of personal growth, extending beyond the physical capability to perform tasks without assistance. As both an educator and a parent, my insights into the development of this critical life skill are deeply intertwined, with each role informing the other.

My approach to nurturing independence has been significantly shaped by watching my children grow from toddlers to the age of ten, particularly during their playtime. These early years provide a fertile ground for teaching autonomy and resilience. Instead of constantly hovering over them, ready to intervene at the slightest wobble, I adopted a more hands-off approach, intervening only when absolutely necessary.

For instance, their natural inclination to climb and explore their environment became a valuable opportunity for them to learn about their own abilities. When my children assessed a wall or staircase they wished to ascend, I resisted the immediate instinct to step in. This deliberate choice allowed them to engage in risk assessment, trial and error, and the development of motor skills on their terms. The goal was not to leave them to fend for themselves but to let them engage with and learn from the environment around them.

In moments of struggle, my approach was to guide rather than to solve. Instead of providing answers, I offered questions such as "How do you think you can come down safely?" This encouraged them to use their own judgement and resources. Such interactions, though deceptively simple, are critical in establishing a framework for independent problem-solving.

Applying these principles to the classroom, I cultivate a similar environment of guided autonomy. I create situations where students are urged to take the reins of their own educational journeys. Rather than simply providing answers, I present challenges that compel them to think critically and solve problems. By promoting decision-making, addressing difficulties, and formulating strategies within a supportive context, students not only learn academic content but also develop the mindset and skills necessary for independent living.

Emphasising independence in teaching and parenting goes beyond transmitting knowledge; it's about instilling a value system. It's a commitment to preparing young people for life's complexities by embedding in them the confidence and competence needed to face the world on their terms. Independence is, essentially, not just a trait we wish to see in our children or students; it's a foundational characteristic of a fully realised individual.

Guided Discovery in the Classroom: Fostering Independence in Learning

The practice of guided discovery in the classroom is a cornerstone of my educational philosophy, particularly in cultivating independent learning among my students. In my classroom, I often assume the role of a guide rather than a lecturer, posing probing questions that encourage students to think critically and explore the material more deeply. This approach, though it may appear indirect, is meticulously crafted to empower students to realise their capability to uncover and understand complex ideas on their own.

This strategy is exemplified in a lesson on French possessive pronouns with my A-level students. During this lesson, the objective was to comprehend the difference between phrases like *la tienne* ("yours") and *le mien* ("mine"). I guided a student through sentences that utilised these structures, prompting her to notice the subtleties in usage. When she was faced with a new sentence construction, such as determining the correct possessive pronoun form for "my pens," I refrained from immediately providing the answer. Instead, I directed her through a series of questions that led her to the correct conclusion, ensuring that she grasped the fundamental grammatical principles. The satisfaction she exhibited was a testament to the effectiveness of guided discovery.

The moments of realisation, when a student's expression lights up with understanding or they smile with pride upon unravelling a complex topic, are profoundly fulfilling. These breakthrough moments, when a student no longer looks to the teacher for answers but begins to look within themselves, are the most rewarding. Such experiences reinforce not only the student's knowledge of the subject matter but also their confidence in their ability to solve problems and learn independently.

In both my roles as a parent and an educator, I am committed to fostering a learning environment where students are encouraged to take initiative and explore. The journey towards independence in learning is not just about accumulating knowledge; it's about developing the skill set to acquire that knowledge independently. I strive to encourage my students to question, analyse, and conclude on their own, thereby equipping them with the tools necessary to not only navigate the academic world but also to approach life with a sense of curiosity and self-assurance.

Emphasising Understanding Over Memorisation: An Educator's Approach

In the age of digital information and smartboards, it might be assumed that rote learning and mere copying would have been phased out of modern classrooms. Yet, the instinctive action of students reaching for their pens as soon as something is written on the board is a testament to how deeply ingrained this practice is in our educational system. Across various subjects, students often equate the volume of notes in their books to the depth of their learning. This notion is fundamentally flawed, and as an educator, I've made it my mission to challenge and change this perception.

In my classroom, I challenge this age-old convention. I emphasise to my students the importance of genuinely engaging with the content, rather than mechanically jotting down words without grasping their meaning. It's akin to judging a chef's cooking skills based solely on the number of recipes they have in their collection, without tasting a single dish they've prepared. I often remind them, "A notebook filled with words is of little value if the mind remains empty." True learning, in my eyes, is not about hoarding information but about understanding it deeply and being able to apply it in real-life scenarios.

To drive this point home, I employ a simple yet effective method: role-playing. Using the universally understood scenario of a tourist in a foreign land, I demonstrate the impracticality of relying solely on written notes. Just imagine being in the middle of a bustling Parisian street, fumbling through a textbook to find the correct French phrase to answer after someone has posed a simple question in French! The comedic description not only entertains but also conveys an essential message: knowledge is most valuable when it's readily accessible in our minds and can be used spontaneously, without needing to refer back to written notes. The class understands that real-world application of knowledge is instant and does not come with the luxury of rifling through pages.

This approach aims to cultivate independent thinkers who prioritise comprehension over rote memorisation. Since this memorable lesson, I have noticed a gradual shift in my classroom. Students are more engaged, they listen more attentively, and their reflex isn't to write but to understand. Their questions are more insightful, and their interactions mirror genuine curiosity rather than a mere desire to complete an assignment. To me, intelligence is not just about what you know but how you apply what you know. And by reshaping these classroom norms, I aspire to nurture students who don't just gather information but truly understand it, ensuring that the knowledge they acquire remains with them long after they've left my classroom.

Championing the Underdogs: The Power of a Positive Attitude

There are classes that shine and others that struggle, often labelled as "challenging." While many teachers might gravitate towards the former, believing them to be more rewarding or manageable, I have always felt a pull towards the latter. It is not out of a misplaced sense of heroism or a desire for praise but from a deep-rooted belief that every class, regardless of its reputation, has a reservoir of untapped potential waiting to be harnessed.

The concept of "choice" in teaching is immensely powerful. When students understand that their teacher has selected, rather than been assigned, to guide them, it can redefine the entire classroom atmosphere. Communicating to these students that I have actively chosen to work with them sows seeds of respect and trust. I stand before them not as an arbitrary figure assigned by administrative logistics but as an advocate for their success, someone who sees past any stigmas and believes in the value they hold.

Admittedly, winning over the hearts and minds of students who have become jaded by past educational experiences is no small feat. Accustomed to doubt and criticism, they may initially meet such intentions with scepticism. The idea that a teacher would seek them out, not out of duty but from a genuine belief in their potential, can be hard to digest. Yet, once the veracity of my claim has been confirmed, the walls they have built over time begin to crumble.

Change is a gradual process. Trust is built day by day, lesson by lesson. Over time, the dynamics within the classroom begin evolving. The once-common defensive postures give way to engagement and laughter, and a sense of worth takes root. Students, previously sidelined, start contributing, finding their voices, and stepping out from judgement's shadow.

This is the heart of my approach – instilling self-belief in students who have been relegated to the margins, changing the narrative (at least in my classroom), redefining "challenging" classes, and transforming them into collectives of "champions" who recognise their own worth and potential. My role is maintaining a positive attitude and a firm belief in their potential.

COACHING VERSUS SPOON-FEEDING

The coaching philosophy in teaching promotes an active approach to learning. Instead of merely absorbing knowledge, students actively engage and test hypotheses and are unafraid to step outside the box. This contrasts starkly with traditional spoon-fed methods, in which students are passive recipients, often memorising information without deep comprehension.

A coach's role is to facilitate understanding, guiding, challenging, and supporting students as they navigate through the learning journey. As a coach, I aim to create a learning environment where students are not only listeners but active participants in their education. They question, ponder, challenge, make mistakes, and, most importantly, learn.

Embracing mistakes is fundamental in this method. Errors are not seen as signs of weakness but as opportunities for growth and reflection. As a coach, I acknowledge their attempts, help them identify where they went wrong, and guide them towards the right path. It's about empowering them to find answers on their own rather than just providing solutions.

Over the years, I have observed that students who are coached rather than spoon-fed develop a deeper understanding of subjects, acquire critical thinking skills, and exude confidence in their abilities. They are not deterred by challenges but see them as puzzles to be solved.

Moreover, the coaching approach better prepares students for real-life situations. The world outside doesn't come with ready answers. It demands problem-solvers, thinkers, and innovators. When students are taught to think independently, analyse, and approach challenges with a problem-solving mindset, they are better equipped to tackle real-world scenarios.

To any educator reading this: I encourage you to consider trialling a coaching methodology. The rewards, both for you and your students, are manifold. It's a shift from merely imparting knowledge to nurturing thinkers, innovators, and leaders.

This strategy of engaging students through guided questions, often termed the Socratic method, stimulates critical thinking and allows students to discover answers for themselves. Instead of merely receiving information, students become active participants in the learning process.

As students embark on this journey of self-discovery, they often arrive at a more profound understanding of the subject matter. Their comprehension is based on their own logic and reasoning, making the knowledge more personal and likely to be retained. This is why I believe the best response a student can hear is not "Yes, that's right," but rather "Why do you think that?"

Fostering such an environment also has a significant impact on a student's confidence. When they arrive at the correct answer through their own deductive reasoning, it boosts their self-belief. It reinforces the idea that they are capable thinkers and they can trust their intellect. One of my sixth-form students once said in a lesson, "It's a painful journey to the answer, but I get there every time."

Additionally, actively addressing the culture of fear around making mistakes sets our students up for success. In the real world, failure is a natural part of growth. By normalising mistakes within the classroom, I am preparing my students to face challenges outside of it. When they understand that errors are not the end but stepping stones, they are better equipped to handle setbacks in their future careers and lives.

The idea that a teacher is more effective in a relaxed environment resonates deeply with me. Every professional, whether in education, business, or sports, tends to perform best when not under unnecessary pressure. Constant observation and evaluation can stifle creativity, spontaneity, and the natural flow of teaching. A balance must be struck so that educators can receive feedback and support without feeling constantly under the microscope.

So, coaching over spoon-feeding information equips students with the knowledge, skills, mindset, and resilience to navigate this constantly changing world. I believe that educational institutions worldwide could benefit from adopting this more holistic teaching methodology. By giving it a chance, they may well be pleasantly surprised by the positive results it yields.

From Year 7 to Year 11

This journey from Year 7 to Year 11 in secondary school is often a roller coaster of emotions, experiences, and personal growth. The transition from primary to secondary education marks the beginning of a new chapter, in which young individuals begin seeking their identities, influenced both by their peers and their educational environment.

Year 7 often begins with a mixture of excitement and anxiety. The sprawling campus, different teachers for every subject, new faces, and the overarching feeling of being the "junior-most" can be daunting. Yet, this year also brings new friendships, new experiences, and a broader academic exposure, turning that initial apprehension into intrigue.

However, as students ascend the academic ladder, the pressures start piling up. Expectations begin mounting from the educational institution, their peer groups, and, most significantly, within themselves. The once wide-eyed Year 7 students, now in Year 10 and 11, begin viewing school as a stepping stone to their future rather than only an avenue for learning.

The looming presence of significant examinations begins casting its shadow. For many, this is the first real taste of academic pressure. The narrative around them often shifts from learning and understanding to grades, percentages, and performance. The joy of learning risks being eclipsed by the fear of underperforming.

Teachers, too, sense this shift. The once lively discussions and curious questions begin taking a back seat. Students are more concerned about "what's going to be on the test" rather than genuinely understanding the subject. Their intrinsic motivation for knowledge is often replaced by extrinsic motivations like grades, parental approval, and societal validation.

At this stage, my role becomes even more crucial. Instead of just imparting knowledge, I become a coach, guiding students in their studies and in managing their anxieties and fears. Emphasising the importance of understanding over rote memorisation, promoting a growth mindset, and offering constructive feedback is vital. Celebrating effort, resilience, and improvement rather than solely focusing on end results fosters a healthier and more holistic approach to learning.

In education, the phrase "All roads lead to Rome" deeply resonates with the pedagogical approach that appreciates and acknowledges diverse thought processes. Teaching and learning are not always linear. As educators, it's paramount to understand and celebrate the myriad of ways students approach problems and convey their understanding.

Moreover, acknowledging a student's unique approach serves to nurture their self-confidence and critical thinking skills. It conveys the powerful message that their perspective matters and there isn't always a singular, predetermined path to understanding or a solution. For instance, in solving a mathematical problem, there can exist multiple valid methods to reach the correct solution, each with its own merit.

Encouraging students to vocalise and demonstrate their understanding transforms the classroom into a dynamic, interactive environment. The learning process becomes mutual and multidimensional, breaking away from a monologue-driven space.

Moreover, by identifying the root causes of misunderstandings, educators can tailor teaching strategies to meet individual students' needs. For example, a student who says, "Yesterday I eated a cake," demonstrates understanding the rule for forming the preterit tense. The example of "eated" illustrates that errors are not necessarily indicative of poor comprehension but might represent a developmental stage in language acquisition. These small detours on the learning path can often provide valuable insights into a student's thought process, allowing educators to provide more tailored guidance.

A paradigm shift occurs when errors are viewed not as stumbling blocks but as stepping stones. Mistakes become opportunities for deeper exploration, clarification, and the solidification of understanding. Recognising and celebrating the effort, logic, or strategy behind an error empowers students to take risks, explore, and think outside the box. Correcting the irregular verb "eat" in the example becomes more effective when acknowledging the student's grasp of the general rule for forming the past tense, emphasising exceptions.

It's essential to remind students, and educators themselves, that setbacks and failures aren't the opposite of success but rather integral components of the journey to mastery. Understanding this concept reduces the fear of making mistakes, fostering a willingness to step out of comfort zones. Valuing the journey and the myriad of experiences it offers becomes as important as reaching the destination.

In conclusion, recognising multiple pathways to knowledge and viewing mistakes as stepping stones to success allows both educators and students to navigate the educational journey with a growth mindset. This approach ensures that the learning process is as valued as, if not more so than, the final outcome.

As Arnold Schwarzenegger aptly said, "Strength does not come from winning. Your struggles develop your strength."

REWARDS AND SANCTIONS

Rewards

In the context of a school setting, the power of praise as a tool for reinforcing school rules cannot be overstated. While some argue that sanctions or disciplinary actions are essential deterrents to undesirable behaviours, praise emerges as a more effective and positive motivator. By acknowledging and rewarding adherence to school rules, students are not merely discouraged from rule-breaking but are actively encouraged to exhibit model behaviours. This approach enhances students' self-confidence, communicating that their efforts are seen, valued, and acknowledged by their educators. Such recognition often fosters a deeper appreciation for both the lesson and the teacher, as students begin to associate their classroom experiences with positive reinforcement.

Nevertheless, like any tool, the power of praise must be wielded judiciously. Overreliance on or excessive distribution of praise can lead to "praise inflation," rendering the praise meaningless over time. If students perceive that praises are handed out without genuine merit or reason, it may devalue the entire praise system. In such scenarios, educators might find themselves cornered, with their primary positive reinforcement tool rendered ineffective, leaving them reliant solely on sanctions. Thus, while praise is an incredible motivator, it is crucial to ensure its sensible and sincere deployment.

Detecting the onset of praise inflation in a classroom requires careful observation and reflection. Here are some warning signs that educators can look out for:

1. **Lack of Impact**: If you notice that your praise no longer generates the same positive response or enthusiasm it once did, it may indicate that students are becoming desensitised to it. This could manifest as indifference, lack of engagement, or minimal effort despite receiving praise.

2. **Expectation Instead of Appreciation**: When students start expecting praise for every action, regardless of its significance or quality, it indicates that they view praise as a given, not as a reward for exceptional effort or achievement.

3. **Decreased Effort in Tasks**: If students begin to put forth less effort yet still expect praise, this may be a sign they no longer see the value in striving for excellence, since they anticipate recognition regardless of the quality of their work.

4. **Peer Resentment**: Pay attention to classroom dynamics. If students express cynicism or resentment when their peers are praised, it could be a sign they perceive the praise as unwarranted or overly frequent.

5. **Feedback Dismissal**: A key symptom of praise inflation is when students become indifferent to more constructive forms of feedback. It is a red flag if they only respond to praise and disregard constructive criticism or suggestions for improvement.

To prevent praise inflation, teachers can employ the following strategies:

- **Be Specific With Praise**: Instead of generic compliments, pinpoint specific aspects of a student's work or behaviour that are commendable. This makes the praise more meaningful and impactful.

- **Balance Praise With Constructive Feedback**: Combine praise with constructive feedback that guides further improvement. This ensures that praise is seen as an integral part of a constructive learning process, not just a reward.
- **Reserve Praise for Noteworthy Efforts**: Ensure praise is given for genuine effort, improvement, or excellence rather than for routine tasks or minimal effort.
- **Foster a Growth Mindset**: Encourage students to value learning and improvement over simply garnering praise. This cultivates an intrinsic motivation to learn.
- **Personalise Praise**: Understand what type of recognition resonates with each student. Public recognition motivates some, while others may prefer quiet, personal acknowledgement.

By being mindful of these aspects, educators can maintain the effectiveness of praise as a positive reinforcement tool and avoid the pitfalls of praise inflation.

Recognising and celebrating student achievement is pivotal in fostering a positive learning environment. One tangible way to acknowledge these accomplishments is by prominently displaying their work on the departmental display board, within the classroom, or in any other designated space within the institution. Such displays serve multiple essential purposes in the educational realm.

Firstly, they provide students with a clear sense of accomplishment. When students see their projects, essays, or artwork showcased for peers, educators, and sometimes even parents to see, it reinforces the idea that their hard work has not gone unnoticed. This external validation reinforces students' belief in their capabilities, bolstering their confidence and encouraging them to strive for similar achievements in the future.

Moreover, showcasing exemplary student work serves as a source of inspiration for other students. Observing the capabilities of their peers often motivates students to push their boundaries and reach similar, if not greater, heights, igniting a spark of friendly competition. It creates an atmosphere where excellence is not just encouraged but celebrated, driving students to put in their best efforts.

Furthermore, the act of displaying student work communicates a powerful message about the school's values. It demonstrates that the institution not only prioritises academic rigour but also places significant emphasis on recognising and celebrating the individual achievements of its students. This fosters a more holistic educational environment where students feel seen, valued, and motivated.

While displaying student work is undeniably beneficial, it's crucial to ensure it doesn't inadvertently create a competitive atmosphere, where only a select few are ever recognised. Striking a balance is key, ensuring that over time, a diverse range of students and achievements are celebrated, fostering inclusivity and a holistic appreciation of various forms of success.

Extrinsic Motivators

In the first couple of years of teaching, novelty and innovation often drive educators to experiment with unique ways to connect with and motivate students. As a fresh educator, I introduced a full-bodied comic character in the students' books – a humorous representation of myself providing feedback through a speech bubble. This engaging and personal evaluation method brought palpable delight and anticipation to students' faces whenever they opened their books. This innovative method was reserved for those who showcased excellent work, emphasising that their hard work was not only recognised but celebrated uniquely.

As captivating as this approach was, it became immensely time-consuming around my third year of teaching. Balancing my personal life with pursuing hobbies and handling the ever-increasing workload at school made it challenging to maintain this practice. The passion of my early teaching years slowly gave way to the realities and demands of daily life, leading to the eventual discontinuation of this special reward system.

This leads me to an essential reflection on extrinsic rewards. While personalised feedback methods like the comic character were effective, it's crucial to recognise that not all students value the standard school system's rewards. Traditional praise or recognition might not resonate with some students, requiring different extrinsic motivators aligning with their personal values or interests. Whether tangible rewards, privileges, or unique experiences, these tailored rewards can serve as powerful motivators for students who might feel disconnected from conventional reward systems. The challenge for educators is to identify and implement these motivators without causing disparity or feelings of favouritism within the classroom. The ultimate aim is to foster an environment where every student feels seen, valued, and motivated to put forth their best effort.

Competitive Spirit: A Teacher's Perspective

My competitive nature has been an integral part of my life for as long as I can remember. In school, my best friends were also my greatest competitors. We constantly strived to outdo each other, but always in a spirit of healthy rivalry. For instance, my friend Gito and I would spontaneously race each other whenever we met. Winning or losing, each race ended with a profound sense of satisfaction from the thrill of competition. Alongside my friends Ricardo, Shazad, Danith, and Fabien, we competed academically across various subjects, each challenge serving as a vital incentive, whether intrinsic or extrinsic.

Alfie Kohn argues in *No Contest: The Case Against Competition* that competition is detrimental to personal and societal well-being.[31] I respectfully disagree, based on my experiences. My five brothers and I shared this competitive spirit, yet it never negatively impacted our bond. Similarly, my friendships have been significantly enriched through daily contests. However, I acknowledge Kohn's point that in the pressured environment of school, competition can sometimes have adverse effects, potentially undermining teamwork and cooperation, which are crucial for personal and societal success.

This competitive spirit extended to my role as a tutor in a British school, where I was responsible for a tutor group – a small assembly of students assigned to a teacher for both academic and personal guidance.

During a particularly memorable "Tutor-Bond Day," designed to strengthen relationships between tutors and Year 9 students, we played a game of Monopoly, which turned into an intriguing display of competitive dynamics. Interestingly, the boys in the group exhibited a pronounced competitive drive, opting for a free-for-all approach in which their primary goal was to outdo everyone else, irrespective of gender. On the other hand, the girls demonstrated a strikingly different strategy by choosing collaboration and alliances, ostensibly to counterbalance the boys' competitive fervour.

This approach divergence aligns with findings from various studies on gender differences in competitiveness and collaboration. Research suggests that men often exhibit higher levels of competitiveness compared to women. A study by Niederle and Vesterlund (2007) in the *Quarterly Journal of Economics* found that men were more likely to enter a competitive environment than women, even when they had similar abilities.[32] This could explain the boys' eagerness to compete individually in the Monopoly game. On the contrary, women tend to prefer collaborative environments and are

---

[31] Alfie Kohn, *No Contest: The Case Against Competition* (Boston: Houghton Mifflin Company, 1986).

[32] Muriel Niederle. Vesterlund, Lise. *Do Women Shy Away from Competition? Do Men Compete Too Much?.* United States: National Bureau of Economic Research, 2005.

more likely to engage in cooperative strategies, as seen with the girls playing the Monopoly game.

The day was undeniably successful, as evidenced by the enjoyable and memorable experience, fostering lasting connections. Many students from that group and I have maintained contact and still fondly recall that day. Unfortunately, such tutor-bonding activities, focusing more on interpersonal connections and less on academic goals, were only implemented a few times in that school before being replaced by more conventional, academically focused programmes. This shift, while understandable academically, underscores a broader trend in education that often overlooks the importance of social bonding and non-academic skill development in favour of more traditional academic pursuits.

In contrast to playing Monopoly with my family, when my children's mother kindly waived property fees, this school session was marked by a ruthless, yet enjoyable, competitive spirit. We played with a no-mercy approach, embodying the game's essence. It was entertaining to see players go bankrupt one by one, a harmless enjoyment in the context of the game. I believe it is somewhat natural for humans to find joy in such competitive scenarios, where they are free from real-world consequences.

This experience illustrates that competition can be a rewarding and bonding experience when managed healthily. It teaches resilience, strategy, and the ability to cope with both victory and defeat. In an educational setting, such dynamics foster a sense of camaraderie and offer valuable life lessons.

Although I opted for the Monopoly game in my tutor group, a variety of other activities were simultaneously underway in each tutor group throughout the school. Here are some examples that teachers can implement in their own tutor groups:

Team Projects: Encourage students to work together on group projects, including science experiments, history presentations, and creative writing assignments. Working towards a common goal helps build camaraderie and teaches teamwork.

Role-Playing Activities: Involve students in role-playing activities, which can be highly beneficial in subjects like history and literature. By acting out historical events or book scenes, students get an engaging and enjoyable learning experience while also gaining an understanding of various viewpoints.

Outdoor Activities: Organise outdoor team-building exercises like scavenger hunts, sports events, or nature walks. These activities can be educational and encourage physical health, teamwork, and a connection with the environment.

Class Competitions: Like the Monopoly game, class competitions in areas like debates, quizzes, and even friendly sports matches foster healthy competitive spirits. Ensuring these competitions are inclusive and focused on team effort is essential.

Creative Arts Projects: Involve students in group art projects, like mural painting or a collaborative music performance. These activities encourage creativity and allow students to express themselves while working together.

Cultural Exchange: Have a day when students share something about their cultural background or a hobby they love. This fosters mutual respect and understanding among classmates.

Problem-Solving Challenges: Organise activities that require problem-solving and critical thinking, like escape rooms (which can be simulated in the classroom) or puzzle challenges. These activities can be both intellectually stimulating and fun.

Community Service Projects: Involve students in community service or charitable endeavours. Such activities help build stronger relationships and educate students about the importance of contributing to the community.

I believe these activities, like the Monopoly game experience, provide memorable learning experiences and strengthen the bond between teachers and students while teaching valuable life skills.

Good-News Calls: Reframing School-Parent Interaction

I naturally gravitate towards life's positive aspects because this outlook significantly benefits my well-being. I often ponder a moment, remembering myself in the students' shoes, facing the board while sitting across from the teacher's desk. I recall my feelings and thoughts – my aspirations, expectations, and hopes for what I could learn and experience. Embracing this perspective led me to prioritise communication with parents and guardians as a crucial aspect of my educator role. Aiming to alter their expectations regarding school calls, I specialise in making calls that celebrate student achievement or positive behaviour. This approach fosters a more constructive relationship with parents and encourages and motivates the students. Apprehension typically begins the moment of introduction. I can almost hear the tension in a parent's voice as they brace for bad news upon learning a teacher is on the line. But as I explain my reason for calling, there's a palpable sense of relief and then joy.

There's a profound satisfaction in sharing good news with a parent about their child. Whether it's acknowledging a student's diligence, their positive contribution to class, or a particularly impressive piece of work, these moments are as meaningful for me as they are for the families. I've seen firsthand the impact of these positive calls. Students often exhibit remarkable turnarounds in their behaviour and approach to learning afterwards, buoyed by the recognition of their efforts.

This strategy of proactive positive outreach serves several purposes. Firstly, it disrupts the negative stereotype often associated with students known for behavioural challenges. When these students and their families are presented with a positive narrative, it reframes their self-image and reveals new possibilities for how they view school and their place within it.

Secondly, affirmation is a powerful motivator. Students feeling overlooked or pigeonholed into a particular role within the school community realise their efforts do not go unnoticed. This recognition validates their hard work and encourages them to sustain, and even build upon, their positive actions. I typically do not inform students prior to calling their parents, especially those accustomed to receiving negative calls from the school. Often pleasantly surprised by these unexpected positive calls, parents invariably tell their children that their French teacher called with good news about them. I don't know about their other lessons, but the attitude improvement in their French lesson is noticeable.

Building parental trust is another successful outcome of these calls, promoting trust and partnership with the school. This fosters a collaborative approach to a child's education, particularly in conversations revolving around more sensitive issues.

Acknowledging a student's progress contributes to their holistic development. It enhances their self-esteem, making them receptive to constructive feedback and improving their overall attitude towards school.

Moreover, these calls strengthen the student-teacher relationship. Students are keenly aware of the significance when a teacher acknowledges and communicates their positive behaviour, especially to their parents. This leads to increased respect and rapport within the classroom.

By regularly calling to share good news, I aspire to transform the perception of school communication into something that is eagerly awaited. However, consistently making these calls became increasingly difficult because of time constraints. This situation is frustrating, especially knowing the profound positive impact such calls have on both the child and their parents. Recognising these challenges, I devised an alternative approach to utilise the time reserved for writing class reports to also write notes in the students' school planners. In the UK, these planners serve as a crucial communication channel between teachers and parents, offering an effective means to convey positive feedback.

Sanctions

Sanctions as a Last Resort and the Value of Discretion

In my experience within the school environment, I view sanctions as an option to be employed judiciously, serving as a last resort. Teaching extends beyond enforcing discipline; it's about cultivating an environment where understanding, personal growth, and a passion for learning are at the core. So, when it comes to sanctions, I exercise a high degree of discretion, ensuring that I am acting in the best interest of all parties involved – the student, the class, and myself as an educator.

So, what is a sanction? Within educational institutions, "sanction" typically refers to a disciplinary action to rectify students' improper or undesirable conduct. These measures are implemented to uphold the school's rules and ensure a secure and conducive learning atmosphere. The nature and severity of sanctions can vary widely, depending on the school's policies and the specific circumstances of the misconduct. Common examples of school sanctions include the following:

Verbal Reprimand: A warning or reprimand given by a teacher or school official to a student for minor infractions.

Detention: Requiring a student to spend extra time in school during lunch breaks, after school, or on weekends, depending on the school and the country.

Suspension: Temporarily excluding a student from attending school for a predetermined period of time. Suspensions can be in school (where the student is isolated but remains on campus) or out of school.

Expulsion: A more severe form of discipline in which a student is permanently removed from the school for serious infractions.

Community Service: Requiring a student to perform a certain number of hours of service to the school or community.

Restitution or Compensation: In cases where property is damaged, students might be required to pay for repairs or replacement.

Behaviour Contracts: Agreements between the student, parents, and school outlining specific behaviour expectations and consequences for not meeting them.

While primarily punitive, school sanctions often aim to teach students responsibility, help them understand the consequences of their actions, and encourage better decision-making in the future. Schools usually follow a progressive discipline policy, under which the severity of the sanction increases with repeated or more serious infractions.

The goal, in my opinion, should never merely be to impose rules but to work towards the most constructive outcome for the student's development. In the heat of the moment, it can be easy to resort to sanctions without fully weighing the situation. However, I am mindful of their gravity and potential impact. Newly qualified teachers, and sometimes even those with experience, can fall into the trap of adhering too rigidly to the rule book, potentially overlooking the unique context of each incident. The challenge is upholding consistency while not losing sight of individual circumstances.

Consider a student who has been consistently putting in effort but occasionally slips up. Issuing a sanction for a minor mistake in such a case could do more harm than good, possibly undermining their motivation and trust in the school system. In moments like these, discretion and professional judgement of the educator are crucial.

Contrast this with an incident involving another student who attempted to cheat during a class test. Although she thought she was being discreet, I observed her more closely than she realised. To avoid alerting her, I pretended to look away or be preoccupied with my own work each time she looked up at me. She used these opportunities to sneak glances at her book for vocabulary. This continued until the test concluded. Despite her struggle with memorising vocabulary and constructing grammatically correct sentences in Spanish, she was clearly a student eager to succeed.

At the end of the lesson, I discreetly requested she remain as the rest of the class left. I gently informed her that I had noticed her looking into her book during the test, deliberately avoiding the term "cheating" to reduce her embarrassment. I then asked her to retake the test during her lunch break the following day; this was her sanction. While I could have simply given her a zero, my goal was to assess what she had learned and what needed to be reviewed, both for her and others who might have made similar errors.

When a student repeatedly misbehaves during my lesson and I have issued more than two warnings, I follow the school policy and impose a sanction. However, if I notice a significant improvement in their attitude for the remainder of the lesson, I might use my discretion to reduce the severity of the sanction. For example, if I had initially assigned a twenty-minute detention at break time, I may reduce it to just ten minutes. Students often request to be excused entirely from the detention, but I rarely consent in order to reinforce the lesson. Nonetheless, when they attend the detention, I sometimes have a brief conversation with them and then let them go after a minute or two. This approach often proves effective in teaching the lesson, but this leniency is rarely extended to students who are repeat offenders.

Maintaining the integrity and intent behind sanctions should uphold the values and objectives of our educational mandate, not detract from them. An indiscriminate approach to sanctions leads to a culture in which they are viewed as arbitrary or punitive rather than corrective and educational. Students may complain about a teacher, saying he always gives detentions "for no reason." To avoid this perspective, I always strive to ensure that my reasoning is understood by the student. I often discuss with students that there is always a reason behind a sanction; however, it may not align with what they perceive as a justifiable reason. They might still reject it, but if someone asks them why they received a detention from me, they won't be able to say they don't know, or worse, that there was no reason.

The most effective method I have found to avoid having to impose sanctions is by clearly explaining to the student, step by step, what I will do if they continue the behaviour I have already reprimanded them for. This approach isn't always successful, as children will be children and often get carried away in their activities. However, I don't face as much backlash from them as I would have had I not taken the time to explain my approach in a step-by-step manner.

Do I believe sanctions are useful and necessary? Absolutely, yes. The reason lies in our need to adhere to basic behavioural norms in society, allowing us to interact respectfully and humanely. Imposing sanctions on children is also a means of establishing boundaries. It's crucial for children to understand limits because, as they grow and enter the workforce, they will encounter various forms of boundaries, be it through laws, societal customs, or self-discipline. Knowing these boundaries makes it easier to navigate them and function within them.

We can all remember moments from our childhood when the fear of sanctions stopped us from misbehaving. For instance, when I was around six or eight years old, I wanted to mimic adults by smoking a cigarette. My younger brother Dominique and I sneaked into our parents' bedroom, closed the door, and crafted our own "cigarettes" from a sheet torn out of a school exercise book. We lit them and pretended to be grown-ups, even imitating their manner of speaking. It was all fun and games until our mother walked in and caught us red-handed within a couple of minutes. The ensuing reprimand was intense, and as the older child, I received the lion's share of it.

Did this incident alone deter me from smoking later in life? Not entirely, but it certainly played a part. I tried smoking a cigarette once as an adult, only to realise I didn't like it. That experience was enough to ensure it was my first and last time putting a cigarette to my lips.

I aim to navigate classroom dynamics with a perspective that is both firm and empathetic, balancing the need for discipline with the understanding that each student's situation is unique. Through experience and an empathetic understanding of my students, I make decisions that are tailored to individual needs and conducive to learning.

Paradoxically, if you ask my students whether I am strict, they will undoubtedly respond affirmatively. I foster a positive atmosphere in my classroom where everyone respects one another and feels comfortable to participate without the fear of being labelled "dumb" for making mistakes. My students understand I have high expectations for their behaviour and their effort. I emphasise that it's the effort they put into their classwork and homework that matters most to me – the results are secondary. The effort students invest invariably determines their outcomes. While my students recognise my strictness on this front, they also appreciate that I am what they call a "fun teacher." For that reason alone, I believe it is unlikely my name would appear on the top list of the strictest teachers at the school.

By using sanctions sparingly and thoughtfully, I find they retain their significance and efficacy. More importantly, this approach allows me to maintain a classroom atmosphere that is fair, respectful, and primed for learning. It ensures the classroom remains a place of growth, where students feel supported in their journey and where both their academic and personal development are the primary focus.

The Importance of Parental Involvement

The influence of family support in a child's educational journey cannot be overstated. Parents and guardians play an instrumental role in shaping a child's attitude, behaviour, and perception towards learning and school. Their involvement, or lack thereof, significantly impacts the child's academic performance, social interactions, and overall well-being.

When parents take an active interest in their child's education, they send a strong message about the value and importance of learning. This can manifest in various ways: attending parent-teacher meetings, helping with homework, or simply engaging in conversations about school experiences. Such involvement promotes students' sense of responsibility and accountability. When children recognise that their parents are invested in their education, they are more likely to exhibit positive behaviours, be more engaged, and strive for academic excellence.

Moreover, the collaboration between parents and educators creates a cohesive front that reinforces appropriate behaviours and academic standards. This united approach pre-emptively addresses potential behavioural issues, rendering sanctions less necessary. When students understand that their behaviour and performance are monitored at school and discussed at home, they often exhibit greater self-discipline and motivation.

However, when parents are not involved, or when there's a disconnect between home and school values, students might feel less accountable. This increases misbehaviours, academic slip, and the likelihood of the school resorting to sanctions.

My Personal Experience

Throughout my teaching career, I have consistently observed that students whose parents maintain regular communication with the school often flourish, reaching their full potential. This parental involvement, which manifests in various forms – be it through consistent attendance at parent-teacher meetings, effective use of the child's school planner for ongoing communication, or other proactive methods – acts as a cornerstone for the child's academic success. Conversely, students who lack this parental engagement often face greater challenges in their educational journey. This correlation is hardly surprising. Especially during the formative primary school years, children look to their parents for guidance, support, and validation. The absence of such a pivotal support system can lead to a profound sense of loss, instability, and increased stress for the child.

Reflecting on my personal experiences post-divorce, I realised the paramount importance of maintaining a strong presence in my children's lives. Amidst the shifting family dynamics, there was a palpable fear that my children might encounter academic struggles or be subjected to societal stigma, despite the increasing normalisation of divorce in Western society since the turn of the millennium. My concerns extended to the educational sphere, where I feared they might be labelled as "children with limited domestic parental support." This label, often tacitly used in educational settings, can inadvertently lead to lowered expectations or biases from educators, which can further impact a child's self-esteem and academic performance.

Moreover, the importance of parental involvement extends beyond the academic realm. It plays a crucial role in the holistic development of a child. Parents who are actively engaged in their child's life foster a sense of security and belonging, critical for their child's emotional and social well-being. They serve as role models, mentors, and advocates, shaping their child's values, attitudes, and behaviours. This involvement also extends to everyday life, where such simple acts as sharing a meal, discussing the day's events, and engaging in leisure activities together can significantly strengthen the parent-child bond and provide the child with a stable and nurturing environment.

Additionally, schools encouraging and facilitating parental involvement often see a positive impact on overall school culture. Such involvement fosters more effective communication between teachers and parents, better understanding of individual student needs, and a collaborative approach to addressing academic or behavioural challenges. It underscores the idea that education is a shared responsibility, not confined within the walls of a classroom but extending into the home and community.

In conclusion, I am fully convinced that parental presence in children's academic life and everyday experiences is an invaluable asset. It lays the foundation for a supportive, enriching environment where children can thrive both academically and personally. As educators, recognising and supporting this vital role of parents can promote more effective teaching and a more inclusive, responsive educational system. Parental involvement is not only beneficial for academic success; it also plays a crucial role in behavioural management within schools. A strong, collaborative partnership between educators and parents significantly decreases the need for sanctions, as the emphasis shifts from mere discipline to holistic development and understanding.

Rewards and sanctions are pivotal in guiding student behaviour in educational settings. Rewards, like praise and personalised gestures, boost student motivation and self-confidence, recognising achievements and reinforcing positive behaviours. But we must always remember their overuse can diminish their efficacy. On the other hand, sanctions, ideally a last resort, serve to correct undesirable behaviours. Their application requires an educator's discretion, taking context into account. The involvement of parents can significantly influence student behaviour, potentially reducing the need for punitive measures. When applied judiciously, rewards and sanctions create a balanced learning environment, fostering both academic growth and behavioural development.

LIFE IN THE REAL WORLD

The importance of students immersing themselves in the real world is something I deeply value as an educator. Human beings have an intrinsic need to engage with the environment around them, a trait crucial for our development throughout history. In the context of modern education, this need translates into the importance of experiential learning opportunities like field trips, geographical explorations, and other forms of outdoor education.

These excursions are far more than mere diversions from daily classroom learning; they are essential experiences in which academic theories are applied and tested in real-world settings. When students step outside the school walls, they enter a broader learning canvas that enlivens education with tangible, multi-sensory experiences. Such real-world engagements are critical for cementing abstract concepts, sparking innate curiosity, and cultivating a genuine appreciation for various disciplines.

Students encounter real-world scenarios that challenge them to think on their feet, adapt, and problem-solve. These experiences not only reinforce their classroom learning but also develop their resilience and adaptability, qualities imperative for personal and professional success.

The old saying that "experience is the best teacher" resonates in education. Children's natural defiance of rules and instructions is often not a sign of rebellion but a reflection of their urge to engage with the world, understanding it through firsthand interaction. This experiential learning allows them to process information profoundly, ensuring that knowledge gained is knowledge remembered.

Collaboration is a critical component of real-world learning. When students collaborate on projects or engage in fieldwork, they encounter a diverse range of perspectives, challenge one another's thinking, and learn to build solutions. This mirrors the collaborative nature of problem-solving they will encounter later in life, preparing them for teamwork and joint initiatives. I will expand on the importance of collaboration in the second part of this book, under the chapter "The Power of Collaboration in Achieving Greatness."

Effective communication and critical thinking are skills refined through real-world experiences. These skills involve listening, interpreting, and interacting with clarity and purpose. Placing students in situations where they must articulate their ideas or justify their reasoning fosters critical thinking. They learn to assess the validity of information, understand its context, and present it convincingly.

Ultimately, the real-world experiences I strive to provide for my students surpass the mere acquisition of knowledge. These experiences are about mastering life skills that are integral to navigating the complexities of life beyond school.

PART TWO

THE EDUCATION SYSTEM

Consider these two numbers: 6,600 and 13,000. What could they possibly represent in the context of this book? Keep them in mind, as their significance will be revealed in the upcoming chapters.

Nelson Mandela and the Power of Education

Nelson Mandela's assertion that "Education is one of the most important weapons in a country"[33] encapsulates the transformative potential of knowledge. This profound statement emphasises that the might of military weapons, as formidable as they may be, pales in comparison to the lasting impact of an educated mind. After all, these instruments of war – tanks, fighter jets, submarines, and even nuclear bombs – were conceived and constructed by individuals armed with education. The true force behind these creations is not just raw materials or technology but the minds that harnessed, applied, and innovated. While these machines can change landscapes and geopolitics, education has the power to alter ideologies, beliefs, and the very course of humanity. It is a tool for progress, a beacon of hope, and a catalyst for positive change.

The aim of this section is to present a critique of the school system from my perspective. I plan to identify what I see as both potential flaws and strengths. In areas where I perceive flaws, I analyse their underlying causes and, where possible, propose relevant solutions. Of course, I am acutely aware that I don't have all the answers, and neither does anyone else. True progress comes from the amalgamation of our efforts and ideas, moving us closer to an ideal solution. With this section, I aim to make my contribution to this collective endeavour.

---

[33] SABC News, "Education is One of the Most Important Weapons: Nelson Mandela," YouTube video, December 11, 2013, https://youtu.be/h0w_PFEl1zs?si=FRcBalgmd2 t0xvof&t=116.

HISTORY OF THE CURRENT ENGLISH EDUCATION SYSTEM

The Current School System's Resistance to Change

Whoever said that landing a man on Mars is easier than changing the school system was very perceptive, in my opinion. This statement is believed to be from billionaire and CEO of the social media platform X, formerly known as Twitter, Elon Musk. I could not find any official and trustworthy sources to confirm that; nevertheless, this statement somewhat aligns with his current stance on education at the time of writing this book. During an interview, Elon Musk shared his vision for simplifying and modernising the education system. He made a striking remark, stating to "make education as close to a video game as possible . . . you do not need to tell your kid to play video games; they will play video games on autopilot all day." His comments highlight the significant challenge of updating an educational framework that has largely remained unchanged for decades.[34] The current system, seemingly anchored in the past, still needs to fully meet the needs and realities of the modern world. This disconnect implies that many aspects of our current education may not be sufficiently equipping

---

[34] My Idol Elon, "Elon Musk's Incredible Speech on the Education System | Eye Opening Video on Education," YouTube video, May 21, 2021, https://youtu.be/YNQDp3v-VGE.

students for the challenges of today and the future. This dissatisfaction with conventional education, and specifically private schools in Los Angeles, led a visionary like Elon Musk to establish a school specifically for his children.

If we truly want to equip our students for success in a rapidly changing world, we need to rethink and rework our approach to education. Just as we have acknowledged the importance of rewards and sanctions in motivating students, it's equally critical to ensure that the system itself is relevant and responsive. Clinging to old ways in a new age will only leave our students at a disadvantage. It's high time for change, even if that change requires challenging deeply ingrained norms.

If Roman philosopher Lucius Seneca were still alive, he would certainly keep reminding us that "we learn not in school, but in life."

The education system in the Western world, which comprises all of North America, Great Britain, and Europe, has been criticised for various flaws. Some of the most common criticisms include a lack of individualised learning, a focus on standardised testing, unequal access to education, and a failure to prepare students for the real world.

Sir Ken Robinson, a well-known educator and writer, has been a vocal critic of today's education system. In his book *Creative Schools: The Grassroots Revolution That's Transforming Education*, he claims that the system is old-fashioned and doesn't equip students for today's world. He explains that our education system was created during times very different from now – the Enlightenment, a period of intellectual growth, and the Industrial Revolution, a time of major economic change.[35]

The fact that many educators have been sounding the alarm for several decades is a glaring sign of urgency. Educator Diane Ravitch has more than once pointed out the deficiencies of the educational system, notably in her book *The Death and Life of the Great American School System*. She argues, "Test scores are not educational outcomes. They are merely a measure

---

[35] Ken Robinson and Lou Aronica, "Chapter 2," in *Creative Schools: The Grassroots Revolution That's Transforming Education* (New York: Viking, 2015)

of one aspect of education, and they are not a reliable or valid measure of educational quality or effectiveness."[36]

In agreement with authors Sir Ken Robinson and Diane Ravitch, the current education system in the Western world is indeed flawed in several fundamental ways. Their criticisms highlight significant issues that resonate with my experiences in school and as an adult in the professional world.

Firstly, the lack of individualised learning in schools is a critical problem. Each student possesses distinct abilities, passions, and learning methods, but the prevailing educational system frequently adopts a uniform strategy for all. This can be especially problematic for students who might not fit into the conventional learning mould. For instance, in my school years, I observed many exceptionally talented classmates in areas like art, music, and practical problem-solving, but these skills were seldom nurtured. Instead, they were often overlooked because their skills didn't align with the standard curriculum.

Moreover, the heavy emphasis on standardised testing is a significant concern. These tests often fail to measure students' true abilities or potential. As Ravitch points out, test scores are not a comprehensive indicator of educational quality or effectiveness. In real-life scenarios, success often depends on skills like creativity, adaptability, and critical thinking, which need to be adequately assessed beyond standardised tests. I recall my own school days, when the focus was predominantly on rote memorisation to pass exams rather than understanding concepts and applying them in real-world situations.

Unequal access to education is another significant issue. Socioeconomic status, geographic location, and other factors can drastically affect the quality of education a student receives. This disparity continues into adulthood,

---

[36] N. Singh, "Review of Diane Ravitch Book, 'The Death and Life of the Great American School System: How Testing and Choice are Undermining Education,'" *Poverty & Public Policy* 4, no. 2 (2012).

when those with better educational opportunities often have advantages in the job market.

Furthermore, the failure of the system to prepare students for the real world is evident. Many graduates find themselves ill-equipped to handle the challenges of adult life, be it in higher education or the workforce. Essential skills, such as managing finances, communicating effectively, and understanding emotional intelligence, should be included in school syllabuses.

In summary, while the Western education system has its merits, it is crucial to address these flaws. A more holistic approach that values individual talents, focuses less on standardised testing, provides equal educational opportunities, and prepares students for real-world challenges would be a significant step forwards. This would benefit students and contribute to a more adaptable, innovative, and equitable society.

Life can feel short for some, but it's important to consider how we can make the most of the time we have. One way to do this is by removing or lowering barriers to a fulfilling life. For children, it's important to consider how much time they have to simply be themselves amidst the demands of school, homework, chores, and other obligations. While different societies have varying expectations for children, it's important to ask ourselves whether we're allowing them enough time to just be kids. By prioritising the things that truly matter and allowing ourselves and our children time to pursue various passions and interests, we can live more fulfilling lives.

History of the Current English Education System

The education system in England, as a crucial part of the larger UK framework, has evolved through the ages to become one of the most globally respected educational models. This system has its roots deep in the country's history. Initially, education was a privilege of the elite, closely tied to the church. Yet, as England entered the industrial age, the need for a more uniform educational structure became apparent, leading to significant state interventions.

The Education Act of 1870 was a watershed moment in English educational history, mandating the creation of elementary schools that would be accessible to all children. The transition to a state-funded, universally accessible system marked the beginning of modern public education in England, reflecting a societal shift towards inclusivity and broader knowledge dissemination. However, this evolution also introduced challenges that are still pertinent today.

One significant impact of these changes was the gradual standardisation of curriculum and teaching methods. While this ensured a consistent educational baseline, it often neglected individual learning styles and creative thinking. Critics like Sir Ken Robinson argue that such a system, primarily focused on academic achievements and standardised testing, limits the development of critical thinking and creativity in students.

Moreover, the historical emphasis on industrial-era skills led to a system that sometimes struggles to adapt to the rapidly changing demands of the twenty-first-century workforce. The digital age requires skills such as adaptability, digital literacy, and innovative problem-solving, areas where traditional educational models may fall short.

This historical context also highlights the ongoing debate about educational equality. While the Education Act of 1870 was a step towards equal access, disparities in quality and resources between schools continue to be a significant issue, impacting the life chances of children from different socioeconomic backgrounds.

The impact of this history is evident in contemporary society. Many adults today, shaped by this education system, may find themselves ill-prepared for the rapidly evolving job market. This misalignment can lead to a workforce that is technically skilled but lacks the adaptability and creative problem-solving abilities crucial in today's world. Conversely, the strengths of the English education system, such as its emphasis on a broad-based curriculum and strong academic foundations, have contributed to a well-educated populace capable of innovation.

To some extent, I cannot fault the English and American education system for being static, as it has evolved over the years. However, the pertinent question remains: Has it evolved sufficiently? Has it progressed in a direction that nurtures the aspects discussed in the first part of this book?

I believe that England and the US, with their remarkable architectural prowess, showcase a perfect blend of history and modern innovation. Walking through their cities, I am constantly awed by the way contemporary structures seamlessly integrate with historic landmarks. This architectural ingenuity reflects a nation that values its past yet boldly embraces the future. In my opinion, if the education system mirrored this approach, blending traditional teaching methods with innovative, forward-thinking strategies, it would significantly enhance the learning experience.

England's place in the world is undisputedly significant. As a global hub of finance, culture, and politics, it naturally becomes a focal point for students worldwide. The country's education system, renowned for its high standards and academic excellence, is a magnet for international students. I feel this is a strength that could be leveraged even further. By integrating a global perspective and embracing diverse teaching methods, the system could prepare students to excel in a rapidly globalising world.

The attractiveness of England's education system to foreign students is undeniable. It's known for diverse perspectives and innovative thinking. England is also a unique cultural experience, offering the opportunity to engage with a diverse, multicultural environment. I strongly believe the system could do more to capitalise on this, perhaps by incorporating more international perspectives into the curriculum, encouraging student exchange programmes, and fostering an environment where global cultures and ideas converge.

In my opinion, the success of both England and the US is the result of John D. Rockefeller's vision for the education system: "I don't want a nation of thinkers; I want a nation of workers." I am advocating to reverse this vision, as I believe that it will elevate humanity more.

Across Continents: The Structure of Schooling in North America and Europe

Schooling structures around the world exhibit a fascinating diversity that reflects the cultural, historical, and social nuances of each region. In North America and Europe, these structures cater to the developmental stages of students, albeit through different educational frameworks.

In North America:

United States:
 Elementary School: Begins with kindergarten and continues up to fifth or sixth grade, serving children ages five to eleven.
 Middle School: This transitional stage includes sixth or seventh through eighth grade, for students aged eleven to fourteen.
 High School: Encompassing ninth through twelfth grade, students aged fourteen to eighteen culminate this period with a diploma.
 Higher Education: Post-secondary institutions include two-year community colleges granting associate degrees and universities offering bachelor's, master's, doctorate, and professional degrees.

Canada:
 Elementary School: Kindergarten through sixth or eighth grade, with the cut-off age varying by province.
 Secondary School: Runs up to grade twelve or thirteen, depending on the region, ending with a high school diploma.

Post-Secondary Education: Mirrors the US system with community colleges, universities, and graduate institutions, though programme lengths can vary provincially.

In Europe:

United Kingdom:

Primary Education: From Reception to Year 6 for ages four to eleven.

Secondary Education: Year 7 to Year 11 for ages eleven to sixteen, culminating in GCSE exams.

Further Education: Covers ages sixteen to eighteen, offering A-levels and BTECs, among others.

Higher Education: Universities provide a range of undergraduate, postgraduate, and doctoral programmes.

Germany:

Grundschule **(Primary School):** Grades one through four for children starting their school journey.

Secondary Education: Students are streamed into *Hauptschule*, *Realschule*, or Gymnasium, each leading to different educational and vocational pathways, with Gymnasium students taking the Abitur exam.

Higher Education: Comprises both traditional universities and Universities of Applied Sciences for varied degree programmes.

France:

École maternelle **(Preschool):** Caters to ages three to six.

École élémentaire **(Elementary School):** For ages six to eleven.

Collège **(Middle School):** Ages eleven to fifteen, ending with the *Diplôme National du Brevet*.

Lycée **(High School):** Ages fifteen to eighteen, culminating in the *Baccalauréat*.

Higher Education: Features universities and prestigious *grandes écoles*, among others.

Italy:

Scuola primaria (**Primary School**): Ages six to eleven.

Scuola secondaria di primo grado (**Middle School**): Ages eleven to fourteen.

Scuola secondaria di secondo grado (**High School**): Ages fourteen to nineteen, concluding with the *Esame di Stato*.

Higher Education: Universities offer a spectrum of undergraduate to doctoral degrees.

While these outlines provide a basic framework, the intricacies within each system reflect the depth and breadth of educational philosophies and practices in each country. Nations like Spain, the Netherlands, and Russia, not detailed here, contribute their unique perspective on education to the global landscape.

It's intriguing to note that despite a century or more of innovation and reform, the fundamental purpose and progression of these systems has remained relatively stable, underscoring the enduring nature of formal education's role in societal development.

The Rhythm of Learning: School Day Variations Across Cultures

Comparing school days across different countries involves examining not only the length and structure of the school day but also the pedagogical approaches and cultural attitudes towards education, which can significantly influence student experiences.

United States: In the US, the school day in both primary and secondary education typically runs from around 8:00 a.m. to 3:00 p.m., though this can vary. The day is divided into periods for different subjects, with a lunch break and a short recess in elementary schools. There's a strong emphasis on extracurricular activities, which are considered integral to student development. However, some argue that the longer day, combined with homework and extracurriculars, can lead to overscheduling and stress among students.

United Kingdom: The UK school day generally starts at 9:00 a.m. and ends around 3:30 p.m., with variations existing. There's a morning break and a lunch period, with younger children often having additional breaks. British schools tend to place a high value on uniformity and structure within the school day, which proponents say can provide a sense of security and order, fostering focus and discipline. Critics, however, suggest that it may limit students' opportunities for creativity and independent learning.

Germany: German school days usually start earlier, around 7:30 a.m., and may finish by lunchtime, especially in primary schools, reflecting a cultural value placed on afternoon family time and recreational activities. This schedule means that the academic sessions are more concentrated, and the school day is typically shorter than in the US or the UK. Some suggest this model allows for a better work-life balance and less stress for students, but others argue that it could lead to a more intense and potentially overwhelming morning session.

France: In France, school starts around 8:30 a.m. and can go until 4:30 p.m., with a longer lunch break than seen in the US or the UK, sometimes lasting up to two hours. This reflects the French cultural emphasis on mealtimes as social, restful periods. French students traditionally attend school for longer days but have a shorter week, with Wednesday afternoons off in many cases. This schedule allows for more in-depth learning periods at school, but it also places a heavy importance on out-of-school learning and support, which can exacerbate educational inequalities.

Italy: Italian primary school days typically start around 8:00 a.m. and end around 1:30 p.m., with secondary school days sometimes running longer.

The school day often consists of a continuous block of lessons with short breaks and no distinct lunch period, reflecting the cultural norm of eating the main meal of the day at home. This schedule supports familial cohesion and a rhythm that aligns with societal norms, but it can also mean that the academic programme must be very focused and condensed, potentially adding pressure to the school hours.

Finland: Finnish school days start around 9:00 a.m. and end by 2:00 p.m. to 4:00 p.m., depending on the day and grade level. With shorter school days and minimal homework, the system emphasises student well-being and independence. Breaks are frequent to encourage play and socialisation. This approach, I believe, reduces stress and burnout, fostering an environment where students enjoy learning.

Denmark: Danish school days typically begin at 8:00 a.m. and finish around 3:00 p.m., featuring a well-rounded curriculum that includes significant time for physical activity. Danish culture prioritises a balance between educational attainment and quality of life, which is reflected in their school day structure, potentially leading to happier, more well-rounded students.

China: In China, the school day often runs from 7:30 a.m. to 5:00 p.m. or later, with additional evening study periods being common. The extended hours focus on academic excellence but can lead to high levels of student stress and competition. The intense focus on education is driven by societal expectations and the high-stakes *Gaokao* exam for university admissions.

Russia: Russian students usually start school around 8:00 a.m. and finish by 2:00 p.m. There's a considerable emphasis on a broad education including the arts and sciences. The shorter school day reflects a traditional approach to education, focusing on depth of knowledge, which may contribute to strong academic performance.

Saudi Arabia: School days in Saudi Arabia typically run from 7:00 a.m. to 1:00 p.m. The system is influenced by religious studies and societal roles, with gender-segregated classes. The schedule allows students to participate in family and religious activities outside school hours, aligning with cultural norms.

Brazil: In Brazil, school hours vary widely, but typically, students attend either a morning session from around 7:00 a.m. to 12:00 p.m. or an afternoon session from around 1:00 p.m. to 6:00 p.m. This split allows for more students to be educated with limited resources invested but can limit extracurricular and holistic educational activities.

Georgia: Older students commonly attend school during the morning shift, which typically starts at around 8:00 a.m. and ends near 12:00 p.m. Meanwhile, younger students often attend school during the afternoon shift, which can run from approximately 1:00 p.m. to 5:00 p.m. This split-shift system allows educational institutions to maximise the use of their facilities and manage teacher workloads more effectively.

Regarding Brazil and Georgia, the shift system provides both benefits and drawbacks for students. On the positive side, it can result in smaller class sizes and more individual attention for students during their respective sessions. It also provides flexibility for families and students who might have other responsibilities or prefer a certain part of the day for formal education.

However, the shift system also poses challenges. It may limit the amount of time available for each student in school, potentially impacting the depth and breadth of the curriculum that can be covered. Additionally, it might affect the amount of time available for extracurricular activities and other forms of enrichment that play a significant role in a student's overall development.

Senegal, Mali, and Ethiopia: The school day timing in Senegal, Mali, and Ethiopia reflects an effort to maximise educational delivery within resource constraints, operating Monday to Thursday from 8:00 a.m. to 5:00 p.m., with a shorter day on Friday. The use of shifts, necessitated by limited resources, may impact consistency and depth of learning, as students receive education in varying environments and time frames. Despite these challenges, the system aims to impart essential knowledge and skills. However, the long hours from Monday to Thursday and the shift system could contribute to student fatigue and potentially affect retention and engagement. Additionally, these timings show an adaptation to local economic and social realities, indicating a tailored approach to education that balances instructional needs with community and infrastructural capacities.

Global Education Review: A Comparative Analysis

The global educational landscape presents a complex relationship between a nation's economic standing and the effectiveness of its education system. This interplay suggests that education is not just a reflection of national prosperity but is also a key driver of it.

The Global Partnership for Education, recognising education as a fundamental human right, is a catalyst for broader human, social, and economic development. Education is championed as the pillar of progress, advancing gender equality, fostering peace, and enhancing life and career opportunities globally. While this concept appears straightforward and easy to implement on paper, the reality paints a different picture.

Let's consider the notion that education is a catalyst for broader human and socioeconomic development. As per UNESCO's data from September 2022, an alarming 244 million children and youth aged six to eighteen were out of school in 2021. Some might view this figure as relatively insignificant in the grand scheme, but I must disagree. To put it in perspective, 244 million is more than half of the population of the twenty-seven European Union countries combined. This staggering statistic highlights the scale of the issue.[37]

When it comes to rankings, methodologies can differ greatly, leading to diverse outcomes. For example, the Best Countries Report by *US News &*

---

[37] Audrey Azoulay, "244M Children Won't Start the New School Year," UNESCO, September 1, 2022, last updated April 20, 2023, https://www.unesco.org/gem-report/en/articles/244m-children-wont-start-new-school-year.

World Report, in collaboration with the BAV Group and the Wharton School, gauges the quality of education by considering factors like the development of public education systems, university attendance, and the perceived excellence of education. In their 2021 rankings, they highlighted a list of ten countries that exemplify educational success according to their criteria.[38]

The United States, often seen at the top in terms of educational resources and innovation, faces challenges like lagging student performance in mathematics and science. The issue has been partially attributed to educational funding not rising in step with inflation, resulting in slipping international rankings over recent decades.

Discrepancies across different rankings underscore the impact of varying assessment metrics and what each study determines as indicative of educational quality.

Another influential global measure of educational success is the Programme for International Student Assessment (PISA), which assesses the abilities of fifteen-year-old students in reading, mathematics, and science. China's performance in PISA has been remarkable, often leading the rankings, with countries like Korea and Finland also consistently showing strong outcomes.[39]

However, many countries still face educational challenges. UNESCO's Education for All Global Monitoring Report frequently points to issues like internal conflict, economic constraints, and insufficient funding as barriers to the development of effective educational systems.[40] Such challenges highlight

---

[38] U.S. News Staff, "Countries With Well-Developed Public Education Systems, Ranked by Perception," *U.S. News,* September 25, 2020, https://www.usnews.com/news/best-countries/slideshows/countries-seen-to-have-well-developed-public-education-systems?slide=12.

[39] "PISA 2022 Results," *OECD,* accessed March 4, 2024, https://www.oecd.org/publication/pisa-2022-results/.

[40] "Global Education Monitoring Report Summary, 2021/2: Non-State Actors in Education: Who Chooses? Who Loses?," *UNESCO,* 2021/2, https://unesdoc.unesco.org/ark:/48223/pf0000380076.

the need for a concerted global effort to prioritise education and address these disparities.

While various reports and studies provide snapshots of educational quality across the globe, it's clear that a comprehensive approach to enhancing educational systems is needed, one that considers economic contexts, cultural values, and the inherent rights of all individuals to quality education. This global view also reminds us that while rankings offer insights, they are only one lens through which to view the multifaceted, evolving narrative of global education. This leads me to pose the following question: Is a country's level of education proportionate to the happiness of its citizens?

Is a Country's Level of Education Proportionate to the Happiness of Its Citizens?

Interestingly, there appears to be little to no direct correlation between education levels and happiness. In some cases, it seems that those nations with less formal education might even lead happier lives. Why might this be? Various factors come into play, such as the absence of educational pressures. The higher the societal stakes, like infrastructure scarcity, job shortages, and intense competition due to dense populations, the greater the pressure on educational attainment. However, people in developing countries often embrace life as it comes and find joy in the simplest of things.

As a native of Haiti, I can attest that there are few people who display more happiness with what little they have than the Haitian populace. This resilience and joy may well be the source of my own positive outlook. Beyond cultural influences, we must consider the role of climate – good weather and sunlight exposure lead to serotonin release in the brain, which elevates mood. The absence of sunlight can result in decreasing serotonin, potentially leading to depression or seasonal affective disorder (SAD) – a fitting acronym, indeed.

So, if the level of education doesn't necessarily equate to a person's happiness, is there a way to forge this connection? After all, knowledge is a profound and beautiful enrichment for the mind.

Educating for Joy: Bridging Learning and Happiness

To explore potential ways to bridge the gap between education and happiness, let's consider some avenues:

Purpose-Driven Education: Aligning educational objectives with personal values and societal needs can enhance the sense of purpose in students. Education that empowers individuals to make meaningful contributions to their communities can promote a sense of fulfilment and well-being.

Life Skills Integration: Integrating practical life skills into the curriculum, such as managing finances, cooking basic meals, and preparing for job interviews, equips students with essential capabilities for adult life. This approach promotes self-reliance and real-world problem-solving, ensuring students are academically prepared and adept at navigating the complexities of everyday life. Such skills are invaluable in fostering independence, confidence, and adaptability to various life situations.

Balanced Academic Demands: Adjusting academic expectations to reduce stress and anxiety, while promoting a love for lifelong learning, can improve the overall educational experience. A balanced approach valuing creativity and personal growth alongside academic achievements may enhance satisfaction.

Community and Collaboration: Promoting a sense of belonging within educational institutions by fostering strong community ties and collaborative opportunities can lead to happier student experiences. Feeling connected and supported is a key component of happiness.

Access to Nature and Play: Incorporating outdoor learning and ensuring that students have access to nature and opportunities for unstructured play can improve mood and well-being. This is especially important for young learners, who benefit greatly from physical activity and environmental education.

Culturally Relevant Education: Education that respects and reflects the cultural background of students can promote a positive identity and enhance engagement. When students see their lives and histories represented in their education, it can increase their sense of worth and joy.

Mindfulness and Well-Being Programmes: Schools that implement programmes focusing on mindfulness, meditation, and general well-being can help students manage stress, leading to increased happiness.

Experiential Learning: Allowing students to learn through experience, such as internships, community service, and field trips, provides a more engaging and often joyous way to learn and apply their knowledge in real-world settings.

Inclusive Environments: Ensuring that education is inclusive and accessible to all, regardless of socioeconomic status, can level the playing field and remove barriers to happiness associated with inequality.

Post-Educational Support: Guidance for life post-education, including career counselling and life coaching, can help students transition smoothly into the next stages of their lives, reducing anxiety about the future and enhancing happiness.

It is important to note that while education itself might not be a direct conduit to happiness, the ways in which it is structured and delivered can have significant implications for the well-being of individuals.

A GLIMPSE INTO GLOBAL EDUCATION

What Are the Experts Saying about the Current System?

Who are the experts, and what justifies them being called "experts"? Experts hold diverse opinions on the current education system: some commend its strengths and successes, while others critique its limitations and challenges.

On one hand, proponents of the current education system praise its capacity to facilitate social mobility and economic growth. They commend its role in providing access to knowledge and opportunities to individuals globally. Advocates argue that education is critical for building strong communities, promoting civic engagement, and developing the skills and knowledge necessary for success in the modern world.

On the other hand, other experts have spotlighted the limitations and challenges inherent in the current education system. They contend that the overemphasis on standardised testing and narrow metrics of academic achievement have led to a devaluation of creativity, diversity, and non-academic skills. Concerns also extend to the impact of technology on education, with some experts suggesting that technology can be a distraction and a barrier to learning, rather than an enhancement tool.

Additionally, ongoing debates persist regarding the best approaches to teaching and learning. Some experts argue that the current system is outdated and in need of significant reform. They advocate for more student-centred and inquiry-based approaches to learning, emphasising the development of critical thinking, problem-solving, and collaboration skills.

As I contemplated writing this book, initially believing my ideas for changing the education system were somewhat unconventional and unique, I soon discovered that I was not alone in my thinking. Sharing my thoughts and exploring the writings of educators like Pasi Sahlberg and Sir Ken Robinson revealed a shared desire for a significant update in the school system. And many advocates before them initiated the battle for educational reform.

Through numerous conversations with friends, colleagues, and educators, I discovered a shared consensus on the need for a profound change in the education system. My quest for literature on this topic led me to discover a wealth of works by educators, researchers, and teachers who shared my belief in prioritising a child's learning and well-being within the education system.

This exploration reinforced my conviction that the current education system requires transformative adjustments. It is heartening to realise I am not alone in my perspective. There are others who envision a more relevant and effective education system.

I have come across several educators who have shared their insights on the subject. I have found their quotes to be informative and thought-provoking, and I am eager to share some of them with you.

One quote that particularly resonates with me is from Sir Ken Robinson, an expert in creativity and education. He once said, "We have to go from what is essentially an industrial model of education, a manufacturing model, which is based on linearity and conformity and batching people. We have to move to a model that is based more on principles of agriculture. We have to recognise that human flourishing is not a mechanical process; it's an organic process. And you cannot predict the outcome of human development. All you can do, like a farmer, is create the conditions under which they will begin to flourish."[41]

Sir Ken Robinson's insightful critique of the industrial model of education deeply aligns with my own observations and experiences as an educator. The industrial model, with its emphasis on conformity and standardisation, often undermines the essence of humanity. Under this system, individuals are not encouraged to think, question, or explore; instead, they are expected to comply and execute predetermined tasks, akin to a cog in a machine. This educational approach, treating individuals more like robots, severely hampers personal development, stifling the pursuit of hobbies, artistic interests, and the individual exploration crucial for holistic growth.

By their very nature, human beings are explorers and creators. We are wired to seek new opportunities, learn, grow, and push the boundaries of what is known and familiar. The traditional educational model, with its rigid structure and focus on rote learning, fails to cater to this innate human propensity for exploration and innovation. It overlooks the fact that learning is a dynamic and individualised process, one that cannot be effectively encompassed within a one-size-fits-all framework.

Children, especially, embody this natural tendency for exploration and curiosity. They are like rivers, meant to flow freely, carving their own paths. This was beautifully illustrated to me during a morning walk when I observed a young boy, about five or six years old, walking with his mother. In a moment of pure, uninhibited curiosity, he stepped aside from the flat comfort of the pavement to climb the ledge of a wall. This simple act was a profound reminder of the intrinsic desire in all of us, especially children, to explore, challenge ourselves, and engage with our environment in novel ways. Even as adults, such actions bring a sense of joy and fulfilment.

This is why I staunchly believe in the philosophy that education should nurture, not stifle, these natural inclinations. It should provide children with

---

[41] Greg Whitby, "Ken Robinson pt 3 (Ken Robinson at TED2010)," YouTube video, April 28, 2014, https://youtu.be/J4p4xeXTTOM.

the space and freedom to explore their interests, make mistakes, and learn from these mistakes. Our role as educators is not to constrain this natural flow but to guide and support it, allowing each child to discover their unique potential and path. In doing so, we honour their individuality and cultivate a generation of thinkers, innovators, and lifelong learners.

In my opinion, the essence of education should not solely focus on imparting specific skill sets or knowledge. Instead, the focus should be on fostering adaptability, critical thinking, and collaborative skills. The world is changing at an unprecedented pace, and technological advancements have accelerated this rate of change. Platforms like YouTube, which allows users to speed up videos, reflect our society's growing impatience and urgency to move quickly to the next task.

This rapid evolution directly impacts the job market. We are witnessing a seismic shift in career landscapes. Jobs that exist today might become obsolete in the next decade, giving rise to entirely new professions. For students currently in secondary education, the reality is that the career path they envisioned may no longer be viable by the time they graduate from university. I've observed this first-hand with students pursuing degrees in industries transformed by technology within a few years, rendering their specific skills less relevant.

This evolving scenario underscores the importance of teaching children not just information but how to learn, adapt, and pivot. Skill flexibility and the ability to enhance one's potential are crucial assets in this context. Education should prepare students for the unknown, equipping them with the ability to face and thrive in a future we can't fully imagine. It's about nurturing an open, curious, and resilient mindset.

In my teaching practice, I focus on project-based learning and group work, in which students collaboratively tackle real-world problems. This approach builds their knowledge base and, more importantly, hones their ability to work in teams, problem-solve, and think creatively. These skills will stand the test of time, regardless of how technology or the job market evolve.

Yong Zhao's insightful words capture a crucial aspect of contemporary education – the importance of nurturing creativity, an entrepreneurial spirit, and global competitiveness in our children. His observation that "the most important thing we can do for our children is to prepare them to be creative, entrepreneurial, and globally competitive" deeply resonates with the core reason behind my decision to write this book. It's a call to action, a reminder that while the traditional education system may not have been originally designed to foster these qualities, it's never too late to pivot and embrace a new direction.

My motivation for writing is rooted in a realistic yet hopeful vision. I fervently believe in the power of positive forces, those that nourish the mind, body, and soul, over negative forces. It is far more sustainable and beneficial to cultivate and foster positivity than to suppress or control the inherent tendencies of human nature. This philosophy aligns with the analogy of the river; you might attempt to redirect its course, but when its waters gather strength, they will carve their own path, often with tumultuous consequences. This natural force is akin to the human spirit, especially in young learners, an unstoppable force that, when guided positively, can lead to phenomenal growth and development.

Considering the ever-growing global population, the prospect of an educational revolution becomes not just a possibility but a necessity. As the number of young minds ready to be shaped and nurtured increases, so does the responsibility to provide them with an education that is relevant, empowering, and in tune with the demands of a globalised world. We don't want a system that only prepares students for a predefined world; we want one that equips them with the skills, mindset, and creativity to shape the world they will inherit.

In this context, the goal of education should be empowering students to harness their innate creativity and curiosity, guiding them to become more than just consumers of knowledge. Turn them into creators and innovators. We must encourage them to think globally, act entrepreneurially, and compete effectively in a constantly evolving world. This is the essence of a true educational revolution – one that embraces change, encourages innovation, and prepares our children for a future that we can imagine but have yet to see.

This book, therefore, is a call to action – an appeal to educators, policymakers, parents, and all stakeholders in education – to embrace change and work towards creating learning environments that are dynamic, inclusive, and forward-thinking. It's a testimony to my belief in education's transformative power; it's a force that, when aligned with the natural course of human development and global trends, can provide extraordinary outcomes for our children and the world at large.

Why Are the Education Systems of the World So Similar?

Numerous factors contribute to similarities in education systems worldwide, including globalisation. The exchange of ideas and knowledge across borders, propelled by globalisation, has led many countries to adopt similar educational approaches and policies. The dissemination of best practices and innovations, including the integration of technology and digital tools into education, further fuels the convergence of education systems. Additionally, international organisations like UNESCO and the OECD play an important role in promoting common educational goals and standards, facilitating the exchange of ideas and practices globally. The historical impact of European colonisation and imperialism has certainly played a significant role in shaping education systems worldwide, leaving legacies that continue to influence various aspects, including education. Recognising and understanding these historical influences is crucial for addressing inequalities and promoting more equitable education systems.

However, the standardisation of education systems worldwide has resulted in a narrow and limited perspective on education, failing to meet the diverse needs of learners. I believe it is important to share best practices and learn from other education systems to improve educational outcomes. Unfortunately, because of historical standardisations, encountering a truly unique education system somewhere has become challenging.

While it may be disheartening to witness experts pointing out flaws in education systems without immediate changes, it's important to remember that change is a gradual process requiring time and sustained effort. Various factors, including political and economic pressures, can hinder the implementation of sweeping reforms, especially when immediate results are not apparent. However, this should not discourage efforts towards progress.

One avenue for effecting change is through grassroots efforts and advocacy. Collaborative endeavours by educators, students, and parents can push for reforms, prioritising student well-being and effective learning. Additionally, policymakers and education leaders can be influenced by research and data showcasing the benefits of alternative approaches. More significantly, the collective voice of the masses, including parents, educators, and students, can exert substantial influence on policymakers, fostering rapid changes.

Maintaining optimism and persistently advocating for change, even in the face of challenges, is crucial. The education of future generations is a matter too vital to relinquish.

What Is the Education System Like in South America?

Education systems in South America are diverse and intricate, varying across countries and regions. While global educational frameworks share certain parallels, such as the emphasis on core subjects, South American schools are increasingly prioritising holistic development. This includes fostering non-academic skills like creativity, critical thinking, and communication.

However, the South American education sector grapples with challenges, especially regarding inequality. The region's pronounced socioeconomic disparities manifest in unequal access to quality education and divergent educational outcomes. Factors like high poverty rates further exacerbate these educational challenges.

In response, numerous South American countries have initiated reforms to enhance educational accessibility and quality. Strategies encompass bolstering educational funding, expanding access to early childhood education, and implementing innovative teacher training programmes. Aligning with global educational trends, there's increasing emphasis on integrating technology and digital tools, which are perceived as vital in enhancing learning experiences and democratising access to educational resources.

Common Points in the World's Education Systems

There are several commonalities in education systems worldwide, although the extent of emphasis and implementation may vary by country or region. Some of these shared features include the following:

1. Core subjects: Most education systems globally mandate students study a set of core subjects, such as language arts, mathematics, science, and social studies.
2. Grade levels: Students typically progress through a series of grade levels, with each level building on the knowledge and skills acquired in the previous one.
3. Standardised testing: Many education systems globally employ standardised testing to evaluate student performance and progress.
4. Teacher training: Most education systems require teachers to undergo some form of training and professional development to attain certification.
5. Curriculum development: Education systems often designate a central authority responsible for developing and updating the curriculum.

6. Emphasis on education as a means of social and economic development: Worldwide, there is recognition of education's crucial role in promoting social and economic development.

Despite these commonalities, it is important to acknowledge significant differences across education systems, particularly concerning access, quality, and available resources for students. Additionally, ongoing debates persist about the optimal approaches to teaching and learning, with various countries and regions prioritising different educational values and goals.

Differences in the Education Systems of the World

Here are some differences observed across education systems worldwide:

1. Access to education: Significant disparities in access to education exist in many parts of the world. Factors such as poverty, gender, ethnicity, and geography can result in certain groups or communities having limited or no access to education.

2. Funding and resources: The level of funding and resources available to education systems can vary significantly across different countries and regions. Some education systems are well funded, with access to state-of-the-art resources, while others may be underfunded, lacking basic resources like textbooks and technology.

3. Curriculum and teaching styles: Education systems may emphasise different subject areas and adopt diverse approaches to teaching and learning. For instance, some systems may prioritise rote learning and memorisation, while others may focus on critical thinking and problem-solving.

4. Standardised testing: While many education systems use standardised testing, variations exist in the types of tests, testing frequency, and the

importance placed on test scores in evaluating student and teacher performance.

5. Teacher training and certification: Requirements for teacher training and certification vary significantly across countries and regions. Some education systems mandate extensive training and certification processes, while others have less rigorous requirements.

6. Cultural values and priorities: Education systems may reflect and reinforce different cultural values and priorities. Some systems strongly emphasise academic achievement, while others prioritise the development of non-academic skills like creativity, communication, and empathy.

Investing in Tomorrow: Rethinking Governmental Commitment to Educational Funding

Reflecting on the current state of educational funding, I find a stark contrast between the swift mobilisation of financial resources in times of crisis and the persistent underfunding in the educational sector. It's striking to consider how governments quickly allocate substantial funds in situations like the 2007–2008 financial crisis, the COVID-19 pandemic, and international conflicts like the war in Ukraine. Yet, when it comes to education, a sector fundamental to the future of any nation, governments fall short in adequately funding it.

I have noticed that long-term investments like education don't receive the same level of attention or urgency as immediate responses for emergencies. This disparity in funding priorities raises critical questions about governmental commitment to the educational needs of future generations. The impact of this underfunding is far-reaching, affecting not just my salary and my colleagues' but also the quality of education we can offer. Without adequate resources, our ability to provide a rich learning environment for our students is significantly hampered.

I strongly believe in the economic argument for investing in education. As an educator, I see education as a crucial driver of economic development. A well-educated population is essential for a nation's growth and innovation. This perspective leads me to question why educational funding isn't viewed as a vital long-term investment. It's frustrating to witness a reluctance to allocate resources to a sector that yields such significant returns over time.

Another aspect I often ponder is the role of international organisations in bridging the educational funding gap. These bodies provide more than just financial aid; they are instrumental in sharing innovative educational models and best practices globally. Examining how different countries prioritise educational funding is enlightening. Nations that invest heavily in education often reap the benefits of a more skilled, innovative, and productive workforce.

Reflecting on my teaching experiences and those of my colleagues, the challenges we face due to stagnant salaries and increased living costs are profound. We marched in the streets, demanding a mere 10-percent increase after a decade-long pay freeze. This demand seems minimal when considering the loss of over 40 percent in purchasing power due to inflation over twelve years. Our struggles are not only about compensation; they represent the broader issue of how little value is placed on the profession that shapes future generations.

In summary, I advocate for a re-evaluation of how we view and fund education. It's time for governments and international bodies to recognise education as a critical long-term investment, crucial not just for individual development but for the prosperity and success of our whole society. This change in perspective is essential for improving our education system and, ultimately, our future.

The Unquantifiable Value of School Trips

Imagine this: In most professions, an eight-hour workday is the standard. Work beyond these hours often commands overtime pay, sometimes at double the rate. Weekend work, particularly on Sundays, can offer even higher financial incentives. Yet, within the realm of teaching, the dynamics are starkly different, especially when organising school trips. Teachers responsible for planning and executing these excursions do so without any additional financial remuneration. They become full-time guardians, responsible for the well-being and safety of each student under their watch from the moment they step off school grounds until their return. This level of responsibility can be daunting; it is a commitment that extends far beyond the confines of a typical workday, and one at which many would baulk.

So why do educators willingly undertake such tasks? The answer lies in the inherent value that these student experiences offer. School trips, particularly abroad, provide an invaluable opportunity for students to gain exposure to different cultures and perspectives. They transcend traditional education, becoming life-enriching experiences that some students might never otherwise have. These trips can profoundly impact young minds, offering them first-hand exposure to diverse ways of life, broadening their horizons, and challenging preconceived notions.

For instance, during a trip to Germany, I witnessed first-hand the transformative impact on my students. Those who harboured prejudices based on historical events, movies, or hearsay were confronted with a reality that starkly contrasted their preconceived notions. They discovered a Germany vibrant with culture, warmth, and diversity, far removed from the stereotypes of perpetually eating bratwurst or harbouring xenophobic attitudes. Such experiences are pivotal in teaching young minds about tolerance, diversity, and the shared humanity that transcends national borders.

Reflecting on my own personal Year 8 experience on a school trip to England, I found it equally transformative. It shattered my own stereotypes of

England as a perpetually rainy country where everyone donned a bowler hat and carried an umbrella. The reality was a revelation – sunny days and diverse lifestyles and attire. It was a lesson in challenging and overcoming stereotypes that has stayed with me throughout my career.

School trips represent more than just an opportunity to see new places. They are a conduit for real-world learning and personal development. Students acquire adaptability, independence, and resilience. They return with enriched mindsets and memories that often last a lifetime. It is an education that transcends textbooks and classrooms, teaching empathy, global citizenship, and cultural appreciation.

Unfortunately, such trips are a privilege not universally accessible. Many schools, particularly in less affluent regions or countries, cannot offer these invaluable experiences. This disparity brings to light a broader challenge in the global education landscape – the unequal distribution of opportunities for experiential learning. Our educator role extends beyond imparting academic knowledge; it encompasses nurturing well-rounded, globally aware individuals.

In conclusion, the decision by teachers to organise and lead these trips, despite the absence of additional financial compensation, is a testament to their dedication to providing students with holistic educational experiences. It reflects a commitment to a kind of teaching that shapes not only knowledgeable but also empathetic and worldly individuals. As we move forwards in the changing world of education, it is crucial to recognise and support the invaluable role of such experiential learning opportunities in shaping tomorrow's citizens.

Where and When Did It Go Wrong?

Pinpointing exactly where things started going wrong in the education system is a difficult question with no single answer, as the challenges and limitations of education systems have evolved and changed over time. However, some experts and scholars point to certain historical and social factors that have contributed to the current state of education.

One factor is the rise of industrialisation and the need for standardised education to meet the demands of the workforce. As the economy shifted from an agricultural to an industrial model, schools became more focused on producing compliant workers who could perform repetitive tasks efficiently, rather than fostering creativity and critical thinking skills.

Another factor is the emphasis on standardised testing and accountability measures that began to take hold in the mid-twentieth century. While intended to improve educational outcomes and track progress, these measures have been criticised for creating a culture of teaching to the test and neglecting the development of other important skills and qualities.

Additionally, many experts point to the limitations of the one-size-fits-all model of education, which fails to meet the diverse needs and abilities of students. This expanded awareness of the importance of personalised and student-centred learning and a recognition of the need for greater emphasis on non-academic skills and qualities such as creativity, problem-solving, and social-emotional development continues to shape contemporary discussions about education reform.

The French education system, for instance, has been criticised for various weaknesses, including a lack of flexibility, a focus on rote learning, and a high-stakes exam culture. According to Francois Dubet, retired sociologist and former director of the School for Advanced Studies in the Social Sciences, "the French education system has a rigid and inflexible structure that does not allow for innovation or creativity."[42]

Educational systems worldwide have been the subject of numerous studies, many of which have identified concerning areas. Combining what I experienced during my teaching years with what I have read and heard, I have

---

[42] Théophile Larcher, "Education: Do French Schools Deserve Their Harsh Reputation?" *The Connexion*, May 18, 2022, https://www.connexionfrance.com/article/Comment/Opinion/Education-do-French-schools-deserve-their-harsh-reputation.

compiled a non-exhaustive list of several aspects of the educational system that I believe need serious, if not radical, revision. Moreover, this has been highlighted in several national and international studies.

Standardised Testing: Overreliance on standardised testing can lead to a narrowed curriculum, teachers "teaching to the test," and undue stress on students.

Lack of Individualisation: Many educational systems follow a one-size-fits-all approach, which doesn't cater to the individual needs, strengths, and interests of each student. In England, applying "differentiation" in lessons is recommended. Still, to be effective or simply feasible, teachers require extra time for planning, more resources, and reduced class sizes.

Teacher Burnout: High demands, inadequate support, and low remuneration can lead to high turnover rates, burnout, and low morale among teachers, resulting in teacher shortages.

Inequitable Resource Allocation: Disparities in funding and resource allocation can exacerbate inequalities in education, with socioeconomically disadvantaged schools often needing more critical resources.

Outdated Curriculum: Some school systems have curricula that have not been updated in years, leaving students unprepared for the modern world's demands.

Insufficient Emphasis on Soft Skills: While academic knowledge is vital, there's a growing recognition of the importance of soft skills (e.g., critical thinking, communication, collaboration). Many school systems need to emphasise these skills sufficiently.

Overburdened Students: In some countries, students face long school days followed by extra tutoring, leading to burnout, mental health issues, and reduced time for recreational activities.

Limited Teacher Training and Professional Development: In various regions, teachers receive limited initial training and few opportunities for ongoing professional development, leading to stagnation and reduced efficacy.

Lack of Real-World Application: Studies have shown that students often need assistance seeing the relevance of what they're learning to the real world, leading to decreased motivation and engagement.

Inadequate Use of Technology: While technology has the potential to revolutionise education, its insufficient or inappropriate use can hinder learning. In some schools, technology is underutilised or used in ways that don't enhance pedagogical goals.

Addressing these challenges requires comprehensive reforms, stakeholder collaboration, and a focus on creating educational environments that cater to the holistic development of students.

Haiti's Classroom Conundrum: Colonial Languages in a Creole Society

The educational challenges in Haiti poignantly mirror the broader systemic issues deeply ingrained in the country's history and societal structure. As a former colony of France, Haiti's ongoing struggle with the language of instruction in education is a stark reminder of the long-lasting impacts of colonialism. This struggle isn't just about language but identity, accessibility, and equality.

Colonial Legacies and Linguistic Hurdles

Haiti's complex history of French colonisation has left a linguistic divide that persists, impacting the heart and soul of its educational system. While Creole is the language spoken by the entire Haitian population and a proud marker of their identity, the education system remains attached to French. This language, emblematic of Haiti's colonial past, is largely inaccessible to the masses, creating a chasm between the language spoken in homes and communities versus the one used in schools. This deep linguistic disconnect presents insurmountable barriers to learning, as children are forced to navigate an educational system in a language that is foreign to their daily lives.

Creole Versus French: The Educational Language Divide

The persistent use of French in academic and administrative settings has effectively marginalised a significant portion of Haiti's population. Imagine being a young student, eager to learn yet faced with textbooks and lessons in a language you scarcely understand. This scenario is a daily reality for many Haitian children, leading to confusion, frustration, and a sense of alienation. This linguistic conflict undermines educational outcomes and exacerbates societal divides, perpetuating a cycle of inequality that echoes through generations.

Educational Outcomes and Societal Impact

This linguistic mismatch has profound and far-reaching consequences. The image of a Haitian classroom where students struggle to comprehend lessons taught in an alien tongue starkly represents squandered potential. Do you remember the story of my friend Jerry, who was punished for writing the wrong word on the board? In Creole, the same phrase would not require any context, which, though required in French, was not provided by the teacher. Many Haitian students reach the precipice of higher education without mastering French, implying that their foundational years, crucial for cognitive and skill development, are marred by linguistic barriers. This not only caps individual potential but also stifles the nation's economic and social progress. The irony is bitter – a country striving to progress yet held back by a colonial legacy that continues to dictate the language of its future.

Comparative Perspectives

Haiti's situation is not unique but reflects a pattern seen in other post-colonial settings, especially in parts of Africa, where education systems are structured around the languages of former colonisers. These systems inadvertently favour students from affluent backgrounds, often urban elites, who are more likely to be fluent in the colonial language. This disparity creates a deeply entrenched social divide, in which language becomes a gatekeeper of opportunity, perpetuating the colonial hierarchies of its birth. It's a global echo of inequality reverberating through countries shackled by their colonial past.

Looking Forwards: Language and Learning

The path forwards for Haiti's education system lies in embracing its linguistic heritage. There is a growing recognition of the need to integrate Creole, the language of the people, into the educational framework. Efforts towards bilingual education models are emerging, but the journey is fraught with challenges. A systemic overhaul is necessary to transform the educational landscape – one that elevates Creole from the language of the streets to a language of learning and intellectual discourse. Such a change has the potential of both enhancing educational outcomes and healing a nation still grappling with the shadows of its colonial past.

In addressing this issue, we see a chance for Haiti to reclaim its identity and empower its youth. It's about giving voice to a culture that has long been silenced, allowing students to learn in their own language. This goes beyond educational reform; it's a step towards national healing and a future where every Haitian child sees themselves reflected in the pages of their textbooks and hears their history and stories in the language that speaks to their souls.

Public Spending on Education as a Share of GDP from 1870 to 2022

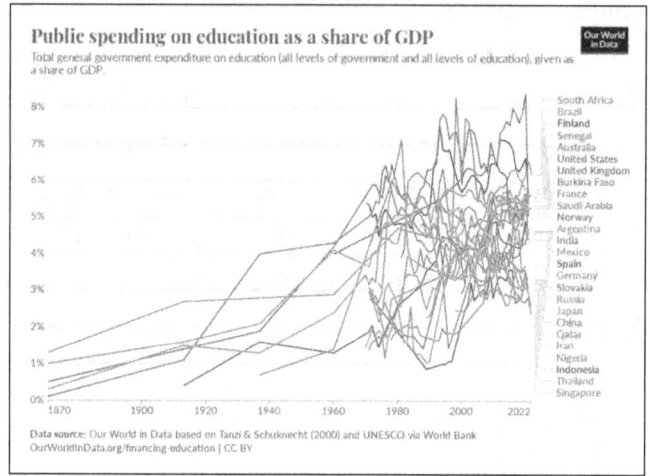

Government Expenditure on Education

After observing some dramatic fluctuation in the world's public spending between 1870 and 2022, let's examine how education was funded in various countries over the last couple of years (2021–2022).[43]

Africa:

South Africa: In 2021, the South African government allocated approximately ZAR 402.7 billion (around USD 27 billion) for education and training, which represented about 16.4 percent of the total government budget.

---

[43] "Public Spending on Education as a Share of GDP," *Our World in Data*, October 24, 2022, last updated July 10, 2023, https://ourworldindata.org/grapher/total-government-expenditure-on-education-gdp?tab=chart&country=USA~GBR~ESP~FRA~NOR~ZAF~NGA~BFA~SEN~QAT~IRN~SAU~ARG~BRA~MEX~IND~IDN~JPN~THA~SGP~CHN~AUS~RUS~SVK~DEU~FIN~DNK.

Senegal: In 2021, the Senegalese government allocated approximately XOF 772.7 billion (around USD 1.4 billion) for education, which represented about 26.5 percent of the total government budget.

Burkina Faso: In 2021, the Burkinabe government allocated approximately XOF 193.6 billion (around USD 350 million) for education, which represented about 17 percent of the total government budget.

Nigeria: In 2021, the Nigerian government allocated approximately NGN 742.5 billion (around USD 1.8 billion) for education, which represented about 6.7 percent of the total government budget.

Middle East:

Qatar: In 2021, the Qatari government allocated approximately QAR 38.1 billion (around USD 10.5 billion) for education and training, which represented about 10.2 percent of the total government budget.

Iran: In 2021, the Iranian government allocated approximately IRR 1,220 trillion (around USD 4.9 billion) for education, which represented about 14 percent of the total government budget.

Saudi Arabia: In 2021, the Saudi Arabian government allocated approximately SAR 193 billion (around USD 51 billion) for education and training, which represented about 20 percent of the total government budget.

North America and Europe:

United States: In 2021, the US federal government allocated approximately USD 66.6 billion for the Department of Education, which represented about 3.3 percent of the overall federal budget. However, education spending is also the responsibility of individual states, and their spending can vary widely.

United Kingdom: From 2021 to 2022, the UK government planned to spend approximately GBP 91.6 billion (around USD 128 billion) on education and children's services, which represented about 15.4 percent of the total government budget.

Finland: In 2021, the Finnish government allocated approximately EUR 6.8 billion (around USD 8 billion) for education, which represented about 11.8 percent of the total government budget.

Denmark: In 2021, the Danish government allocated approximately DKK 141.4 billion (around USD 22.6 billion) for education, which represented about 17.7 percent of the total government budget.

Norway: In 2021, the Norwegian government allocated approximately NOK 166.4 billion (around USD 19.2 billion) for education, which represented about 10 percent of the total government budget.

France: In 2021, the French government allocated approximately EUR 76.6 billion (around USD 90 billion) for education and research, which represented about 18 percent of the total government budget.

Germany: In 2021, the German federal government allocated approximately EUR 20.9 billion (around USD 24.7 billion) for education and research, which represented about 5.2 percent of the total federal budget.

Canada: From 2021 to 2022, the Canadian government planned to spend approximately CAD 33.5 billion (around USD 26.4 billion) on education, which represented about 13.5 percent of the total government budget.

Slovakia: In 2021, the Slovakian government allocated approximately EUR 2.3 billion (around USD 2.7 billion) for education and science, which represented about 5.7 percent of the total government budget.

Spain: In 2021, the Spanish government allocated approximately EUR 2.5 billion (around USD 2.9 billion) for education and vocational training, which represented about 2.3 percent of the total government budget.

Russia: In 2021, the Russian government allocated approximately RUB 1.4 trillion (around USD 19 billion) for education, which represented about 4.5 percent of the total government budget.

Asia/Eurasia:

China: In 2021, the Chinese government allocated approximately CNY 1.4 trillion (around USD 216 billion) for education, which represented about 4.5 percent of the total government budget.

Australia: From 2021 to 2022, the Australian government planned to spend approximately AUD 34.2 billion (around USD 25.4 billion) on education and training, which represented about 4.2 percent of the total government budget.

Singapore: In 2021, the Singaporean government allocated approximately SGD 13.5 billion (around USD 10 billion) for education, which represented about 20 percent of the total government budget.

Thailand: In 2021, the Thai government allocated approximately THB 500 billion (around USD 16 billion) for education, which represented about 14 percent of the total government budget.

Indonesia: In 2021, the Indonesian government allocated approximately IDR 536.1 trillion (around USD 37 billion) for education and culture, which represented about 20 percent of the total government budget.

India: From 2021 to 2022, the Indian government planned to spend approximately INR 93,224 crore (around USD 12.6 billion) on education, which represented about 3.4 percent of the total government budget.

Japan: In 2021, the Japanese government allocated approximately JPY 5.4 trillion (around USD 49 billion) for education, which represented about 3.5 percent of the total government budget.

South America:

Argentina: In 2021, the Argentine government allocated approximately ARS 729.2 billion (around USD 7.5 billion) for education, which represented about 3.3 percent of the total government budget.

Mexico: In 2021, the Mexican government allocated approximately MXN 820.9 billion (around USD 41 billion) for education, which represented about 11.7 percent of the total government budget.

Brazil: In 2021, the Brazilian government allocated approximately BRL 142.6 billion (around USD 27 billion) for education, which represented about 3.8 percent of the total government budget.

In assessing the impact of financial investment on global education systems, a general trend emerges from the 2021 rankings[44]: countries that allocate a significant portion of their budgets to education tend to achieve higher standings. This pattern suggests a positive correlation between the amount of funding dedicated to a country's education system and the perceived quality of that country's education system on a global scale.

This commitment to education is especially apparent in the case of Singapore, which, despite its small size, makes substantial investments in education, correlating with its impressive position in the global rankings.

Conversely, countries with lower education funding, such as Argentina, find themselves placed lower in the rankings. This suggests that lower investment levels may be linked to lesser performance in the global education arena.

However, it is important to note that while funding is a critical component, it is not the sole determinant of educational success. Other factors, including the efficient use of funds, the educational policy landscape, cultural values surrounding education, and historical investments in educational infrastructure, also play significant roles in shaping educational outcomes.

---

[44] Organisation for Economic Co-operation and Development, "Education at a Glance 2022: OECD Indicators," accessed April 19, 2024, https://www.oecd-ilibrary.org/sites/9149c2f5-en/index.html?itemId=/content/component/9149c2f5-en.

THE SINGULARITY OF THE FINNISH SCHOOL SYSTEM

Is the Finnish School System the Best One?

*O*n what grounds do agencies like PISA claim the Finnish school system is the best one?

The concept of the "best" school system worldwide is subjective and can vary based on evaluation criteria. However, international assessments and studies, such as the Programme for International Student Assessment (PISA), offer insights into the academic performance of students in various countries.

Based on PISA and similar rankings, several countries consistently stand out:[45]

1. **Finland**: Often praised for its education system, Finland emphasises teacher training, student well-being, and a holistic approach to

---

[45] OECD, *PISA 2022 Results (Volume I): The State of Learning and Equity in Education (How did countries perform in PISA?)*, OECD iLibrary, last visited March 5, 2024, https://www.oecd-ilibrary.org/sites/9149c2f5-en/index.html?itemId=/content/component/9149c2f5-en.

education. Their system features less homework, fewer tests, and a strong emphasis on creativity, critical thinking, and problem-solving. Finland's teachers are highly respected and well paid.

2. **Singapore**: Renowned for its rigorous curriculum and high academic standards, Singapore consistently ranks at the top in international assessments. Their education system is structured and disciplined, and it places a strong emphasis on math and science.

3. **Japan**: The Japanese education system emphasises hard work, discipline, and rote learning, resulting in students excelling in math and science. The cultural value placed on education is reflected in the high performance of Japanese students.

4. **Canada**: Canadian students, particularly in provinces like Alberta and British Columbia, excel in reading, mathematics, and science. Canada's approach to multiculturalism and equity in education has garnered recognition.

5. **Estonia**: Often overlooked but high-performing, Estonia places a strong emphasis on student-centred learning and boasts a well-developed vocational education and training system, earning accolades in PISA rankings.

6. **South Korea**: Known for its intense academic pressure and long study hours, South Korea places a significant emphasis on education. Their students consistently outperform in reading and mathematics.

While these countries consistently perform well in rankings, it is essential to acknowledge that what works well in one cultural and societal context might not be as effective in another. Each system has its strengths and weaknesses, shaped by various factors, including culture, economic conditions, societal values, and historical contexts.

Finland Emphasises Teacher Training

The Finnish education system commands global attention, particularly for its remarkable success in international assessments like PISA. This achievement is largely attributed to the country's distinctive approach to teacher training, which has become a subject of interest for educational reformers and policymakers, including those in countries like England. The Finnish model of teacher training encompasses several key aspects:

Rigorous Selection Process for Teacher Candidates:

- Finland bestows a level of prestige and respect akin to medical or legal professions upon its educators. According to the Finnish National Agency for Education, only about 10 percent of applicants gain acceptance into teacher training programmes. This stringent selective process ensures that only the most motivated and capable individuals embark on a career in teaching.

Contrast With English Teacher Training:

- The journey to becoming a teacher in England encompasses various routes, including the Postgraduate Certificate in Education (PGCE), School Direct training, and the Teach First Leadership Development Programme. Contrasted with Finland's selective process, England allows a broader range of individuals to enter the profession. The shift towards inclusivity is notably evident, with opportunities for aspiring teachers who might not have accessed the profession two decades ago when I began my career. The shift is partly a response to the challenges that the education system has faced over the years, prompting measures to address teacher shortages and maintain a robust educator presence.

- Teacher training in England often faces criticism for its perceived brevity and a pronounced emphasis on "on-the-job" training. This approach may lack the comprehensive exploration of pedagogical theory emphasised in Finnish programmes.

Teacher Training in France:

- The French system requires prospective teachers to complete a master's degree followed by a competitive examination known as the *Concours* to determine their placement in teaching positions.
- French teacher training is known for its dual emphasis on subject-matter expertise and pedagogical skills. However, criticism has been directed at its perceived emphasis on theory over practical classroom experience. Many of my university classmates, now teaching in France, share this sentiment, underscoring the limited exposure to practical aspects during their training programmes. Reflecting on my own school years in France, I don't recall having a trainee teacher in my class, highlighting the potential gap in practical teaching.
- Recent scrutiny through an undercover documentary aired by one of the country's leading television channels revealed challenges within the French education system, shedding light on a significant shortage of teachers. A report by the French press platform AFP revealed that 48 percent of secondary schools and high schools are facing a shortage of at least one full-time teacher.[46]

---

[46] Le Parisien, "Rentrée scolaire : il manque un professeur dans la moitié des collèges et lycées, selon le Snes-FSU," *Le Parisien*, September 11, 2023, modified September 12, 2023, https://www.leparisien.fr/societe/rentree-scolaire-il-manque-un-professeur-dans-la-moitie-des-colleges-et-lycees-selon-le-snes-fsu-11-09-2023-CEZ5TNLHN5FB5PTCCXF6UPKWWI.php.

Balance and Perspective:

- While the Finnish model is exemplary in its rigorous selection process and comprehensive training, it is tailored to Finland's unique cultural and educational context. Directly applying this approach to countries like England or France, each with their own distinct educational traditions and societal needs, would likely lead to challenges. For instance, the Finnish model's emphasis on pedagogical theory over standardised testing might not align with the more diverse and exam-oriented educational environment in England. Similarly, the French system's theoretical approach provides a strong foundation in educational theory but may lack the practical experience that English routes offer.

Master's Degree Requirement

In Finland, the required master's degree for all teachers sets a high bar for educational qualifications. This extensive education, including both bachelor's and master's degrees, provides Finnish teachers with a deep understanding of content and pedagogical skills, ensuring their preparedness for the complexities of teaching.

In contrast, the English education system does not universally require a master's degree for teaching. While there are routes like the PGCE (Postgraduate Certificate in Education) that include postgraduate study, they're not equivalent to a full master's programme. This difference may impact the depth of academic and pedagogical training English teachers receive compared to their Finnish counterparts.

On the other hand, the French system also emphasises high academic qualifications for teachers. In France, secondary school teachers are required to hold a master's degree and pass a competitive national exam: the *Capes* or *Agrégation*, depending on the teaching level. However, this system focuses more on subject-matter expertise than pedagogical training, differing from the Finnish model's balance of both.

Pedagogical Training and Research Emphasis

Finnish teacher training is distinguished by its dual focus on subject content and pedagogical skills, complemented by a research requirement. This instils a research-oriented mindset in educators, nurturing critical thinking and reflective practice.

In England, particularly in programmes like the PGCE, there is a focus on pedagogical training, but the depth of exposure to research methodology may differ from the Finnish system. English teacher training is often critiqued for its practical orientation at the expense of theoretical depth. Striking the right balance is a formidable task when dealing with the dynamic, changing nature of individuals and society. The prolonged delay in substantial adjustments has contributed to the worsening of educational challenges over time.

The French approach, like Finland's, significantly emphasises academic rigour. However, it is frequently characterised as heavily theoretical, with a notable absence of practical, in-classroom training during the initial stages of teacher education. This imbalance between theory and practice differs from the Finnish model, which integrates both seamlessly.

Continuous Professional Development

Continuous professional development (CPD) is a cornerstone of the Finnish education system, providing teachers both time and resources for ongoing learning. This approach highlights the value of lifelong learning in the Finnish educational culture.

In England, while continuous professional development is encouraged, the responsibility to pursue and fund these opportunities often falls on individual teachers or the school. Unlike the systemic support seen in Finland, the systemic backing for CPD in England is less pronounced.

The French system also recognises the importance of CPD for teachers. However, akin to England, pursuing these opportunities often lies with individual educators. The allocation of time and resources for such development is not as integrated into France's institutional framework as it is in Finland's.

The Finnish teacher training system stands out for its comprehensive approach, seamlessly integrating academic rigour, pedagogical expertise, and a robust commitment to continuous professional development. This distinguishes it from the English system, which, while flexible, is less academically intensive; and the French system, which emphasises academic qualifications but follows a distinct path in pedagogical training and continuous professional development.

Trust and Autonomy

With its demanding training, Finnish society places a high level of trust in teachers' expertise. This is evident in the significant autonomy granted to teachers within the classroom. While there is a national curriculum, teachers are entrusted with the freedom to devise their teaching methods and materials. This trust is well founded, a direct result of the comprehensive training they undergo. The combination of well-prepared teachers, coupled with trust and autonomy, fosters an environment conducive to delivering high-quality education.

Lack of Trust and Autonomy in England's Education System: Andreas Schleicher, the director of PISA, noted that mistrust of teachers in England hampers educational progress. This lack of trust permeates the system, giving rise to bureaucracy and the need to control, increasing teacher workload and diminishing autonomy.[47] Despite initial attempts to address this challenge by hiring more teaching assistants, the issue remains unresolved.

Impact of Ofsted Inspections on Teacher Autonomy: The proposal for no-notice Ofsted inspections has faced criticism for its likelihood of putting undue pressure on teachers. Teachers might be compelled to tailor lessons with an eye on potential inspections, fostering an environment overly fixated on data gathering and promoting a culture in which "every lesson counts." This approach reflects a deeper issue of distrust in teachers, contrasting with countries like Estonia, which maintain a lighter culture of inspection.

Challenges in the English Education System Structure: The English education system, with its division between local authority ("maintained") schools and academies, is seen as fragmented and incoherent. This division fails to yield significant improvements in educational outcomes and perpetuates ambiguity within the system. Disparities in governance structures and financial management between these two types of schools gives rise to transparency issues, further complicating the roles of teachers and school leaders.

Issues With Regional Schools Commissioners and Free Schools: The eight Regional Schools Commissioners (RSCs) in England, tasked with various aspects of school management, face criticism for their perceived opaqueness and potential detachment from the best interests of pupils and parents. The increasing number of academies and the complexities of their admissions systems further exacerbate these issues.

Teacher Autonomy and Job Satisfaction: Autonomy, defined as a teacher's perception of their ability to make decisions related to their work, significantly influences job satisfaction. A lack of autonomy in instructional decisions and classroom management has been cited as a contributing factor in teacher resignations. Prescribed lesson plans, standardised tests, and data collection often drive instructional decisions, limiting teacher autonomy. This situation

---

[47] "Pisa Chief: 'Mistrust of Teachers Holds England Back'," *TES*, December 6, 2019, https://www.tes.com/magazine/archive/pisa-chief-mistrust-teachers-holds-england-back.

is compounded by political and cultural conflicts, leaving teachers uncertain about addressing controversial topics.

Building Trust as a Path to Autonomy: Earning trust is essential for achieving teacher autonomy. Developing mutually trusting relationships with colleagues, supervisors, and other stakeholders can empower teachers with greater autonomy in their work. Trust is fundamental to allowing teachers the freedom to innovate and exercise professional judgement in their teaching methods.

Student Well-Being in the Finnish School System

The Finnish education system's success isn't solely measured by academic achievements or rankings in international assessments. An integral part of the system's ethos is its emphasis on student well-being, ensuring that schools are not just places of academic learning but also environments that foster holistic health and happiness.

Start of Formal Education

In Finland, formal education commences at the age of seven, allowing the early years of childhood to be dedicated to play and exploration. This approach stands in contrast to England, where formal education begins at four to five years of age, and France, where children often start attending *école maternelle* (preschool) as early as three. The English and French systems place a greater emphasis on early academic learning compared to the Finnish model.

It's widely recognised that humans require the longest period of nurturing of any species to attain independence. I firmly believe that the most effective nurturing occurs when provided by parents in an environment that grants children the freedom to explore their creativity, various interests, and talents without the constraints typically associated with school life, such as sitting still, being quiet, asking for permission to use the bathroom, not running, wearing a uniform, and adhering to a strict daily schedule.

Starting formal education at age seven seems more appropriate to me. By this age, children typically develop their senses, agility, and speech, and they have a grasp of social behaviour. Such a foundation paves the way for a smoother transition into the structured environment of formal schooling.

School Schedule and Breaks

Finnish students enjoy the benefits of shorter school days and frequent breaks, fostering relaxation and socialisation. In contrast, a typical school day in England is longer, often running from 8:30 a.m. to 3:00 p.m. or later, with relatively shorter breaks. Similarly, French students face longer school days, traditionally operating on a six-day week, although recent changes have altered this schedule. I recall having lessons on Saturday mornings during my secondary school days. Both the English and French systems place less emphasis on regular, extended breaks compared to their Finnish counterparts.

Reflect on your own school days – sitting for an entire hour, or even two for double lessons, without the opportunity to stand up and stretch. Breaks were only during the interchange between classes. In the next class, it was the same routine: sit down, stay still, and be quiet. One reason why teachers might not consider students' discomfort is that they themselves have the freedom to move around the classroom, sit at their desk, and drink water without asking for permission.

Considering this, I make a point to allow my students a few minutes to relax and move around at the end of the first hour of a double lesson. The positive impact this has, along with the students' appreciation, reaffirms the value of such breaks. In single-hour lessons, this practice isn't as necessary since students naturally transition to their next class. Nonetheless, I do permit students to stand and stretch when needed, particularly if they are coming from a lengthy session.

This approach is even more crucial for neurodivergent students, who often find it challenging to remain seated for extended periods. The effort required for them to maintain self-control and conform to typical classroom behaviour can be both immense and exhausting. By the end of the school day, those who manage to avoid sanctions for misbehaviour are often worn out.

I have noticed similar tendencies during staff meetings, when both myself and my colleagues often become fidgety. This restlessness appears to be a natural reaction to staying inactive for too long. If such movement can alleviate discomfort for adults, it stands to reason that it would be beneficial for students as well.

Fidgeting in children offers several benefits, particularly in terms of learning and psychological well-being. Here are some key advantages:

It enhances concentration: Many children find fidgeting aids in maintaining focus and concentration, particularly during lengthy or less engaging tasks. It acts as a self-regulation tool, keeping the brain stimulated and alert.

It reduces stress and anxiety: Fidgeting can serve as a coping mechanism for managing stress and anxiety. Engaging in small physical activities provides a mild sensory stimulus, offering a calming effect and alleviating feelings of anxiety.

It improves learning styles: For children with learning differences, such as ADHD, fidgeting can be a beneficial way to channel energy and enhance learning. It helps them process information and engage with educational material according to their learning style.

It has physical health benefits: Certain forms of fidgeting, especially those involving movement like leg shaking or walking, contribute to a child's physical activity levels. This can promote increased activity and potentially support better physical health.

It boosts creativity and cognitive function: Research suggests that light physical movement associated with fidgeting can enhance creativity and cognitive function. The continuous movement helps keep the mind active and engaged.

It regulates emotion: For some children, fidgeting becomes a method for regulating emotions and handling overwhelming situations. It offers focus or distraction, helping them to manage emotional responses more effectively.

It provides sensory input: For children with sensory processing issues, fidgeting provides essential sensory input. This helps them stay grounded and process sensory information more effectively.

It is important to note that excessive or disruptive fidgeting may require attention, as it could potentially be a sign of underlying issues. However, in many instances, fidgeting is a natural and beneficial aspect of child development, contributing to the advantages enumerated above and more.

Free Nutritious Meals

Finland's commitment to student well-being and educational equality is epitomised by its practice of providing free nutritious meals for all students. This inclusive approach guarantees that every child, regardless of background, can access healthy food, which is essential for learning and overall development. Moreover, the communal aspect of these meals nurtures a sense of togetherness and social skills among students.

In England, although free school meals are offered, they are typically restricted to certain age groups or families meeting specific income criteria. This structure may create disparities among students and potentially impact the learning capabilities of those who do not qualify but still face food insecurity. The French approach, emphasising the quality and cultural significance of meals, offers heavily subsidised, but not free, lunches. While this ensures high-quality meals, it doesn't address the issue of equal access to the extent seen in Finland.

Inclusion of Physical and Artistic Education

Physical and artistic education are vital for well-rounded development, offering benefits like channelling energy, improving blood circulation, and enhancing mental sharpness with increased oxygen flow to the brain.

Finland distinguishes itself with a diverse range of physical activities and a strong emphasis on arts and crafts, contributing to students' physical, cognitive, and creative development. This inclusive approach ensures that various interests and talents are nurtured, providing students with a more engaging and holistic educational experience.

In England, while physical education is part of the curriculum, there is often a predominant focus on traditional sports. Recent funding cuts have adversely impacted the variety and quality of these offerings, particularly in artistic education. This reduction can limit students' exposure to a broad spectrum of physical and creative activities crucial for their overall development.

France mandates physical education and places significant importance on artistic and cultural education. However, the range of physical activities might not be as diverse as Finland's, potentially limiting students' exposure to different forms of physical expression. While the French system excels in its cultural and artistic offerings, incorporating a broader range of physical activities could further enhance the benefits for student development.

Health Services

The comprehensive health and dental services offered in Finnish schools exemplify a profound commitment to holistic student well-being. Regular health and dental check-ups, along with easy access to counselling and psychological services, ensure that students' physical and mental health needs are addressed proactively. This preventative approach aims to address issues before they escalate into significant problems.

In contrast, health services in English and French schools are generally more limited. In England, while there are school nurses and some health services, the system lacks the integrated and comprehensive nature seen in Finland. Similarly, French schools provide health education and some services, but the scope is not as extensive. In my opinion, both countries could potentially benefit from adopting a more integrated approach to health services in schools, mirroring the Finnish model, and enhancing overall student well-being.

Minimal Homework

Finland's approach to homework is another aspect in which the country's commitment to student well-being is evident. By minimising homework, Finnish schools provide students with more time for play, relaxation, and family interaction – essential components for healthy development. This approach recognises the importance of a balanced lifestyle for children, in which academic learning is balanced with leisure and rest.

In England and France, the scenario is notably different. Both countries tend to assign more homework, contributing to additional stress for students and reducing time for other essential activities. In England, the ongoing debate over homework's effectiveness and impact on children's well-being persists. France faces a similar situation, with a growing awareness of the need for a balanced approach, yet students continue receiving significant homework loads. Adopting a Finnish-like approach could potentially alleviate stress and improve the overall well-being of students in these countries. However, implementing such a change in systems deeply ingrained in tradition requires the collective commitment of educators, parents, and policymakers. Those in positions of power, elected to represent our interests, should be open to experimenting with methods proven effective in other contexts. True change begins with the courage to take the first step, leading the way, adjusting and evolving as we progress – the essence of evolution in education.

As parents, we understand the strain excessive homework can place on our children's well-being because we experienced it ourselves. I strongly advocate limiting the amount of homework given to children. However, for such a change to be viable in England, where I practise my profession, comprehensive reform is imperative. This reform should provide teachers with more time for planning and teaching, and reducing the number of students in each class is essential to ensure teachers can effectively address individual students' needs.

A Holistic Approach to Education in the Finnish School System

By now, it's probably evident that I hold the Finnish education system in high regard. In my view, this system exemplifies many of the effective methods and approaches I deeply value in the teaching profession. Finland's approach to education is holistic, emphasising the development of the whole child – cognitively, emotionally, socially, and physically. Rather than focusing narrowly on academic achievement, Finnish schools prioritise creating well-rounded individuals equipped with the skills and knowledge needed to thrive in the broader contexts of life and society. Here's how this holistic philosophy manifests in the Finnish education system:

Curriculum Design

The Finnish National Core Curriculum stresses not just subject knowledge but also transversal (cross-curricular) competencies. These include thinking and learning to learn, cultural competence, interaction and expression, multiliteracy, ICT (information and communication technology) competence, working life and entrepreneurship, and participation and building a sustainable future. This multidimensional curriculum ensures that students aren't just memorising facts but developing essential life skills.

Emphasis on Social and Emotional Learning (SEL)

Finnish schools' integration of SEL into their curricula is a progressive approach, fostering emotionally intelligent, self-aware, and socially adept individuals. This contrasts with England and France, where SEL is not as systematically embedded in the curriculum. While there are efforts in these countries to address SEL, they often lack the comprehensive and structured approach seen in Finland. This Finnish emphasis on SEL could serve as a model for England and France, highlighting the importance of emotional intelligence alongside academic achievement.

School Culture and Environment

The community-oriented and cooperative learning atmosphere in Finnish schools stands in stark contrast to the often individualistic and competitive environments prevalent in schools in England and France. While initiatives to encourage cooperative learning do exist in these countries, the implementation and emphasis can vary significantly from one school to another. Embracing a more consistent and student-centred approach, akin to that of Finland, could greatly benefit schools in England and France. Such an approach would likely enhance interpersonal skills and cultivate a stronger sense of community among students. In the chapter titled "Paradoxes," I will delve deeper into my perspectives on cooperative learning and its implications.

Arts, Crafts, and Real-World Learning

The Finnish system's significant emphasis on arts, crafts, and real-world learning is notably different from the more academically focused curricula in England and France. In these countries, subjects like music, art, and crafts are often seen as secondary to core academic subjects. Integrating more practical, hands-on learning experiences, as seen in Finland, could enhance the educational experience in England and France, making it more engaging and relevant to real-world scenarios.

Less Emphasis on Exams

The minimal use of high-stakes testing in Finland presents a stark contrast to the exam-centric systems in England and France. These countries could learn from Finland's approach, which reduces student stress and fosters a love for learning rather than just rote memorisation. A shift towards continuous assessment and project-based learning, as practised in Finland, could benefit students in England and France by providing a more holistic evaluation of their abilities and fostering a deeper understanding of subject matter.

Ethics, Philosophy, and Life Skills

Finland's inclusion of ethics, philosophy, and life skills in the curriculum is a forward-thinking approach that prepares students for navigating complex real-world scenarios. In England and France, while life skills are addressed, the approach is not as comprehensive as in Finland. Enhancing the focus on these areas could provide students in England and France with a more rounded education, equipping them to handle the moral and ethical dilemmas of modern life.

An All-Inclusive Approach to Education

Broad Curriculum

Finnish schools offer a curriculum encompassing many subjects, ensuring students receive a well-rounded education. This broad approach contrasts with the systems in England and France, where there's often a stronger emphasis on traditional academic subjects. In England, for example, the focus on core subjects like mathematics, science, and languages sometimes overshadows the arts and physical education, especially in the face of standardised testing pressures. While known for its rigorous academic curriculum, France also tends to prioritise traditional academic subjects, though with a vital inclusion of arts in the general curriculum. Integrating a broader range of subjects, as Finland does, could help students in England and France develop a more diverse set of skills and interests.

Social and Emotional Learning

The Finnish emphasis on SEL is critical to their educational success, fostering well-rounded individuals capable of handling various life challenges. In comparison, England and France have begun to recognise the importance of SEL, but still, its integration into the curriculum is less deeply ingrained than in Finland. The Finnish model could inspire England and France to embed SEL more fully into their educational frameworks, benefiting students' emotional and social development.

Real-World Learning

Finnish education's incorporation of real-world experiences offers practical knowledge and hands-on learning, a significant shift from the more traditional, textbook-focused approaches common in England and France. This experiential learning could be more extensively adopted in England and France to complement and enhance traditional academic learning, providing students with a more engaging and applicable education.

Inclusive Education

Finland's inclusive education model is commendable, promoting mutual respect and understanding among students with diverse needs. While England and France have made strides in inclusive education, the Finnish approach serves as a model for further development. Emulating Finland's inclusivity could help England and France foster more equitable and supportive educational environments for all students.

Personal Critical Opinion

From a personal standpoint, the Finnish education system's broad curriculum, focus on SEL, real-world learning, and inclusivity present a holistic and effective approach to education. These aspects are not just about academic proficiency but about preparing students for life in a broader sense. Adopting similar strategies in England and France could significantly enhance the educational experience, helping to nurture well-rounded, capable, and empathetic individuals who are better prepared for the complexities of the modern world. The Finnish model underscores the idea that education should be a journey of comprehensive development, not just a path to academic success.

Reduced Emphasis on Homework and Tests

Homework Philosophy

The Finnish philosophy of assigning less homework and adhering to shorter school days, maintaining a balance between academic, leisure, and family time, is a refreshing contrast to the approach in many other education systems, including England and France. In these countries, there's a significant emphasis on homework, often resulting in students spending long hours on assignments outside school. This approach can lead to stress and reduce time for other important developmental activities. From my perspective, the Finnish approach recognises the importance of holistic development and acknowledges the need for students to have time for play, relaxation, and family engagement, which are vital for their overall well-being.

Minimal High-Stakes Testing

Finland's minimal reliance on high-stakes standardised testing is unique compared to the education systems in England and France, where such exams play a significant role in the educational process. For example, the focus on GCSEs and A-levels in England can create a high-pressure environment for students. Similarly, the *Baccalauréat* exam is a pivotal moment in a student's educational journey in France. Finland's approach, emphasising continuous and formative assessments, reduces stress and allows for a more rounded evaluation of a student's abilities and progress. This method could benefit students in England and France by fostering a less stressful learning environment and allowing for more individualised assessment.

Focus on Continuous Assessment

The continuous assessment method in Finnish schools, relying on teacher observations and feedback rather than standardised tests, aligns with a more personalised educational approach. It enables teachers to understand and cater to the individual needs of each student. In my experience, this approach is more effective in supporting student development than relying heavily on standardised testing. It builds a trust-based system in which teachers, given their rigorous training, are trusted to make educational decisions. In contrast, in England and France, the heavy reliance on standardised testing can sometimes overshadow the individual learning journey of students.

My Thoughts

Based on my analysis and experience, the Finnish model's reduced emphasis on homework and high-stakes testing, as well as its focus on continuous assessment, present a more compassionate and effective approach to education. It recognises students as whole individuals, not just as vessels for academic content. Adopting aspects of this model in England and France could lead to more well-rounded, less stressed, and happier students who are academically equipped for the various challenges of life. This philosophy underscores the importance of looking beyond traditional academic achievements to nurture students so that they are capable of thriving in all aspects of life.

Creativity, Critical Thinking, and Problem-Solving in the Finnish School System

Finland's education system is lauded not just for its academic achievements but also for its distinctive emphasis on skills that prepare students for real-world challenges. Creativity, critical thinking, and problem-solving are pillars of this approach. Here's a closer look at how these competencies are interwoven into the Finnish educational experience.

Interdisciplinary Learning

Finnish schools often adopt thematic or project-based learning in which students explore a topic from various angles. For instance, a project on "water" might incorporate elements from chemistry (properties of water), geography (water bodies), history (historical significance of rivers), and art (depicting water through various mediums). This integrated approach requires students to think critically, draw connections between disparate pieces of information, and employ creative solutions.

Example: In some Finnish schools, students might undertake a project on sustainable living. They would delve into the science of renewable energy and the economics of sustainability, and then they might be tasked with designing a sustainable model house, integrating their knowledge from various subjects.

Learning Environments

Finnish classrooms are increasingly being designed to be flexible and adaptable, allowing for group collaboration, individual research, and hands-on experimentation. Traditional rows of desks are often replaced by movable furniture, open spaces, and resource-rich corners, fostering an environment where creativity and innovation can thrive. The *Innova* classrooms, found in many Finnish schools, are spaces designed for adaptability, with movable walls and a variety of technological resources, enabling varied pedagogical approaches.

Assessment Methods

Rather than relying solely on standardised tests, Finnish teachers employ a variety of assessment methods. These might include portfolio assessments, in which students showcase their best work, or open-ended projects that require creative problem-solving.

Example: A student might be assessed on their ability to create a multimedia presentation on a given topic, weaving together visuals, text, and sound in a cohesive and creative manner.

Emphasis on Arts and Music

Arts, crafts, and music aren't sideline activities in Finnish schools – they're integral. Such subjects naturally foster creativity and offer students alternative mediums to express themselves, innovate, and view the world from different perspectives.

Example: Students might be tasked with creating an art installation using recycled materials, a lesson that fosters creativity while also teaching sustainability.

Problem-Based Learning (PBL)

Many Finnish schools use PBL, in which students are presented with a complex problem and must employ research, collaboration, and critical thinking to arrive at a solution.

Example: In a mathematics class, instead of directly teaching a formula, a teacher might present a real-world problem that requires students to derive or employ the formula as part of the solution.

Teacher Training

Teachers in Finland receive high-quality training, with a strong focus on developing students' critical thinking and problem-solving skills. This training equips them to design lessons that are not just informative but also thought-provoking and challenging.

Example: As part of their training, teachers might be exposed to case studies in which they design lesson plans around hypothetical (or real) current events, requiring students to critically evaluate information, debate, and draw informed conclusions.

Teachers in Finland: Respected and Well-Compensated Professionals

The quality of an education system can't surpass the quality of its teachers. Recognising this, Finland places significant emphasis on its educators.

Teachers in Finland are not merely seen as facilitators but as pivotal pillars of the education system. Their high status in Finnish society and the considerable attention given to their professional development play crucial roles in the success of the nation's educational model. Teaching is one of the most sought-after professions in Finland, with only a fraction of applicants being accepted into teaching programmes. For example, primary school teaching programmes can have more than ten applicants for each available spot. This competitive selection ensures that only the most passionate and capable individuals enter the teaching profession.

Once selected, teacher candidates undergo a rigorous, research-based master's programme, typically spanning five years. This extensive training equips them with deep content knowledge, pedagogical skills, and the ability to conduct educational research. As a result, Finnish teachers are not just educators but also contributors to educational scholarship.

Finnish teachers enjoy a great deal of autonomy. While there is a national curriculum, it serves more as a guideline, allowing teachers the freedom to decide how best to achieve the desired learning outcomes. This trust in teachers' professional judgement encourages innovation and responsiveness to the unique needs of their students. Even after their initial training, teachers in Finland are provided with ample opportunities for professional growth. The government invests in regular in-service training, ensuring that educators stay abreast of the latest pedagogical research and best practices.

Teachers in Finland hold a status comparable to other professionals like doctors and lawyers. This respect stems from the public's trust in the education system and the recognition of teachers' extensive training and crucial societal role. Such societal respect bolsters job satisfaction and attracts high-quality candidates to the profession.

While Finnish teachers' salaries may be comparable to those in other OECD countries, when adjusted for the cost of living, their compensation becomes highly competitive. Furthermore, the non-tangible benefits, such as job security, an optimal work-life balance, and societal respect, contribute to the profession's allure.

Finnish schools cultivate a collaborative environment, allowing teachers more time for essential tasks like curriculum planning, student assessment, and collaboration with colleagues. This collaborative spirit facilitates the sharing of best practices and continuous improvement.

The relatively low student-to-teacher ratio in Finnish schools enables teachers to better understand and address individual student needs, fostering a positive and supportive classroom environment where teachers can effectively guide students in their learning journey.

In summary, the success of the Finnish education system is inextricably linked to its teachers. Through rigorous selection, high-quality training, professional autonomy, continuous development, and societal respect, Finland has created an environment where educators can thrive, directly benefiting the students they serve. The reverence and support for teachers underline Finland's belief that a nation's future lies in the hands of its educators.

Given Finland's sustained success and its distinctive system, one may wonder why England has not attempted to emulate these elements. While administrative roles such as Head of Department, Head of Year, and Assistant or Deputy Headteacher are crucial for effective school management, they may not appeal to educators like me who find fulfilment in direct classroom teaching. These roles often involve increased administrative duties and may limit one's independence, particularly when there's pressure from higher-ups to achieve specific yearly school objectives. Despite their significance, such positions may not align with the preferences of those who cherish the direct engagement with students in the classroom.

What Can We Learn from PISA's Top School Systems?

Emphasis on Teacher Quality

Across the globe, many top-performing countries prioritise teacher quality, mirroring Finland's well-documented emphasis on educator excellence. For instance, Singapore's National Institute of Education delivers intensive training, ensuring only the most distinguished graduates join the teaching ranks, akin to Finland's high entry standards for teacher training programmes. Japan, like Finland, invests significantly in its educators, providing extensive initial training and continuous professional development. Similarly, Canada decentralises its educational system, emphasising pedagogical skills and deep content knowledge in teacher training across provinces. Estonia's requirement of teachers holding a master's degree echoes Finland's commitment to in-depth, university-level education for its educators. Finally, South Korea's strategy of attracting the best academic performers into the teaching profession and subjecting them to rigorous training aligns with Finland's approach of making teaching a prestigious and selective career choice. While each country has unique nuances, their collective emphasis on teacher quality closely parallels the Finnish model, reinforcing its global significance.

In contrast, the weakness of schools in England and France is evident in the prevalence of classes led by substitute teachers, cover supervisors, and even students lacking qualified teacher status.

The Situation in England

According to a June 2023 report from *The Guardian*, England is facing an unprecedented exodus of teachers from the profession.[48] The Department

---

[48] Anna Fazackerley, "Schools across England face unprecedented struggle to hire English teachers as recruitment crisis grows," *The Guardian*, June 17, 2023, last updated April 20, 2023, https://www.theguardian.com/education/2023/jun/17/schools-across-england-face-unprecedented-struggle-to-hire-english-teachers-as-recruitment-crisis-grows.

for Education's recent workforce survey indicated that almost 9 percent of the teaching workforce, equating to 40,000 teachers, resigned from state schools in the past year. This is the highest number since data collection began in 2011, coupled with an additional 4,000 teachers retiring. The number of unfilled teaching positions surged to over 2,300, a stark contrast to the 530 vacancies a decade ago. Sick leave among teachers has seen a notable increase, with over 3 million sick days taken last year, marking a 50 percent increase from pre-pandemic levels in 2018–2019.[49] The National Foundation for Educational Research's Jack Worth called for measures to enhance teacher retention by reducing workload and augmenting pay competitiveness. Unfavourable working conditions and diminished pay were cited as reasons for many teachers' departures, while the Labour Party criticised the government's policies for the crisis.[50]

However, the Department for Education highlighted a recent influx of nearly 48,000 teachers entering the profession, marking an increase from the preceding year. There has also been a growth in the number of teachers in state schools, aligning with the rising student population.[51]

A separate survey commissioned by the Department for Education revealed that 60 percent of educators and school leaders believe that student misbehaviour adversely impacts their health, with classroom disruptions costing teachers six minutes per half-hour lesson. The article also touched upon the increasing number of students eligible for free school meals, which now includes nearly one in four pupils, a reflection of growing household poverty and changes in government benefit provisions.[52]

---

[49] Fazackerley, "Schools across England."
[50] Fazackerley, "Schools across England."
[51] "School Workforce in England," *Gov.uk*, June 8, 2023, last updated December 15, 2023, https://explore-education-statistics.service.gov.uk/find-statistics/school-workforce-in-england.
[52] Jack Dyson, "'Wake-up' Call for Schools as Weeks of Lessons Lost to Misbehaviour," *Schoolsweek*, June 8, 2023, https://schoolsweek.co.uk/wake-up-call-for-schools-as-weeks-of-lessons-lost-to-misbehaviour/.

The education sector in England grapples with significant challenges related to teacher availability, as the number of both vacant teaching positions and temporarily filled roles have been on the rise, especially in the recent two years. This upwards trend suggests difficulties in recruiting and retaining permanent teaching staff.

The departure of educators from the teaching profession in England is multifaceted. One of the prominent concerns is the inadequate salary structure for teachers, which has remained stagnant since 2011. This financial stagnation culminated in a significant teachers' strike across the country in 2023, persisting for several months.

Additionally, the teaching profession grapples with diminished respect from various quarters, including students, parents, and broader societal attitudes. Erroneous assumptions persist that teaching roles come with extensive holidays and shorter working days, undermining the substantial effort and long hours educators consistently invest. These misconceptions and challenges have undoubtedly impacted the morale and commitment of many in the teaching profession, accentuating the necessity to address and rectify these issues for the benefit of the education system.

The Situation in France

In September 2022, France faced a shortage of 4,000 teachers, a number that improved slightly to 3,100 by September 2023. This shortage spanned across primary and secondary schools, college, and *classe préparatoire* (preparatory class). In the context of the French educational system, *classes préparatoires* or *classes préparatoires aux grandes écoles* (CPGE) are two-year courses designed to prepare students for the entrance exams to the prestigious higher education institutions in France known as *grandes écoles*. These institutions cover diverse fields such as engineering, business, public administration, and literature and humanities.

The demanding curriculum of a *classe préparatoire* focuses on subjects like mathematics, physics, literature, or economics, depending on the student's chosen specialisation. These classes are known for their rigorous workload and high expectations, and students prepare for competitive exams at the end of the two-year (or three-year, for those opting to repeat a year) programme to secure admission to their desired *grandes écoles*.

Curriculum and Pedagogy

Singapore prioritises depth over breadth in its curriculum, placing a strong emphasis on critical thinking and the practical application of knowledge. Japan's "Zest for Life" policy uniquely integrates academic learning with essential life skills and values. Across the provinces in Canada, curricula are designed to focus on core competencies, including critical thinking, problem-solving, and communication skills. Estonia's curriculum stands out for its integration of technology and a commitment to student-centric learning approaches. South Korea adopts a rigorous and balanced curriculum, promoting both academic excellence and character education.

Quality in Education

In Singapore, the "Every School a Good School" initiative is a notable effort to ensure quality education across all institutions. Japan's commitment to distributing educational resources fairly ensures that all students, regardless of socioeconomic background, have access to quality education. In Canada, provinces prioritise inclusive education, ensuring that students of diverse backgrounds, including indigenous communities, receive quality instruction. The Estonian education system minimises the impact of socioeconomic status on student performance. And there's a strong emphasis on equal educational opportunities in South Korean schools, with support programmes implemented for disadvantaged students.

Parental Engagement, Adaptability, and Forward-Thinking

In leading school systems worldwide, active participation and adaptability to evolving trends are paramount. For instance, in Singapore, collaboration among schools, parents, and the community is fostered by groups like the Parent Support Group. Japan emphasises a close partnership between local communities and schools, while in Canada, school boards and parent-teacher groups play pivotal roles in shaping educational approaches. Estonia experiences high involvement from parents and the community, and in South Korea, parents actively engage, even investing in additional educational resources for their children.

Simultaneously, these nations exhibit a forward-thinking approach. Singapore shifts its educational focus from mere grades to real-life skills, embracing a philosophy of continuous learning. Japan adapts its schools to be more globally oriented and tech-savvy. Canadian schools regularly update their curricula, incorporating contemporary subjects like computer skills and environmental awareness. Estonia leads the way in using technology in schools, and South Korea endeavours to alleviate exam pressure on students, prioritising creativity, moral values, and overall student well-being.

While the education systems in the United States and Canada share some commonalities, each reflects distinct social, cultural, and political contexts. Both countries organise their curricula around core subjects such as language arts, mathematics, science, and social studies, with students progressing through grade levels, building upon acquired knowledge and skills.

A key difference lies in the funding mechanisms. In the US, education is predominantly funded at the state and local levels, often through property taxes, leading to significant disparities in funding and resources across districts. In contrast, Canada's education funding falls primarily under provincial jurisdiction, resulting in a more uniform distribution of resources across regions within a particular province.

In recent years, both countries have increasingly emphasised technology and digital literacy, reflecting a global trend. Recognising the increasing significance of technology across various fields, educators consider digital literacy essential for students to navigate and thrive in the twenty-first century. This emphasis aligns with the importance of remaining updated in a rapidly evolving world.

PARADOXES

The Human Connection: Elevating Social Skills in Education

The essence of our existence as humans is intricately linked to our ability to form and maintain interpersonal relationships. We build our lives around communities, cities, towns, villages, and tribes, and our daily interactions invariably involve others. This web of human connection underscores the central role of social skills in our lives. These skills are the currency with which we navigate our social world. They allow us to communicate with clarity and empathy, facilitating our connections with friends, relatives, colleagues, and beyond. The art of building, maintaining, and nurturing these relationships is, therefore, a critical measure of success in any societal context.

Yet, despite their importance, social skills often take a back seat in the traditional educational setting. Young children, whose instinct is to engage and interact – to be social as their nature dictates – sometimes face the paradoxical reality of the classroom, where spontaneous conversation is often quelled. The emphasis in education has historically been placed on academic and cognitive development, literacy, numeracy, and scientific understanding. While these are undeniably important, they are but one facet of a child's holistic development. Social competence, the ability to forge and sustain meaningful relationships, is equally vital. It equips children with the skills needed to cooperate, share, empathise, and collaborate, laying the groundwork for both academic and life success.

In the real world, the absence of strong social skills can be the Achilles' heel of even the most academically accomplished individuals. Children learn the delicate art of conversation through interaction, the unspoken eloquence of body language, the grace of cooperation, and the joy of shared experiences. Research continually affirms that many relationships, both personal and professional, stumble not from a deficit of knowledge or skill but from a shortfall in effective communication. The ability to navigate the social landscape with dexterity is perhaps one of the most valuable gifts we can bestow upon the next generation.

With this understanding, it seems only logical that social skills should receive greater emphasis in our education systems. They should be nurtured with the same intention and rigour as reading, writing, and arithmetic, for they are the skills that ultimately determine how we relate to the world and to each other. The ability to navigate the complex social landscapes of our modern world is a necessity. For what good is knowledge if one cannot share it? What is the value of insight if one cannot communicate it? Integrating social skill development into the very core of educational curricula, making it a centrepiece rather than a mere footnote in the narrative of our children's education, is imperative. This is the primary reason I praise the Finnish and Danish school systems.

The Power of Collaboration in Achieving Greatness

Does any truly successful individual reach the pinnacle of their field entirely on their own? Across various domains, from sports and music to literature and politics, there's a recurring theme: the indispensable role of collaboration. Let's delve into some well-known examples.

Lionel Messi, often touted as one of the greatest footballers of all time, dazzles with incredible skill. While writing this book, he won the Ballon d'Or for the eighth time, making him the most frequent football player recipient. Yet, even he relies on his teammates' passes, strategies, and support to score those iconic goals.[53] Similarly, despite his undeniable talent, basketball legend Michael Jordan often credited his teammates for the Chicago Bulls' six championship titles. Their collective effort, combined with Jordan's prowess, was the recipe for their success.[54]

Visionaries like Jeff Bezos and Warren Buffett didn't build their empires single-handedly in the business world. Bezos, the founder of Amazon, had many engineers, marketers, and other professionals helping transform his vision into the global powerhouse it is today. Likewise, Warren Buffett, one of the most successful investors in history, has consistently emphasised the importance of the teams behind the companies he invests in.

These examples present a simple yet profound truth: No matter how talented or visionary an individual might be, the synergy of teamwork amplifies their potential and paves the way for extraordinary achievements. Fusing individual brilliance with collaborative effort is often the key to unparalleled success.

An anecdote from my youth captures the essence of a collective undertaking and the incredible results it can produce. During my teenage years, I had a classmate of Chinese descent. He lived in a modest flat, often brimming with relatives and, occasionally, family friends. The apartment was a hive of activity, with every member playing a role in the family's grocery

---

[53] Sky Sports. "Ballon d'Or 2023 recap: Inter Miami and Argentina captain Lionel Messi wins men's Ballon d'Or for record eighth time." Sky Sports. Accessed February 28, 2024. https://www.skysports.com/football/live-blog/11095/12996706/ballon-dor-2023-recap-inter-miami-and-argentina-captain-lionel-messi-wins-mens-ballon-dor-for-record-eighth-time.

[54] MJ23 His Airness Forever, "After Winning the Championship, Michael Jordan Gave Credit to Teammates (1992.06.14)," YouTube video, June 17, 2022, https://www.youtube.com/watch?v=vT5vSrEy6VQ.

shop. Despite his school commitments, my classmate dedicated his after-school hours and weekends to the family enterprise.

A second shop sprouted in another part of the neighbourhood in what felt like a blink of an eye. By our graduation from secondary school, a third, larger establishment had been inaugurated, dwarfing the combined size of the other two. Interestingly, their living situation had not changed; they remained in that tiny apartment. However, the dynamics shifted as their growing prosperity allowed other family members to find their own homes.

The most striking aspect of this story was not their shared living quarters; many families worldwide cohabitate with extended kin. I experienced that in my childhood. What was truly remarkable was the shared vision and collective sacrifice they exemplified. Their unanimous decision to pool financial and labour resources was a calculated strategy aiming for long-term self-sufficiency for all involved.

While such a living arrangement might appear challenging, even unthinkable, to many in the Western world, including regions like the United States, Canada, and Europe, one cannot help but marvel at the outcome of such collective effort. Although unconventional by specific cultural standards, this approach showcases a powerful model of success rooted in collaboration, shared vision, and mutual sacrifice. It's a testament to the idea that when individuals unite with a common purpose, they can achieve milestones that might seem impossible when approached alone.

In the domain of employment, the dynamics of collective strength become even more apparent. No matter how skilled or tenacious an individual employee may be, they often find themselves somewhat powerless when faced with institutional challenges or discrepancies. Yet, by joining forces with fellow employees to form a union, they and their colleagues can create a collective voice powerful enough to negotiate, advocate, and sometimes even challenge their superiors. This united front reinforces the age-old wisdom "United we stand."

Historically and geopolitically, the strategy of creating division to weaken an entity is not new. Many nations have aimed to fragment the populace of their adversaries, understanding that internal strife and division can incapacitate a country far more effectively than external force. It is akin to introducing a virus that disrupts the system from within.

Similarly, when we examine the architecture of various institutions, be they companies, organisations, corporations, or governments, they all stand on the foundational principle of teamwork. A court case, for instance, isn't just fought with one lawyer but with a battery of attorneys, each bringing a unique skill set and crafting a harmonised defence. Advisory boards, financial teams, and other specialised groups emphasise an institution's reliance on collective wisdom and effort.

Steve Jobs, the visionary behind Apple, once rightly noted in an interview, "No matter how smart you are, you need a team of great people."[55] This attitude encapsulates the core of our discussion. Our successes are seldom solo journeys. Behind every achievement, there's often a mentor recognising our potential, an opportunity given to hone our talent, or guidance provided to access resources and courses beneficial for our growth. Our triumphs are interwoven with the contributions and faith of others, painting a mosaic of combined efforts and mutual support.

In wrapping up this exploration of the dynamics of individuality versus collective strength, it is pertinent to reflect upon the words of Dr Jordan Peterson, a thought leader who has delved deeply into the intricacies of human nature and societal constructs. During an enlightening interview, he observed, "Whatever you are, you are not a unitary spirit that's under your own dominion. You're something like a loose unity of a multiplicity of spirits,

---

[55] Epistles Written, "'no matter how smart you are, you need a team of great people.' - @ stevejobs," YouTube video, April 1, 2022, https://www.youtube.com/watch?v=ielsajw1j8k.

many of which are doing their own things, which you're striving to bring into some form of unity."[56]

Peterson's insight encapsulates the essence of our discussion. Even within ourselves, we are not singular entities but a confluence of various experiences, emotions, and aspirations. This internal plurality mirrors our external interactions, in which our successes and endeavours are seldom achieved in isolation but are often the result of collaborative synergies. It stresses the value and necessity of unity and collaboration, both with others and within ourselves. As we journey through life, embracing teamwork and collective effort, both internally and externally, is vital to achieving holistic success and balance.

Nurturing Social Skills: The Role of Early Childhood Interactions

The foundation of robust social skills is most effectively laid in the earliest years of a child's life. I am a firm proponent of the idea that this critical learning begins at home. For children, especially those without siblings, the role of parents in cultivating social interactions is paramount. Parents need to create opportunities for their children to interact with peers, which can often be facilitated through playdates and community or group activities. These early interactions are not just about play – they are the building blocks for social development and emotional intelligence.

Well-developed social skills in children are linked to social competence, cognitive development, and mental well-being. Socialisation allows children to hone their communication skills, understand emotional cues, and develop problem-solving abilities. During these formative interactions, children learn to negotiate, share, empathise, and cooperate, skills that are invaluable throughout life.

---

[56] WordToTheWise, "RESPECT YOURSELF - Powerful Life Advice | Jordan Peterson," YouTube video, August 18, 2019, https://www.youtube.com/watch?v=nT-tVPpXlzk.

As children grow, those who are socially adept tend to navigate the school environment with greater ease. The "popular" kids, often idolised in school culture, usually have well-honed social skills. They are the students who engage effortlessly with their peers, participate actively in school life, and often attract the admiration of their classmates. While popularity is a complex dynamic and not always an accurate measure of social proficiency, it's evident that those with strong social skills have an advantage in the social arena of school.

However, it's essential to recognise that social dynamics in childhood and adolescence are nuanced. While some may envy the socially adept, this sentiment often stems from a desire to be understood, accepted, and connected with, which are basic human needs intrinsically tied to our social nature. In cultivating a child's social skills, it is crucial to instil empathy and inclusiveness, encouraging them to reach out and connect with those who may struggle socially.

The investment in a child's social education yields lifelong returns. A child proficient in social skills is ready to continue developing those skills with each new encounter and challenge they face as they mature. It equips them for professional success, as the workplace increasingly values emotional intelligence and the ability to work within diverse teams.

Learning Through Play: The Childhood Foundations of Social Development

Reflecting on my childhood, I recognise the experiences I shared with my friends and siblings were a rich source of learning about the world. Through play and interaction, rather than structured lessons from adults, I discovered and made sense of the environment around me. Children are natural explorers, and they assimilate knowledge by watching, imitating, engaging, and posing an endless stream of questions. In these dynamic interactions and casual observances, the roots of valuable social skills are planted and begin to flourish.

Many youngsters' initiations into the world beyond their immediate family begins with day care or nursery. This new landscape of peers provides a fertile ground for developing the art of socialisation. Children are cast into a diverse mix of ages, learning to navigate and adapt to different maturity and ability levels. In this melting pot, children's social aptitude begins to take shape, and we can observe the unfolding of their personalities.

The advantages of mingling with peers of varying ages are manifold. Children who play with others their own age learn to cooperate, share, and resolve conflicts. They start to understand the nuances of fairness, the give-and-take of friendships, and the simple joy of shared experiences. Meanwhile, interactions with older children can challenge them, sharpening their problem-solving skills and fostering traits like resilience and adaptability.

Conversely, when children find themselves in the company of those younger, they are often thrust naturally into leadership positions. This boosts their confidence and instils a sense of responsibility. Acting as mentors, even in such an informal capacity, allows them to practise patience, guidance, and care, traits essential for any well-functioning adult in society.

I try to nurture an atmosphere in the classroom that mirrors the complexities of the wider world so I can arm my students with the social tools they need for the future. The beauty of this approach lies in its simplicity: by allowing children the space to play, lead, follow, and teach each other, I deliberately facilitate a natural learning process. The skills learned in these early years – empathy, leadership, and cooperation – are the very ones we hope to see in the adults of tomorrow. Thus, it becomes clear that the most accurate form of preparation for the "real world" is not found solely in books or lectures but in the lively and unstructured world of children's play. I will explore the importance of gaming in learning in the chapter called "Gaming."

The Symbiosis of Social Skills and Success

Can someone with underdeveloped social skills achieve success? I am confident that the answer is a resounding yes. This is a comforting thought, as the alternative could lead to a society steeped in antisocial tendencies. However, it's essential to acknowledge that social competence is a significant predictor of success in life. In the contemporary job market, soft skills, attributes that allow someone to interact effectively and harmoniously with others, are increasingly recognised as crucial for employability.

Through my observations, children struggling with social skills often exhibit challenging behaviours at school. Communication, a core component of social skills, encompasses the words we choose, our tone, our body language, and the ability to listen and respond appropriately. Mastering these elements can foster empathy, reduce misunderstandings, and ensure that individuals can advocate for themselves and achieve satisfying interactions.

Furthermore, social skills are inextricably linked to emotional intelligence. This concept has gained prominence through the work of psychologists Peter Salovey and John D. Mayer. Emotional intelligence is a nuanced form of social intelligence that empowers individuals to be aware of and understand their own emotions and those of others, using this awareness to guide their actions and communications. In essence, it's the capacity to navigate the social environment by tuning in to emotional cues and adjusting one's approach accordingly.

Emotional intelligence, therefore, is not merely an academic concept; it is a practical skill that has tangible impacts on an individual's ability to succeed in life after school – in real life. While someone may not initially possess strong social skills, the capacity to develop emotional intelligence offers a pathway for overcoming these challenges and thriving in various life situations. The good news is that emotional intelligence and social skills can be cultivated and developed, paving the way for success – even for those who may start with a social skills deficit.

The Essence of Communication: Connecting Across Cultures

My passion for languages is deeply intertwined with my love for communication. The joy of connecting with people, regardless of their origin or tongue, is a profound motivation that has led me to immerse myself in the pursuit of learning different languages. Each new language learned acts as a key, unlocking a multitude of cultures, each with its own set of narratives, emotions, and wisdom. My affinity for languages is rooted in the profound satisfaction derived from connecting with others, understanding their stories, and sharing their experiences.

When we think of communication, the act of speaking often springs to mind first. We picture conversations, debates, or even monologues. However, focusing solely on speech overlooks the complex mosaic that constitutes human communication. Writing, for instance, is an equally dynamic form that empowers us to convey complex ideas, evoke emotions, and record thoughts for posterity. It's a potent medium through which we can reach the minds and hearts of those with whom we communicate.

Yet, the spectrum of communication is complete only through including listening and observing. These skills are just as vital as speaking or writing, if not more so. A skilled listener gains trust, becoming a sanctuary for the thoughts and feelings of others. Through attentive listening, one can grasp not only the words spoken but also the emotions and intentions woven within them. It is an act of respect and care, often leading to deeper and more meaningful relationships.

Observation is another silent yet eloquent participant in the dialogue between beings, allowing a keen observer to discern unspoken signals: a furrowed brow signalling worry, a quick smile indicating joy, or a restless gaze hinting at distraction. This perceptive ability allows one to read the room, adapt responses to each interaction's subtleties, and pre-emptively address or resolve misunderstandings.

In our interactions, the synergy of speaking, writing, listening, and observing creates a comprehensive approach to communication. This diverse array of skills enables us to connect effectively, minimise misunderstandings, and nurture relationships in every sphere of life. For me, languages are about building bridges between hearts and minds, transcending boundaries, and fostering understanding in our increasingly interconnected world.

MICROPOLIS

School as a "Micropolis": Preparing Youth for the Urban Life

picture the school environment as a miniature city, a "micropolis" bustling with life, interaction, and the pursuit of knowledge. This microcosm, with its intricate structures and dynamic social fabric, mirrors the larger workings of urban life. Within its confines, the school houses a complex system akin to a city's infrastructure, governance, and community life.

At the helm, the school's administration mirrors a city council, shaping the educational landscape through decisions much like urban policies shape city living. Teachers assume roles akin to city workers, each contributing to guiding the youth – the city's heartbeat. Students are the vibrant inhabitants of this "micropolis," each on their unique journey, with ambitions and dreams as diverse as the citizens of any metropolis.

Extracurricular clubs and societies in schools echo the myriad of community groups in a city, nurturing special interests and fostering a sense of belonging among their members. Similarly, the disciplinary systems within schools serve a parallel purpose to law enforcement in cities – maintaining order and promoting a safe, productive environment for all. School-shared spaces, like playgrounds and cafeterias, function as public squares where young minds learn the art of social interaction. Here, they practise the give-and-take of community living, from the simple act of sharing a bench to navigating the complexities of group dynamics. These spaces are training grounds for life beyond the school gates. In contrast, public spaces in cities offer a broader stage for social and civic engagement.

Moreover, schools, like cities, are hubs of diversity, offering a range of subjects that introduce students to the spectrum of professional roles sustaining a city. From arts to sciences, technology to trades, schools expose students to various disciplines, helping them carve out potential paths for their future careers.

The concept of the school as a "micropolis" posits that education should extend beyond mere academic instruction. It should embrace a comprehensive curriculum inclusive of vital life skills, ethical values, and societal norms to accurately reflect the more extensive world. By mirroring society more effectively, schools could better prepare students for their eventual transition into adulthood and urban life. This approach might positively influence youth, potentially reducing their encounters with the judicial system after completing their mandatory schooling years.

The Controversial Metaphor: School as a Prison?

Drawing a seemingly far-fetched parallel between schools and prisons reveals some stark resemblances upon closer examination, a comparison noted by others before me. I aim to delve deeper into this analogy by highlighting additional details. The strict adherence to schedules, the punctuated sound of bells marking transitions throughout the day, and the controlled environments all echo the regimented structure of a prison.

Consider the daily assemblies in schools, akin to the systematic headcounts of inmates. There is a similar echo of discipline, an expectation of orderliness, and a collective gathering that underscores conformity and uniformity. Within the school cafeteria, parallels continue to unfold. Like prisoners, students are often allotted a brief window to consume their food before moving swiftly to the next segment of their day. The hurried mealtimes reflect a broader theme of strict time management and control over individual leisure within both institutions.

The short breaks peppered between academic periods do little to dispel the comparison. They are like the allotted prison recreation times; moments when movement and freedom are permitted yet heavily circumscribed and supervised, with teachers or other support staff on duty. School rules that govern student behaviour often mirror the rigid regulations of prison conduct, controlling the natural impulses of students to socialise and move freely. The prohibition of running in corridors, akin to movement restrictions within prison facilities, constrains the natural tendencies of energetic young individuals.

Modern school architecture often includes surveillance systems, echoing the omnipresent eyes that monitor inmate behaviour, ensuring safety but also enforcing a watchful environment. Even more concerning is the presence of isolation rooms utilised for disciplinary action in schools, uncomfortably resembling the solitary confinement cells in prisons.

Perhaps the most direct comparison lies in the educational "sentence," the predetermined number of years students are required to attend school, much like the fixed terms served by inmates. This parallel draws attention to the mandatory nature of attendance and the perception of education as an obligation rather than a privilege or a journey of enrichment.

Despite these disconcerting similarities, it is crucial to underline that schools are fundamentally designed to be places of empowerment, learning, and growth rather than prisons' punitive and corrective purposes. While structure and rules are indispensable for order and safety, the challenge lies in crafting frameworks that support, rather than constrain, the educational journey.

Indeed, the similarities can be shocking, but can anyone reject these similarities? An ideal "micropolis" should strike a balance, borrowing the best from cities and refining the rigidity that mirrors prisons to create a nurturing environment for young minds. In reimagining the "micropolis" of school, the aim should be to blend structure with freedom, control with creativity, and discipline with encouragement, transforming the space into one that liberates rather than confines the spirit of learning and exploration.

The Homework Debate: Balancing Education and Well-Being

Homework, a term that often sparks contentious debate among students, parents, and educators alike, remains a fundamental aspect of education. Should you survey students regarding their views on this after-school practice, an overwhelming consensus might emerge: homework feels like a collective effort by teachers to monopolise students' leisure hours. Officially, homework refers to tasks assigned by teachers for students to complete outside of regular class time, within the confines of students' homes and during what would otherwise be their downtime.

Educational policies, especially during critical exam periods like the GCSEs and A-levels, can significantly invade students' free time, turning holidays into periods of revision rather than relaxation. However, it would be incorrect to assume I am against homework. I assign it in accordance with school policy, recognising its purpose and potential benefits. Like any educational tool, the key to its effectiveness lies in moderation. Excessive homework or assignments without clear educational goals can be counterproductive, diminishing students' motivation and infringing on their crucial time for rest, play, and exploration – activities equally vital to a child's development.

Supporters of homework argue that it reinforces classroom learning, instilling discipline, time management skills, and autonomy. In this context, discipline refers to the ability to follow a structured plan, advantageous for managing future work responsibilities. However, homework can also be a significant stressor, leading to adverse effects such as anxiety, depression, and strained relationships with peers and family. The undeniable impact of homework on student well-being includes potential issues like fatigue, weight loss, and other health issues.

Another critical consideration is the role of homework in exacerbating social inequalities. Not all children come from homes conducive to academic study. A child with limited support at home, whether due to parents' educational backgrounds or economic constraints, is at a distinct disadvantage compared to peers who have access to help, whether from family or tutors.

In the context of primary education, the benefits of homework are even less tangible. Young children's brains are wired for interactive play and social engagement rather than for completing written assignments. The Finnish education system, with minimal homework, serves as an example that minimises the risk of creating negative attitudes towards learning.

We must ask ourselves: If we struggle to make school an engaging and enjoyable experience for children, how can we extend the school day into the home with homework? Many children resent school when their experiences are characterised by obligation rather than inspiration. As educators, our mandate is to impart knowledge and kindle a passion for learning. It may be time to reconsider both the amount and quality of homework we assign and our objectives in doing so. While some students eagerly seek additional work, expressing a desire to improve, others may benefit more from revisiting classwork or engaging in one-on-one sessions to address areas of difficulty.

MY CASE AGAINST STANDARDISATION IN TEACHING

In many contemporary education systems globally, a predominant model often employs a one-size-fits-all approach. The concept of placing thirty students, all of a similar age, in one classroom and expecting uniform absorption of information, progress, and excellence is fundamentally flawed. Despite sharing birthdates within the same twelve-month span, these students bring vastly different experiences, backgrounds, interests, and capabilities to the learning environment.

At the heart of this system is the expectation that classes, typically around thirty pupils grouped primarily by age, should absorb information at a similar pace. They are subjected to a uniform curriculum, with instructors typically employing a singular teaching methodology. This approach inherently overlooks the uniqueness of each student. While managing larger groups with standard procedures may be convenient, it inadvertently diminishes the individuality and specific interests of each student. By demanding homogeneity, the education system may suppress the diverse talents, inclinations, and potential breakthroughs that arise from recognising and cultivating individual strengths.

Furthermore, with few exceptions like those in Finland, most educational establishments follow an inherent hierarchy of subjects, dictating certain subjects as "core subjects," typically including mathematics, sciences, and the primary language of the nation. This hierarchy sends a message that pursuits outside of these core areas are of lesser significance, limiting exposure to a diverse set of disciplines and perpetuating the notion that success and intelligence are narrowly defined by proficiency in these select areas.

Arguably, the most compelling argument against standardised teaching lies in the nature of humanity itself. Humans, regarded as highly intricate beings, exhibit immense diversity in cognition, interests, and abilities. Given this complexity and individuality, teaching a group of thirty human beings the same way raises questions about realistic expectations for uniform learning, understanding, and output. This not only sets unrealistic standards but might lead to unwarranted stress, loss of interest in learning, and a misplaced sense of inadequacy among students.

The age-old adage cautions against putting all our eggs in a single basket, emphasising the importance of diversification to safeguard against unforeseen challenges. Applied to the education system, this highlights a potential oversight in endorsing and practising standardised teaching. By confining students to a uniform curriculum and pedagogy, we are metaphorically placing the diverse talents, aspirations, and potentials of our students into one constrained educational "basket." This approach risks suppressing individuality and enthusiasm for learning and may have catastrophic consequences for holistic educational outcomes. The commitment to standardised teaching, within the existing educational framework, appears to be a grave miscalculation, jeopardising the holistic development of future generations.

In essence, the standardisation of teaching practices contradicts the very nature of human variability and individual potential. While offering administrative ease and a semblance of uniform progress, it risks stifling the true potential of many students, favouring conformity over the nurturing of individual talents and passions. In an era that increasingly values diversity and personalisation, it's imperative to critically examine whether our education systems, through standardisation, are doing justice to the complex potential of every student.

FEAR OF FAILURE

Fear of Failure: The Power of Experiential Learning

The fear of making mistakes often paralyses us, preventing us from attempting new actions and exploring the boundaries of our capabilities. Although this fear is well intentioned, particularly when instilled by caring guardians, it can stymie the growth and development of young minds. Mistakes, after all, are not merely errors; they represent profound learning experiences.

Reflecting on my childhood brings to mind the rich variety of experiences I was privileged to have. The absence of constant parental surveillance allowed me and my siblings freedom to test the limits of our environment. Like many children, we climbed trees and cycled freely, feeling the rush of wind against our faces and, yes, the occasional pain from a fall. We indulged our curious minds, experimenting with melted candle wax and observing its varying effects on different parts of our hands. The magical dance of molten plastic dropping from burning sticks became another source of fascination.

However, our adventures weren't solely about playful exploration; they also stirred the edges of our imaginations. The discovery of woodlice, those armoured warriors of the insect world, inspired vivid war scenes reminiscent of the tales and cartoons we had absorbed. They became formidable adversaries in our imaginative play, with us raining down melted plastic "bombs" from our makeshift weapons.

Yet, as with all experiential learning, there was a spectrum of outcomes. One particular experiment stands out starkly in my memory. In a moment of youthful curiosity, I tested the effect of the molten plastic on my hand, much like I had done with candle wax. The pain was immediate and intense, leaving not just a mark on my skin but on my psyche as well. To this day, the scar on my left hand serves as a tangible reminder of that incident.

The lesson here is not about the recklessness of youth but about the invaluable lessons embedded in every experience, whether pleasant or painful. While the protective instinct of parents and educators is natural and commendable, there is merit in allowing children to navigate their world, to stumble, fall, and rise again. In every scrape, bruise, or burn, there's an indelible lesson etched, teaching resilience, caution, and the boundless potential of experiential learning.

Fear of Failure: Experiences as a Parent

Guiding my children through life, I always emphasised the value of hands-on experiences. The philosophy of allowing children to confront challenges head-on, within the boundaries of safety, is deeply ingrained in my parenting approach. While it may seem counterintuitive, especially in a world that increasingly cocoons children, there's merit in letting them grapple with the real-world scenarios they'll ultimately face as adults.

When my children encountered obstacles, whether stumbling in play or facing a challenging situation, I consciously held back the immediate instinct to swoop in and assist. By giving them the space to self-soothe and find their own solutions, I wasn't just teaching them resilience but also the value of patience. This skill is rapidly eroding in today's instant-gratification culture, and it's crucial for our young ones to understand the importance of waiting, reflecting, and enduring.

Our interactions were full of fun and insightful dialogues, games, and hands-on lessons. One particularly memorable experience was teaching my younger son how to drive at age seventeen. This wasn't just about the mechanics of driving but a holistic lesson in anticipation, safety, and situational awareness. While I posed hypothetical scenarios about potential hazards, I also nudged him towards situations where he might make a mistake. I believed these mistakes would be invaluable in his driving education.

One aspect of driving that vividly exemplifies this approach is aquaplaning. It's a term most drivers are familiar with, but few truly understand it until they have experienced it first-hand. Aquaplaning, or hydroplaning, occurs when a vehicle's tyres lose traction with the road because of excess water, causing the driver to momentarily lose control. My own driving instructor hadn't dwelt on it, and no amount of verbal instruction can truly capture the sensation or the panic one might feel when it happens. So, while ensuring safety, I believed it was essential for my son to recognise the signs and learn the correct response through experience, rather than just theory.

As parents and educators, while our protective instincts are valid, it's essential to strike a balance. Offering children the space to fail, learn, and grow arms them with practical knowledge and resilience that classroom lessons or overprotective parenting can never provide.

Fear of Failure: Cultivating Patience in the Age of Instant Gratification

Patience, as I have emphasised, is more than a virtue; it's a crucial component of the learning process. The contemporary world, with its myriad of conveniences, often gives the illusion that knowledge and rewards are just a click away. While technology has certainly revolutionised access to information, there's an inadvertent side effect – the erosion of the patience to delve deep and truly understand subjects.

Consider the traditional library, an institution that stands as proof of the painstaking process of seeking knowledge. Once, to satiate one's curiosity or to complete a research task, one had to journey to these treasure troves of information. Navigating the maze of shelves, discovering the right book, and then poring over its pages to unearth the needed knowledge was a journey in itself. This experience wasn't just about finding an answer; it was about the entire process of seeking, the trials and tribulations of not immediately finding what you're looking for, and the eventual euphoria of discovery. These experiences were rich in lessons about perseverance, patience, and the joy of earned knowledge.

Contrast this with today's digital era, when a quick online search often yields immediate answers. While the convenience is undeniable and has its own set of advantages, it has also led to a culture in which depth, exploration, and the journey of learning are sometimes overlooked.

In my role as an educator, I have always believed in equipping students not just with answers but with the skills to find them on their own. When posed with questions, rather than offering direct solutions, I guide them gently towards the route to discovery. This methodology serves a dual purpose. First, it instils a sense of accomplishment in students when they arrive at the answer themselves. Second, it fosters an inherent ability to independently navigate problems, seek solutions, and relish the journey of learning.

The essence here isn't to undermine the benefits of our rapidly advancing digital age but to blend the best of both worlds. While immediate answers have their place, the art of patient exploration, of truly immersing oneself in the process of learning, is an invaluable skill that we must continue to nurture in the generations to come.

Fear of Failure: The Greenhouse versus the Forest

Drawing parallels between the growth of plants and the nurturing of young minds offers a vivid and thought-provoking perspective on the nature of our educational system. The current global academic framework often mirrors a greenhouse, a controlled environment where conditions are optimised to ensure predictable, uniform growth. In this setup, every plant (or student) is given a set amount of water, light, and nutrients, ostensibly ensuring that each one flourishes. However, while this approach guarantees a certain standard of growth, it doesn't necessarily prepare these plants for the vast, unpredictable wilderness outside.

The outside world, with all its unpredictability, challenges, and opportunities, is more akin to a sprawling forest than the confines of a greenhouse. In the forest, plants are subjected to the whims of nature – variations in sunlight, unpredictable rainfall, competition for nutrients, and the ever-present threat of pests. Yet, it's in these exact conditions that many plants thrive, adapting and growing resilient in the face of adversity. Similarly, when children are exposed to challenges, failures, and the need for adaptability early on, they develop resilience and resourcefulness that are hard to cultivate within the sheltered confines of a structured system.

Now, consider pets that have been domesticated and kept indoors throughout their lives. They are cared for and protected, and their every need is attended to. But because of this, they often lose their innate wild instincts, their ability to fend for themselves, and their resilience to the unpredictability of the outside world. In much the same way, when students are overprotected, when their every setback is cushioned, and when they're shielded from the consequences of their mistakes, they might be ill-equipped to navigate the real world with its myriad of challenges.

Of course, this isn't a call to abandon our educational systems or to thrust students unprepared into the wilderness. Rather, it is an invitation to re-evaluate and perhaps reimagine the ways in which we nurture our young minds. Perhaps there is merit in blending the protection and care of the greenhouse with the challenges and unpredictability of the forest. By doing so, we could be raising not just academically accomplished individuals but also resilient, adaptable, and resourceful human beings ready to face the world in all its complexity.

Embracing Failure as a Stepping Stone to Success

Historical accounts and biographies of accomplished individuals often highlight their moments of triumph, their breakthroughs, and their ground-breaking innovations. But what's often overlooked are the numerous failures, setbacks, and heartbreaks that predated their successes. Every path to success is littered with obstacles, detours, and dead ends. It's how individuals navigate these challenges that truly defines their character and eventual achievements.

Consider the following illustrious names: Bill Gates, J.K. Rowling, Steven Spielberg, Walt Disney, and Michael Jordan. Each of these individuals, despite their eventual accolades and impact on society, faced significant hurdles along their respective journeys. Gates's first venture, Traf-O-Data, was a commercial failure. Rowling was rejected by numerous publishers before Harry Potter enchanted the world. Spielberg was turned down multiple times by film schools. Disney's first animation company went bankrupt. Yet, each of these setbacks served not as deterrents but as motivators, propelling these individuals to persevere, refine their craft, and relentlessly pursue their dreams.

When a promising business in which I had invested failed because of the devastating effects of the lockdown on businesses, I lost almost $100K. However, I emerged spiritually stronger, with experiential knowledge that has better prepared me for similar events in the future. I've learned to diversify my investments. Even though it's a piece of advice I had often heard throughout my life – never put all your eggs in one basket – I had to experience it to better grasp the meaning of it.

This perspective on failure is both enlightening and liberating. It reframes setbacks not as endpoints but as crucial feedback mechanisms, necessary detours that provide valuable insights for future endeavours. It encourages a mindset in which failure is not feared but embraced as an inherent part of the journey towards success.

In understanding this, we must redefine our perception of success. It's not a singular, isolated moment of achievement but a culmination of experiences, learnings, and, most importantly, relentless attempts. The road to success is paved with failures, each serving as a stepping stone, bringing one closer to their aspirations. The stories of these iconic individuals remind us that in the pursuit of our dreams, it's not about how many times we fall but how many times we get back up and keep pushing forwards.

In this whirlwind of instant gratification, the concept of persistence, perseverance, and dedication seems to be getting diluted. The journey, which often teaches more than the destination itself, is bypassed for the immediacy of results. Our modern world may have armed us with tools to get things instantly, but it has concurrently weakened our muscle for patience, resilience, and appreciation of the process.

Such an environment is particularly challenging for the younger generation, who, thanks to platforms like Instagram and TikTok, are exposed to curated snippets of other people's lives, mostly portraying success, luxury, and happiness. This can inadvertently create an illusion that success is easy, immediate, and accessible to all at the click of a button.

However, reality paints a different picture. True success is the fruit of labour, persistence, and oftentimes multiple failures. Each setback, each stumble, is an opportunity to learn, grow, and come back stronger. In bypassing the struggles, the trials and tribulations, and heading straight for success, individuals miss out on invaluable life lessons that no textbook or online course can teach.

Failure should not be a term associated with negativity but instead should be embraced as a part of one's journey towards success. It's the lessons we learn in our moments of despair, the strength we discover in our weakest times, and the resilience we build when faced with challenges that truly mould our character.

Today's fixation on instant gratification robs us of the essence of life – the journey. It's high time we recalibrate our understanding of success and failure, appreciating the winding road with its ups and downs, rather than just yearning for the destination.

The journey towards success is absolutely paved with failures, missteps, and lessons. It's through these experiences that we truly learn and grow. Embracing failure as part of the learning process not only helps us to overcome challenges but also instils a growth mindset. It teaches us that the path to success is iterative, demanding both patience and persistence. Every mistake is an opportunity to evolve, refine our strategies, and come back stronger. When we shift our perspective and see failure as a stepping stone rather than an endpoint, we become unstoppable in our pursuit of success. After all, it's not the number of times we fall that defines us but the number of times we rise again, fortified with new knowledge and renewed determination.

GAMES ARE A WASTE OF TIME?

The Educational Power of Play: Reassessing the Value of Games

The general perception of games as trivial pursuits is an intriguing paradox when considering the powerful educational potential they hold. Traditional educational models have long emphasised structured learning and curricula, often relegating games to the status of playful indulgence rather than a viable instructional tool. The assumption that serious learning cannot coexist with the seemingly light-hearted nature of games has persisted in many educational philosophies.

Yet, when one pauses to reflect on the essence of what makes a game so engaging, it becomes clear that these elements are synonymous with effective learning principles. Games inherently demand problem-solving, strategic planning, critical thinking, and adaptability from their players. The unpredictability and governed chaos within games challenge players to devise creative solutions, develop strategies, learn from errors, and continuously adapt – skills that are invaluable in the larger theatre of life.

Roger Caillois's seminal work on the categories of games elucidates this further. Competitive games, or "Agon," fuel motivation and the desire for achievement, much like the pursuit of academic excellence. Chance-based games, or "Alea," teach the art of navigating uncertainty and making decisions in fluid situations. Mimicry, found in simulation games, allows students to step into roles and contexts, applying theoretical learning to lifelike scenarios and witnessing the practical impacts of their decisions.

The category of "Ilinx," seeking vertigo or sensory distortion, may initially seem incongruent with the learning process.[57] Yet, when we consider educational activities that disrupt students' equilibrium or challenge their sensory perceptions, we uncover an opportunity to teach about balance, the laws of physics, and the workings of the human body. These experiences can also be insightful for exploring how our senses can be deceived – a lesson valuable for critical thinking.

Games excel in offering immediate feedback, a feature that is crucial for learning. The opportunity to quickly realise and correct mistakes means that the learning process is active and ongoing. This quick loop from action to reaction enables learners to recognise their missteps promptly and adjust accordingly, mirroring the scientific method's cycle of hypothesis, experiment, and refinement.

The true paradox lies not within games themselves but within our perceptions of their role in education. Games are mistakenly seen as mere distractions when they can, in fact, serve as dynamic and potent educational mediums. If harnessed wisely, games can significantly enhance the educational experience, marrying the joy of play with the rigours of learning.

The Strategic Engagement of Educational Games

In the sphere of education, games hold a particularly unique and compelling position. They straddle the line between structured learning and spontaneous play, offering a blend of motivation that is both intrinsic, drawn from the joy

---

[57] Tom Brock, "Roger Caillois and E-Sports: On the Problems of Treating Play as Work," *ResearchGate*, January 2017, https://journals.sagepub.com/doi/10.1177/15554120 16686878.

of play, and extrinsic, linked to the rewards of formal learning. To combat this paradoxical approach to games in education, here are a few points to consider regarding their potential:

Differentiated Learning: Games naturally accommodate various learning styles, meeting the needs of visual, auditory, and kinaesthetic learners alike. This versatility ensures that educational games can offer multiple entry points for understanding and engagement, depending on individual preferences and strengths.

Safe Environment to Fail: One of the greatest gifts games give learners is the freedom to fail. Unlike the high stakes often associated with classroom assessments, games treat failure as part of the learning curve, an opportunity rather than a setback. They encourage students to experiment, take risks, and learn resilience, all within the low-pressure context of play.

Real-World Application: Through simulations and role-playing, games allow students to experience complex real-life scenarios in a controlled environment. By managing a simulated economy or navigating social interactions within a game, students can apply theoretical knowledge in practical, often impactful ways.

Peer Learning: Educational games have a collaborative edge, especially in multiplayer settings. They can foster constructive competition and cooperation, prompting students to share insights, discuss strategies, and engage in problem-solving together.

Tracking Progress: With the integration of technology in educational games, tracking progress becomes seamless and insightful. Real-time analytics help both educators and students identify areas for improvement, tailor learning experiences, and celebrate growth.

Adaptability: The adaptability of many modern educational games ensures they remain challenging yet accessible. As students' abilities grow, the game's difficulty can scale accordingly, providing a continuously fitting level of challenge without leading to frustration.

Engagement: Let's face it: games are fun! And an engaged student is more likely to be an active participant in their learning process. By making learning entertaining, educational games capture and sustain attention much longer than traditional methods might.

Let the Children Play

Let the Children Play: How More Play Will Save Our Schools and Help Children Thrive by Pasi Sahlberg and William Doyle is a seminal work that delves into the significance of play in a child's education and overall well-being. This is an important book, and I aim to provide you with a critical analysis, which only reflects my opinion of it.[58]

Crisis in Education:

Sahlberg and Doyle pinpoint a pressing concern within today's educational landscape: the increasing "play deficit." As schools in numerous countries, including the United States, shift towards maximising classroom instruction and structured activities, the valuable essence of free, spontaneous play is being diminished. The consequence of such an approach is profound. When children are stripped of their inherent right to play, not only are they robbed of physical activity but they're also denied the chance for creativity, exploration, and the journey of self-discovery. This sentiment is aptly captured by the authors when they state, "In many schools today, children are being deprived of both the time and the spaces to flex and develop their creative muscles, to discover who they are and what they are passionate about." This poignant observation underlines how the contemporary education system, with its intense focus on metrics and results, often overlooks the intangible yet invaluable benefits that arise from unstructured play. By prioritising test

---

[58] Pasi Sahlberg and William Doyle, *Let the Children Play: How More Play Will Save Our Schools and Help Children Thrive* (New York: Oxford University Press, 2019).

scores, there's a risk of fostering an environment where students are drilled more on "what to think" rather than "how to think."[59]

The Finnish Model:

As a counterpoint to the crisis, Sahlberg and Doyle introduce readers to the Finnish educational ethos, offering a refreshing departure from the test-driven environments prevalent in many nations. At the heart of the Finnish approach lies a reverence for the child's pace and style of learning. By delaying formal education until the age of seven, Finland emphasises the importance of letting children be children, granting them the liberty to play, explore, and cultivate their curiosities. Once they embark on their educational journey, the environment remains more relaxed and student-centred. The authors encapsulate this unique approach with this observation: "In Finland, we believe that children must have time to be children. The role of school is to help children grow and develop, not to put them under continuous pressure."[60] Through this lens, the Finnish model doesn't just prioritise academic excellence but underscores the importance of holistic development, instilling a genuine love for learning that isn't bound by the confines of a classroom or a syllabus.

By contrasting the "play deficit" seen in many parts of the world with the Finnish paradigm, Sahlberg and Doyle present a compelling case for reimagining the purpose and approach of education to truly benefit the child's overall development.

Benefits of Play:

In their exploration of play, Sahlberg and Doyle underscore its multifaceted advantages. Play isn't merely a leisure activity; it serves as a fundamental

---

[59] Sahlberg and Doyle, *Let the Children Play*, 197-214.
[60] Sahlberg and Doyle, *Let the Children Play*, 217-222.

driver for a child's cognitive, emotional, and social growth. Drawing upon a myriad of research, the authors emphasise that through play, children hone their problem-solving skills, cultivate their creativity, and foster emotional resilience. For instance, Sahlberg and Doyle note, "When children play, they are not just having fun; they are shaping their brain, learning social skills, and preparing themselves for the challenges of adulthood."[61] This statement encapsulates the essence of play, reminding readers that beyond immediate enjoyment, play serves as a preparatory ground for life's various challenges, fostering adaptability and resilience.

Structured versus Unstructured Play:

Sahlberg and Doyle also differentiate between two types of play: structured and unstructured. While both have their merits, the authors particularly extol the virtues of unstructured play. Structured play, like organised sports or board games, is guided by rules and often adult-led. In contrast, unstructured play is spontaneous and driven by a child's imagination, allowing them to explore, create, and navigate their world without predetermined constraints. The authors argue that it is in the unstructured moments of play that children truly discover themselves and the world around them: "They are having fun while they learn."[62] This perspective illuminates the significance of freedom in play, wherein children, without explicit guidelines or expectations, can genuinely express themselves and learn organically.

The Global Movement:

Highlighting a beacon of hope, Sahlberg and Doyle discuss an emerging global movement that recognises and champions the role of play in education. Across various cultures and educational systems, there's a gradual shift

---

[61] Sahlberg and Doyle, *Let the Children Play*, 42-55.
[62] Sahlberg and Doyle, *Let the Children Play*, 222.

towards integrating more play-centric methodologies. Schools are beginning to understand and embrace the profound impact of play on students' well-being and academic success. Around the world, educators are beginning to understand that the key to learning isn't more work but more play, the authors observe.[63] This burgeoning shift underscores a collective acknowledgement of play's inherent value, emphasising its role not as a peripheral activity but as a central component of holistic education.

Strengths:

Pasi Sahlberg and William Doyle's *Let the Children Play* stands out not merely as an opinion piece but as an earnest call to action, supported by substantial research and global perspectives. One of the foundational strengths of the book lies in its *research-backed arguments.* The authors meticulously gather evidence from diverse sources, ensuring that their advocacy for play in education isn't just based on sentimental value but is rooted in empirical findings. This rigorous approach lends credibility to their arguments. As they state, "The benefits of play aren't just anecdotal; they're scientifically proven,"[64] reinforcing the idea that their assertions aren't whimsical but grounded in evidence.

Further bolstering their narrative is the *global perspective* they adopt. By offering insights into various educational systems around the world, Sahlberg and Doyle provide readers with a comprehensive view of the state of play in education. This worldly viewpoint drives home the idea that the "play deficit" is not a localised issue but a global concern. The Finnish model, lauded for its efficacy, serves as a prime example, yet the authors also pull in examples from other nations, illustrating the universality of their arguments.

Lastly, the *practical insights* offered throughout the book distinguish it from being purely theoretical. Sahlberg and Doyle understand that for

---

[63] Sahlberg and Doyle, *Let the Children Play*, 197–214.
[64] Sahlberg and Doyle, *Let the Children Play*, 52.

real change to occur, stakeholders at all levels, be they educators, parents, or policymakers, need actionable steps. By providing these practical recommendations, the authors bridge the gap between theory and practice. They don't merely highlight problems; they offer solutions, making their work not just an analysis but a blueprint for change.

In summary, *Let the Children Play* draws its strength from its well-researched foundation, its inclusive global viewpoint, and its practical, actionable insights, ensuring that its message is both resonant and implementable.

Criticisms:

While *Let the Children Play* by Pasi Sahlberg and William Doyle is a compelling read, offering profound insights into the world of education and play, I would argue that the book, though well intentioned, may not take into account the entirety of the educational landscape.

One of my significant criticisms is the *feasibility of replicating the Finnish model* in diverse global contexts. The Finnish education system, with its emphasis on play and delayed formal schooling, is undoubtedly commendable. However, it is also evident that it thrives within a unique sociocultural and economic framework. The challenges faced by education systems in larger nations, with more diverse populations and varied socioeconomic challenges, might not always align with the solutions presented by the Finnish model. A direct transplantation of this system could ignore underlying systemic issues that are unique to different countries.

Another point of contention is the *pressure on schools to meet standardised testing benchmarks.* In countries where school funding or teacher evaluations are tied directly to student performance on standardised tests, which is the case in countries like England and France, there's a tangible discouragement to deviate from test-focused curricula. Sahlberg and Doyle criticise the overemphasis on testing yet may not explore deeply enough the systemic reasons behind this focus. Therefore, I understand that without addressing the broader structural factors at play, promoting play-based learning can become challenging.

Furthermore, while the book praises the virtues of play, it might be perceived as *oversimplifying the complex web of educational needs*. While play is undoubtedly beneficial, I feel the narrative could have been more nuanced, acknowledging that not all academic challenges can be resolved merely by introducing more playtime. There might be a myriad of other educational strategies and techniques that can complement play to provide a holistic educational experience.

Re-evaluating the Approach to Play:

The societal inclination to dismiss play as frivolous or counterproductive is deeply ingrained, manifesting in phrases that caution against "playing around" or "playing the fool." Such expressions, laden with negativity, betray a broader cultural ambivalence towards play, especially among adults. This scepticism towards play, viewing it as a mere diversion rather than a vital development component, is a disservice to children and adults alike. Adults are often just children conditioned to suppress their inherent desire for play. When given the opportunity to engage in playful activities, many adults hold back, perhaps out of fear of judgement or a deeply internalised belief that play is unbecoming of adulthood. I have noticed in many staff training sessions that when game activities are announced, many of my colleagues visibly show their discontent, a stark contrast to the enthusiasm such an announcement would elicit in a classroom setting.

A visit to Bubble Planet in London, an exhibition that marries art and science in a bubbly interactive playground, demonstrated this observation. Surrounded by the joyous abandon of children diving into pools of plastic bubbles, the hesitance of adults to join in was stark. They stood on the sidelines, assuming the role of supervisors rather than participants. This reluctance to engage in play limits adults' experiences and implicitly reinforces the notion that play is not a serious endeavour.

This sentiment is mirrored in the educational policies of numerous British schools, where I have observed children's play being systematically constrained. Across the many schools I have worked in, a familiar scene unfolds: the limitation of children's playtime by institutional policies. Staff members patrol corridors and playgrounds. Children's movements and activities are closely monitored, even during supposed free periods, breaks, and the freedom to be. The prohibition against sitting on tables or engaging in unstructured play reflects an institutional hesitation to embrace play's educational and developmental potential fully.

The consequences of such restrictions are not trivial. Poor behaviour in schools, often attributed to various factors, can frequently be traced back to a fundamental source of frustration: the lack of freedom. This is not just about physical constraints within school premises but extends to the limitations placed on children's choices regarding activities, inhibiting their natural inclinations towards curiosity and exploration.

However, in the face of these challenges, there lies an extraordinary opportunity. The advancements in technology and understanding of child development at our disposal equip us to forge an educational system unlike any before. In this environment, play is a core component of learning. In *Let the Children Play*, Pasi Sahlberg and William Doyle emphasise the transformative power of play in education. It is a call to action for educators, parents, and policymakers to recognise play as a crucial element of childhood and a fundamental right of every child. It is about fostering an educational culture that values freedom, creativity, and the intrinsic joy of discovery.

By re-evaluating our approach to play, we have the opportunity to create a setting that nurtures creativity, resilience, and happiness. This paradigm shift requires us to challenge long-held beliefs about the value of play and embrace a more holistic view of education, one that prepares children for the complexities of life not through restriction and supervision but through freedom and exploration.

In envisioning a future where play is central to our educational ethos, we unlock the potential to nurture academically proficient, emotionally intelligent, innovative, and, importantly, happy generations. The key lies in our willingness to let go, to rekindle the joy of play within ourselves, and to champion its place in the lives of the children we guide. By letting the children play, we unlock the door to a future where education nurtures the whole child, preparing them for tests and, more importantly, for life.

How Impractical Are These Ideas in English Schools?

Although Pasi Sahlberg and William Doyle's ideas, particularly those presented in *Let the Children Play*, are compelling and have shown effectiveness in the Finnish context, their direct applicability to English schools and schools in other countries can be debated because of several distinct challenges and contextual differences, which I will lay out below.

Diverse Demographics: English schools, especially in urban areas, serve a highly diverse student population. This diversity encompasses various socioeconomic backgrounds, ethnicities, languages, and cultures. Adapting a model like Finland's, which operates within a more homogeneous context, might not address the specific needs and challenges faced by English schools.

Standardised Testing Pressure: The English education system places significant emphasis on standardised testing, such as SATs, GCSEs, and A-levels. These tests not only influence students' futures but also affect school rankings and reputations. Schools might find it challenging to balance an increased emphasis on play with the pressures of ensuring students perform well in these high-stakes exams.

Curriculum Rigidity: The National Curriculum in England is prescriptive in many ways, defining what should be taught at each key stage.

Finnish schools, in contrast, have greater autonomy over their curriculum. Implementing Sahlberg and Doyle's ideas in England would require significant changes to the existing curriculum, which might face resistance from multiple stakeholders.

School Funding and Resources: Finnish schools are well funded, with resources for special education and support services. In contrast, especially in the wake of austerity measures, many English schools have faced budget cuts, leading to larger class sizes and fewer resources. Emulating the Finnish model would require significant investments in school infrastructure and resources.

Cultural Differences: The societal value placed on education, the role of teachers, and parental expectations can differ between countries. In Finland, teaching is a highly respected profession with rigorous entry requirements. English schools, while having many dedicated professionals, face challenges in teacher recruitment and retention. Implementing a model that relies heavily on teacher autonomy and expertise might be challenging without addressing these underlying issues.

School Start Age: One of the features of the Finnish system is the later school start age, with formal schooling beginning at seven. In England, formal schooling starts at age four or five. Advocating for a later start might face opposition from parents and policymakers who are accustomed to the current structure.

While I find the ideas presented by Sahlberg and Doyle valuable, these specific challenges highlight the complexities of directly applying the Finnish model to English schools and, by extension, to any other country. It stresses the need for a holistic understanding of the local educational landscape and adapting global best practices to fit specific contexts. As with everything, one must act with moderation to achieve an optimal result. It is doubtful countries would change their habits and systems overnight to introduce more play into their curriculum. The world is a village dotted with different colours, landscapes, and customs. We cannot and should not entirely copy what our neighbour is doing. However, we can certainly be inspired by what they do well and strive to reproduce it in our own setting, in appropriate proportions.

Final Thoughts

In concluding the exploration of games as effective learning tools, nature itself provides ample evidence. Both in the animal kingdom and among human toddlers, play, essentially a form of a game, is a cornerstone of learning and development.

In the wild, young lions and tigers often engage in playful "hunting" with their siblings, mock-pouncing and playfully biting without causing harm. This behaviour goes beyond mere enjoyment; it's practice. They are essentially rehearsing the actual hunting techniques they will employ as adults, refining the stalking, pouncing, and biting skills crucial for survival. Similarly, young dolphins, known for their playful demeanour, play with seaweed or other marine objects, pushing them with their snouts or flippers and chasing after them. Beyond amusement, this play aids in developing motor skills, coordination, and a deeper understanding of their environment. Birds, especially species like ravens and crows, engage in mid-air stunts, twisting and turning in the sky, appearing playful but enhancing their aerial proficiency. These acrobatics teach them evasion tactics and, in some instances, skills to nab moving prey during flight. Even domestic animals, like puppies, have purpose in their playful activities. Play-fighting helps establish social hierarchies and, importantly, teaches them "bite inhibition," ensuring communication and interaction without inflicting harm as they grow.

Drawing a parallel with human toddlers, games play a similar instructional role. Classic games like peekaboo and hide-and-seek, for instance, do more than elicit giggles. They are instrumental in helping toddlers grasp the concept of object permanence, understanding that things continue to exist even when out of sight. When toddlers engage with building blocks, stacking them high or knocking towers down, they receive hands-on lessons about balance, gravity, cause and effect, and spatial relationships. Role-playing games, in which children might pretend to be a doctor or play house, offer insights into the adult world and societal roles, promoting empathy and understanding. Physical games, like tag or chase, are foundational for the development of motor skills, coordination, and spatial awareness.

In essence, games are far from frivolous pastimes. They are fundamental tools for learning, both for animals and humans. They offer a safe haven to practise vital life skills and understand complex concepts, enabling physical, cognitive, and social development. Many cultures and societies rightly recognise play as the true labour of childhood. And for many animals, it's an integral aspect of survival and adapting to their environments.

GENIUSCIDE

C hildren, in their purest form, embody boundless imagination and unadulterated genius. Every child possesses an innate ability to perceive the world without the limitations and biases that often constrain adult perspectives. Hand a child any object and they can effortlessly transform it into a multitude of things, limited only by the expanse of their imagination. This creativity is not learned; it is their natural state of being. Many of us, during our youthful days, embraced this boundless imagination, allowing everyday objects to become fantastical tools of exploration and discovery. Such uninhibited creativity is a hallmark of genius, representing the capability to envision and innovate beyond the ordinary.

Yet, as we transition into adulthood, this spark of imagination seems to wane. The very societal structures we have established and the educational concepts that we have embraced appear to contribute significantly to this decline, promoting conformity over creativity. Our formative years, ideally meant to nourish and encourage our innate talents, often end up stifling them. The question arises: Have we become so entangled in the responsibilities and routines of adulthood that we've lost touch with the wonders of our childhood?

Recall the resourcefulness of a child's mind. Faced with obstacles, children often devise ingenious solutions. Whether it's contriving a way to access a forbidden treat or devising a strategy to clamber out of their cribs in the hush of night, they demonstrate unparalleled determination and creativity. As adults, even with our fully developed brains, many of us find ourselves stymied by challenges, lacking the imaginative solutions we once conjured effortlessly. It's almost as if the structures we have erected to educate and socialise our young have inadvertently chipped away at their innate genius, replacing wonder with routine and curiosity with complacency. It is imperative to ask if our education system and societal expectations, in their current forms, are maintaining this unfortunate transformation from child prodigies to constrained adults. The pressing question then becomes this: Are we, through our established systems, unknowingly perpetrating a "geniuscide"?

Creative Mischief: The Ingenuity of Childhood

There's a certain ingenuity in the way children often manage to outwit adults, an attribute we sometimes fail to recognise as a mark of intelligence. It's not the defiance that should be the focus but rather the creativity that rule bending and breaking inevitably inspires. The more restrictive the environment, the more inventive and resourceful kids become. Whether it's fabricating elaborate excuses for incomplete homework or finding the perfect hideaway for prohibited activities, their resourcefulness is boundless.

This relentless drive to innovate and push boundaries isn't exclusive to children; it's a fundamental human trait. As adults, we navigate life's challenges, sometimes bending the rules, in what can be seen as a survival mechanism inherent to all living beings.

Allow me to illustrate with a personal anecdote from my school days, a time when technology was on the cusp of becoming a ubiquitous part of our lives. I was in Year 11, and Hewlett-Packard had just released their revolutionary 48-series calculators. These devices weren't just calculators; they were more like handheld computers, programmable and capable of communicating wirelessly with each other via infrared signals. It was this particular feature that my classmates and I decided to exploit during a chemistry assessment in our lecture theatre. Mr Litman, our teacher, was known for spacing us out in the room to prevent any cheating. Knowing this, we concocted a plan to use our calculators as a means of silent communication.

The anticipation was electric, the planning meticulous. Some students even purchased these expensive calculators just to be part of the scheme. Though I couldn't afford one, I was deeply involved in hatching the plan. On the day of the assessment, Mr Litman was vigilant, as usual, his eyes sweeping the room. But it seemed he had no need to worry; everyone was absorbed in their work, calculators clicking away. Our message relay system worked flawlessly, until one student received an unexpected message: *je vous ai grillés*, which translates as "I busted you." The message circulated, sowing confusion until, collectively, our gazes turned to Mr Litman and his unmistakable grin. We had been outsmarted in our own game. He had no idea of our plan; however, the students' messages began appearing on his own calculator, which he started using at some point. We were unlucky on that one. Everyone who was using a calculator with infrared communication capabilities had to sit a different test. While my classmates were disappointed at being caught, we unanimously accepted the fact that the way that we were caught was very funny.

This episode, while it could be dismissed as mere mischief, showcases the strategic thinking of students and the perceptive acumen of a teacher who turned the tables on us. It's a memory etched in my mind, influencing how I now address the inevitable attempts at cheating in my own classroom. I advocate for creating a learning environment where failure is not dreaded but seen as a step in the learning process. The impulse to cheat often stems from the fear of failure, the terror of appearing inadequate. By redefining failure as a natural part of the journey towards understanding, we can perhaps quell the need for students to resort to such measures and instead encourage them to embrace the learning process with honesty and integrity.

Observing My Children

Observing children at play is akin to watching master artists at work. Their canvas is the world around them, and their tools range from toys to everyday household objects. I have often been amazed at the ingenuity of my children, absorbed in their games, constructing marvels that often defy adult logic. Their seamless fusion of disparate objects into a single, coherent narrative or structure reveals a level of imaginative capability that leaves one in awe. At times, I find myself yearning to delve deep into their minds, hoping to catch a glimpse of the origin of such imagination.

What they've managed to create with their toys often transcends the original intent of those items. For instance, the marvels they have sculpted using LEGOs are not just structures but testimonies to their innovative capabilities. If the creators of LEGO were to see the architectural wonders birthed by my sons, they would undoubtedly be taken aback. My children don't just stop at LEGOs; their canvas is far more expansive. They seamlessly integrate Jenga bricks, Play-Doh, and an array of other toys into their creations. But what truly astounds me is their ability to find potential in everyday household items. Kitchen cutlery becomes a part of their grand designs. A spoon isn't just a spoon – it might be a bridge, a flagpole, or a digger's arm. Books morph into stepping stones to imaginary worlds. An empty box isn't mere trash – it's a castle, a car, or a secret treasure chest. Chairs and pillows? They are not mere objects of utility but become crucial elements of their fantastical realms.

This kind of imaginative alchemy, turning ordinary objects into extraordinary tales and structures, demonstrates the boundless potential within every child. If nurtured and encouraged, this kind of creative thinking could revolutionise how we approach problem-solving, design, and innovation in adulthood. The challenge lies in preserving and nurturing this innate talent as children navigate their journey into the grown-up world.

Storytelling, a natural human ability, finds its most vivid and spontaneous expression in children. They might not be seasoned authors like Agatha Christie or cinematic maestros like Steven Spielberg, but children weave tales with an authenticity and imagination that's unparalleled. Take the example of my godchild, Luna. While playing with my sons, all aged between four and seven, Luna showcased not just her ability to craft a narrative but also her natural leadership skills. She orchestrated an entire play, meticulously guiding the boys, showcasing a directive that many adults spend years in universities trying to cultivate. Such raw leadership abilities in children are a testament to our intrinsic social nature.

This innate ability isn't just limited to storytelling or leadership. Children, with their unrestrained creativity and instinctual skills, echo the evolutionary wisdom that has allowed humanity to thrive. Humans, with our physically fragile constitutions, might not have survived the challenges of prehistoric times if not for our remarkable brains. Our success as a species isn't attributed to brute strength but to collaboration, understanding, and our ability to construct societal frameworks. This collaborative instinct, evident in Luna's natural leadership, stems from the very same cerebral prowess that helped our ancestors evade extinction.

If this is the legacy and potential we are inheriting, shouldn't our focus be on fostering it? By allowing children to nurture their creativity and freeing them from restrictive constructs, we might both preserve and amplify these natural instincts. By "opening the box" for them, as it were, we provide an environment where their innate genius can truly flourish. The outcomes could be revolutionary.

Before stepping into the structured world of formal education, children possess an imagination that is raw and unfiltered. It is as if they view the world through a prism untouched by societal biases or restrictions. Schools, though vital in many aspects, sometimes act as aggressive moderators, refining this untamed creativity to fit within specified boundaries. This intense modulation often suppresses the very essence of childlike ingenuity.

One might ponder, why do so many children resist the idea of school? It's not just the early morning start, because, as many parents can attest, children often rise with the sun, brimming with energy and curiosity. The resistance might stem from the same root many of us felt in our school days. That underlying discomfort, or sometimes outright rebellion against school, was not just juvenile sulkiness but may have been an instinctive pushback against an environment that seemed determined to curb our natural inclinations.

The root of the problem seems to be the lack of evolution in our educational structures. While our world metamorphoses rapidly, adapting to new technologies, ideologies, and challenges, our foundational approach to education remains eerily static. This is a true paradox. The content, methodology, and even physical spaces of learning have witnessed only incremental changes over decades. It's an incongruence that doesn't escape even the youngest minds. If we aim to truly harness the genius within our children, it might be time to reimagine and revolutionise the very spaces and ways in which we educate them.

Classroom Projects

Whenever I assign class projects, I deliberately prioritise student autonomy in how they present their work. In my classes, while the core topic remains consistent, the medium of presentation is fluid and open-ended, ranging from live role-plays and video recordings to PowerPoint slides and handmade posters. This choice offers a window into their distinct talents, creativity, and passion, and the results have consistently been nothing short of enlightening.

The beauty of this method lies in the unique surprises each child brings to the table. The quiet student, who hardly speaks during lessons, has astounded me with their theatrical flair in a live role-play. Another, who often shies away from vocal contributions, unveiled a stunning artistic talent, crafting a poster that vividly brought to life the ambiance of Paris during *la fête de la musique*. These moments of revelation don't just celebrate individual talents but also infuse a dynamic energy into the classroom. With each student offering a distinct perspective, the class remains engaged, curious, and captivated throughout.

Monotony can dull even the most alert minds. When subjected to repetitive, homogeneous content, the brain soon seeks respite, often by drifting off. While adults might have honed the skill of feigning attention, children are still mastering self-control and attention regulation. For them, a monotonous classroom can be an ordeal. I try to diversify my teaching methods and allow my students to express themselves in varied ways. This approach not only caters to different learning styles but also ensures that the spark of curiosity remains undimmed in every young mind.

The Sieve Purpose

Creativity, universally acclaimed as a core virtue, often finds itself relegated to the sidelines in practice, akin to many a politician's earnest vow. This inconsistency between appreciation and application becomes most apparent within the confines of our educational systems. Comparable to a sieve, the education system functions as a filtration mechanism through which every member of society, particularly those aspiring to leadership roles, is expected to pass. This filtration, however, isn't always about refining the best qualities. Often, it's about homogenisation.

But what does this sieving process really achieve? When you pass something through a sieve, you anticipate a uniform outcome. The attire students wear is referred to as a "uniform" precisely because it promotes uniformity and consistency among them. Like any sieve, it's designed to filter out the "unwanted" bits. In this metaphorical filtration, the casualties are often a child's innate qualities: their unique thought processes, inherent creativity, personal inclinations, ideological beliefs, and even some aspects of their daily lives, like dietary habits. While this might seem like a grim perspective, one cannot help but ponder the true intent behind public education. Is its primary goal really enlightenment and holistic development? Or does it lean more towards creating a standardised, easily manageable populace?

If this assertion feels exaggerated, consider a hypothetical scenario in which public education ceases to exist overnight. The immediate aftermath would see the streets flooded with youth, no longer bound by the structured schedules of school. Their unchecked energies and curiosities could very well lead to unpredictable, possibly chaotic outcomes. The sheer thought of such a scenario is the premise for a dystopian narrative, but the question it prompts is crucial. Is our education system's primary role to cultivate minds or to control them? The distinction is critical, and the implications profound, as it can put the ingenuity of childhood at stake.

The Evolving Landscape of SEND Education in England

In England, the approach to Special Educational Needs and Disabilities (SEND) education stands out globally for its progressive nature. Despite certain imperfections, the country's consistent efforts to improve the educational experience for SEND pupils are commendable. This journey, while noble, is fraught with complex challenges.

England has seen a notable rise in SEND pupils, with numbers in 2023 nearing 1.5 million.[65] This increase partly stems from expanded criteria for SEND categorisation, a positive step towards recognising the diverse needs of students and promoting inclusivity.

This surge, however, raises critical questions about the future of SEND education in England, primarily regarding resource allocation. The growing number of SEND pupils escalates the demand for specialised equipment, learning materials, and facilities. Schools must adapt, potentially straining budgets and highlighting the need for additional funding. It's crucial that

---

[65] "Special Educational Needs in England," *Gov.uk*, June 22, 2023, last updated July 20, 2023, https://explore-education-statistics.service.gov.uk/find-statistics/special-educational-needs-in-england.

these resources are not only available but also effectively used to cater to the varied needs of SEND students.

Another key factor is teacher training. The rising number of SEND pupils calls for enhanced professional development for educators. Comprehensive training should include strategies for diverse learning needs, behavioural management, and inclusive teaching techniques. Additionally, it's vital to focus on the emotional and mental well-being of educators in this demanding field, ensuring they have the necessary support to perform their roles effectively.

Maintaining, and ideally enhancing, the overall quality of education is also paramount. Schools face the challenge of providing tailored support for SEND pupils while upholding high academic standards for all students. This balance is essential to ensure that education quality remains high and that each student, regardless of their needs, receives a fulfilling educational experience.

From a teacher's perspective, I recognise the immense challenge of managing a class that includes pupils with significant SEND needs. Their behaviour can disrupt lessons, unintentionally affecting their own learning as well as that of their peers. This situation underscores the need for more support, both in terms of human assistance in the classroom and improved non-human resources.

Consider children with autism, who require specific support. Depending on where they fall on the spectrum, their needs can place considerable demands on a class teacher. Often, teachers lack both the resources and specialised expertise to address these needs effectively, leading to frustration for the child, the class, and the teacher. In such cases, inclusivity without adequate support structures may not be the best approach. Instead, creating an environment with appropriate support, customised schedules where necessary, and adaptable policies is essential. Parents, the ultimate decision-makers for their child's well-being, must be empowered to play a significant role in this process.

Empowering Parents in Navigating Their Child's Education

The role of parents in SEND education is pivotal. Acknowledging their insights and concerns is key to creating a supportive and effective learning environment. Therefore, it is essential to empower parents with full responsibility and decision-making authority over their child's educational journey, especially concerning mental health and well-being.

Flexible School Attendance:

Granting parents more autonomy in determining their child's need for school breaks is a critical step. Similar to adults taking leave from work for mental health, children, often more vulnerable, may need occasional breaks from academic demands. Current policies, which can lead to investigations by school authorities or social services for missed school days, may hinder parents from acting in their child's best interest. A more flexible approach to school attendance, within reasonable limits, could prevent potential crises and ensure children receive necessary physical, mental, and emotional rest. This flexibility also challenges the prevailing focus on high attendance percentages, recognising that well-being should take precedence.

Reduced Timetables for Individual Needs:

Further empowering parents involves the potential for reduced timetables. Recognising that each child is unique, with individual strengths, challenges, and capacities, is crucial. A full timetable can be overwhelming for some students, impeding their ability to thrive in the school environment. Making reduced timetables more accessible and stigma-free allows parents to collaborate with schools in tailoring an educational path that aligns with their child's specific needs. Parents are often the most attuned to their children's requirements and should have a significant voice in these decisions.

In both scenarios, the key is fostering a collaborative approach among parents, educators, and authorities. This collaboration requires open communication, mutual respect for different perspectives, and a united commitment to the child's best interests. Such a partnership can lead to more effective, individualised education strategies that respect and respond to the unique needs of each SEND pupil.

Walt Whitman's "To the States"

Walt Whitman, the quintessential American poet known for his free verse and celebration of self, democratisation, and the American landscape, offers a poignant caution in his exhortation "To the States." The phrase "Resist much, obey little"[66] encapsulates a sentiment that resonates through ages, particularly in the context of power systems, including education.

Rejection of Authoritarianism:

At the surface level, Whitman's quote warns against the dangers of blind obedience to authority. In the context of the education system, it could be seen as a plea against rote memorisation, standardisation, and a one-size-fits-all approach. By urging entities – be they states, cities, or institutions – to "resist" and not merely "obey," Whitman highlights the importance of critical thinking, a value that should be at the core of any educational institution.

The Permanence of Enslavement:

Whitman's assertion "Once fully enslaved, no nation, state, city, of this earth, ever afterward resumes its liberty"[67] paints a bleak picture of the irreversible

---

[66] Walt Whitman, *Leaves of Grass* (Electronic Classics Series, Pennsylvania State University, 2007-2013), 27.

[67] Whitman, *Leaves of Grass*, 27.

nature of oppression once it takes root. This might be seen metaphorically in the context of education: once an individual's love for learning is squashed, or once they are confined within the boundaries of what is deemed "acceptable" knowledge, it becomes exceedingly difficult to reignite that passion or to step beyond those boundaries.

The Individual Versus the Collective:

It's noteworthy that Whitman addresses not only "the States" but also "any one of them" or any city. This decentralisation serves as a reminder that the collective is composed of individuals. Each educational institution, teacher, and student has a role to play in resisting oppressive forces. It's a call for both systemic change and individual agency.

Historical Context:

When reading Whitman's words, it's essential to remember the era in which he wrote. The nineteenth century was a period of significant change in America, marked by the Civil War, the abolition of slavery, and the tumultuous path towards civil rights. While Whitman's words carry universal weight, they are also a direct product of the struggles of his time. This makes his caution more urgent and relevant.

Implications for Modern Education:

Whitman's caution to resist blind obedience rings particularly true in today's age of standardised testing, curriculum controversies, and the commercialisation of education. There's a need for educators, students, and stakeholders to question, challenge, and refuse to accept the status quo merely because it's been handed down. Resistance, in this context, becomes a tool for ensuring that education remains a dynamic, evolving space that genuinely seeks to empower its beneficiaries.

Walt Whitman's "To the States" is not just a cautionary note for nations and cities but a broader commentary on the human tendency to acquiesce in the face of authority. It reminds us that true liberty, whether of nations or minds, lies in the continual act of questioning, challenging, and resisting forces that seek to homogenise or oppress. The education system, as a crucible for young minds, ought to take this advice to heart, ensuring that it fosters a spirit of inquiry and critical thinking rather than mere obedience.

It's amusing that the school system is often criticised, but when mentioning one was homeschooled or wants to homeschool their children, people suddenly view that as irresponsible.

Homeschooling

Criticism of parents who choose to homeschool their children can stem from various concerns or misconceptions. Some of the common reasons include the following:

1. **Socialisation Concerns**: There's a widespread belief that homeschooling limits children's social interaction with peers, which is essential for developing social skills and emotional intelligence.
2. **Educational Adequacy**: Some critics question the ability of parents to provide a comprehensive and well-rounded education, particularly in specialised subjects or higher grade levels.
3. **Lack of Professional Teaching Expertise**: Professional educators undergo training and certification, leading to doubts regarding the teaching effectiveness of parents who may not have this background.
4. **Regulatory Oversight**: Public and private schools are subject to educational standards and accountability measures, while

homeschooling often has less oversight, raising concerns about educational quality and consistency.

5. **Exposure to Diverse Perspectives**: Schools are seen as environments where children are exposed to diverse ideas and viewpoints, which some believe might be limited in a homeschool setting.

6. **Success Metrics**: There are questions about how homeschooling impacts long-term academic and career success. However, research in this area offers varied conclusions.

7. **Personal Bias or Misconceptions**: Some criticism may stem from personal biases or misconceptions about what homeschooling entails, often based on stereotypes or anecdotal evidence rather than comprehensive data.

The debate surrounding homeschooling often centres around various concerns, some rooted in misconceptions. In contrast, others stem from legitimate questions about its effectiveness and impact. Exploring these concerns in depth can provide a more nuanced understanding of the homeschooling landscape.

Socialisation is often at the forefront of homeschooling criticisms. The common belief is that homeschooling confines children within their family circle, limiting their exposure to diverse social settings. Critics argue that regular interaction with peers in a school environment is crucial for developing social skills and emotional intelligence. However, this perspective overlooks the variety of social interactions homeschoolers can and often do engage in outside the home. Activities like sports teams, community events, and homeschooling networks provide ample opportunities for socialisation. Research has shown that homeschoolers can achieve well-rounded social development, often participating in more mixed-age interactions than their traditionally schooled peers.

The adequacy of the educational experience provided at home is another point of contention. Critics express concerns over whether parents can offer a broad and balanced curriculum, especially in specialised subjects or advanced study. While it is true that not all parents possess expertise in every subject, homeschooling often employs a variety of resources, including online courses, tutors, and cooperative classes with other homeschooling families. Studies have indicated that homeschooled children can perform as well as or better than their public school counterparts in standardised tests. For instance, in the United States, homeschooled students often score above average on the SAT (Scholastic Assessment Test) and ACT (American College Testing).

Questions about the lack of professional teaching expertise are also raised in discussions about homeschooling. Traditional educators undergo specialised training and certification, leading to scepticism about the teaching capabilities of parents without this background. However, this viewpoint does not account for the individualised attention homeschooling allows. Parents can customise the learning process to suit their child's distinctive style and speed of learning, which is especially advantageous for children with special educational requirements or those who are exceptionally talented. Moreover, the success of homeschooling does not appear to depend heavily on parents' formal teaching qualifications.

Regulatory oversight is a valid concern. Public and private schools operate under established educational standards and accountability measures, while homeschooling often enjoys more autonomy. This flexibility offers advantages and challenges; it permits personalised education but also brings up questions regarding the uniformity and thoroughness of the learning experience. Different countries and states vary in their regulation of homeschooling, with some requiring regular assessments and others having minimal oversight.

The exposure to diverse perspectives is a critical aspect of education. Schools are seen as melting pots where children encounter various ideas and cultures. There's a worry that homeschooling may shelter children from these experiences. However, many homeschooling families prioritise exposing their children to multiple viewpoints and cultures through travel, community involvement, and diverse curricula, providing a richer experience than state schools can offer.

Success metrics for homeschoolers are an area of ongoing research. Concerns revolve around the effect of homeschooling on long-term academic and career achievements. Data from countries like the US and England show that homeschooled students frequently go on to succeed in higher education and careers. In the US, for instance, homeschooled students represent a growing percentage of college entrants, often outperforming their traditionally schooled peers in academic achievements.

Lastly, personal bias and misconceptions frequently colour the homeschooling debate. Many criticisms are based on outdated stereotypes or isolated cases rather than comprehensive, objective data. While addressing valid concerns about homeschooling is essential, acknowledging the accomplishments and creative approaches within the homeschooling community is equally important.

In conclusion, while these homeschooling concerns are not unfounded, they often stem from a lack of understanding of homeschool education's diverse and adaptable nature. The success of homeschooling in various countries, as evidenced by standardised test scores and college admissions, challenges many of the criticisms levelled against it. However, it is essential to continue monitoring and researching homeschooling outcomes to ensure that all children receive a quality education, irrespective of the setting.

Risks of Being a Male Teacher

Every profession has its own set of advantages and disadvantages. In the case of teaching, there are several disadvantages alongside the many positive points I have discussed extensively in previous chapters. One of the most significant challenges is the risk of false allegations or misinterpretations of innocent words or behaviours. These can be perceived as harmful or unsafe by students and their parents, posing a severe concern to educators.

Male teachers, particularly in countries like England and the US, find themselves traversing a labyrinth of challenges. These range from professional and legal risks to mental, social, cultural, and digital concerns, each adding layers of responsibility and vulnerability to their role. One of the most pressing challenges is the heightened sensitivity to misconduct allegations, especially those involving students. Even when baseless, such accusations can rapidly escalate, often amplified by the media's eagerness to sensationalise, leading to potential reputation damage and severe disciplinary consequences. The need for child protection is unquestionable; students must feel safe and supported in their educational environment. But there is also a pressing need for fairness, ensuring that misunderstandings do not lead to irreversible harm to a teacher's career and reputation.

Legally, the weight of responsibility on teachers' shoulders is heavy. They are custodians of their students' safety and well-being, accountable for adhering to safety protocols and acting in the best interest of their charges. Any deviation, even accidental, from these established guidelines can have serious legal ramifications. Moreover, compliance with child protection laws, while imperative, often treads a fine line, placing teachers in vulnerable positions in which even minor oversights can lead to significant legal issues.

The profession also takes a substantial mental and emotional toll. Teachers routinely deal with work-related stress and the looming spectre of burnout, compounded by concerns about mental health. Additionally, the threat of physical violence, though less common, remains a real and unsettling risk within school environments.

Socially and culturally, male teachers often confront misconceptions and biases that colour perceptions of their actions. Misinterpretations can detrimentally impact their reputation, and entrenched gender stereotypes, particularly prevalent in primary education, can adversely impact their reputation and effectiveness as educators.

In today's digital world, using social media and digital communication tools presents a minefield – inappropriate usage can lead to accusations of professional misconduct. Furthermore, the rise of cyberbullying targeted not only at students but increasingly at teachers by students or parents poses a new and distressing challenge.

These complex risks highlight the need for comprehensive support systems and policy reforms. Such measures are crucial to protect teachers and maintain the integrity and effectiveness of the educational system. Despite these challenges, teaching remains among the most rewarding and impactful careers. It offers a unique opportunity to shape young minds and guide students towards becoming remarkable individuals. For those aspiring to join this noble profession, it is an invitation to a journey filled with potential challenges and immense satisfaction and purpose. The role of a teacher is to be a beacon, a guide, and sometimes a guardian, capable of inspiring and moulding future generations into the best versions of themselves. The daily thank-you, the annual birthday card, and any kind gesture of help with a task helps override the rare negative cases that one may encounter.

There are two crucial aspects educators must navigate with utmost care. They are safeguarding procedures and the maintenance of professional boundaries with students.

Awareness and adherence to safeguarding procedures are paramount. Educators must be well versed in these protocols, designed to ensure students' safety and well-being. This involves being alert to potential signs of abuse or neglect, understanding the proper channels for reporting concerns, and creating a safe and supportive learning environment. The responsibility to safeguard extends beyond the classroom, encompassing all aspects of student interaction and welfare.

Equally important is the establishment and maintenance of professional boundaries with students. This encompasses not only physical boundaries but also emotional and social ones. Teachers must navigate the delicate balance of being approachable and supportive while ensuring that relationships with students remain within the professional realm. This includes being mindful of communication methods and content, particularly in the digital age, when interactions can extend beyond the traditional classroom setting. It's crucial to remember that a child may take your words literally, even when you mean no harm. For instance, a child with autism might not just hear your words but also vividly visualise them, becoming more sensitive to the message conveyed. This heightened sensitivity can significantly impact how they interpret and react to the information. Both safeguarding and maintaining professional boundaries are integral to upholding the trust and integrity that form the foundation of the educational profession. Observing these principles will protect your students and yourself, ensuring a respectful, safe, and productive learning environment.

A Promise No Longer Assured? The Evolving Promise of Education

In the past, there was a prevailing notion: excel in school if you wish to secure a respectable job and avoid the pitfalls of unemployment or underemployment; earn a college degree and you're almost guaranteed a well-paying position. This view held for many years. However, the landscape of education and employment has drastically shifted. A few decades ago, possessing a university degree might have been synonymous with the promise of a lucrative job. Today, that's no longer a given. I have encountered numerous individuals, including former students, who chose a different path. Opting to plunge into the workforce after sixth-form college, many found remarkable success regardless of their A-level results. They have become homeowners and entrepreneurs and have built fulfilling lives with their families. Their trajectories starkly contrast the prevailing notion that tertiary education is the sole route to prosperity.

Additionally, the financial implications of pursuing higher education must be addressed. Universities have a hefty price tag, particularly in England

and the US. Thus, students and their families are increasingly weighing the potential returns on this significant investment. In an age of increasing student debt and various perceptions of the value of formal education, it's essential to consider diverse paths to success.

My children opted against the university route. I wholeheartedly respected and supported their decisions, recognising that their futures were on the line. My primary concern was the pursuit of their passions and finding what resonated with them. Today, both are gainfully employed, earning commendable salaries, and are forward-thinking in their aspirations. Above all, they have found contentment in their chosen paths. Contrarily, I am acquainted with several individuals possessing university degrees yet struggling financially, reliant on state benefits or earning modest incomes that don't reflect their educational background. It's becoming clear that the assumed path of public education leading directly to financial and professional success is no longer as linear or guaranteed as it once was.

Have you ever wondered about the educational backgrounds of some of the world's most successful individuals? Consider Bill Gates and Larry Ellison. These industry titans left college without completing their bachelor's degrees. Their narratives aren't isolated incidents. The annals of business and innovation are filled with stories of individuals who've achieved monumental success without the traditional badge of a college degree.

The broader lesson here isn't to diminish the value of public education but to emphasise that it's no longer the only pathway to success in our contemporary world. While formal education provides a structured approach to knowledge and skill acquisition, life beyond the classroom often values agility, creativity, and intrinsic intelligence. These qualities can't always be gauged by academic achievements or the name of an alma mater.

Indeed, the foundations built by formal education can offer an edge when combined with these innate traits. But it's essential to understand that success in today's fast-evolving world is multi-layered. It's a blend of education, passion, resilience, and often a bit of uncertainty.

Although there have been advancements in teaching methods and technology, the traditional classroom setup of students facing the front and receiving information from a teacher remains the norm. However, there has been a push towards more collaborative and interactive learning environments, with group work, peer-to-peer learning, and project-based learning gaining popularity in many schools. It is important to continue exploring and implementing new approaches to education that better suit students' needs and learning styles.

Standing Over Dry Land: Charting a New Course for Education in a Dynamic World

The Choluteca Bridge in Honduras and the world education system can be metaphorically compared, placing compelling focus on outdated aspects needing revision to serve their intended purpose.

The Choluteca Bridge, formerly celebrated as an engineering wonder, was constructed to endure the most severe weather. However, in 1998, Hurricane Mitch dramatically changed the landscape around it. The river it was designed to span changed course, rendering the bridge useless. It now stands over dry land, a bridge with no river to cross, symbolising a well-intentioned design that failed to adapt to unforeseen changes.

Likewise, the global education system, initially crafted for a bygone era, frequently needs more tools to effectively navigate the fast-evolving context of the twenty-first century. Like the Choluteca Bridge, many educational frameworks were robust and effective in the context for which they were created. They were meant to prepare students for a world where knowledge was less accessible, careers were more linear, and technological advancements were relatively slow. However, just as the river shifted its course, leaving the bridge redundant, the world has shifted too, leaving traditional educational models outdated.

Today's world is marked by rapid technological advancements, a dynamic job market, and a wealth of information at our fingertips. In many cases, the education system still focuses on rote learning, standardisation, and preparing students for a stable, predictable professional path. This approach needs to align more with the reality of a world that values creativity, adaptability, and lifelong learning. Just as the Choluteca Bridge stands isolated from the river, the current education system often stands isolated from the realities and needs of the modern world.

The Choluteca Bridge and the worldwide education system symbolise well-planned structures that have yet to adapt to their evolving surroundings. They represent the need for foresight, flexibility, and continual evolution to remain relevant and practical. For the education system, this means a shift towards skills like critical thinking, adaptability, and digital literacy with an emphasis on learning how to learn, ensuring that it bridges the gap between the learners of today and the unpredictable, dynamic world they face.

Reflecting on the Impact of Traditional Education: A Call to Educators and Policymakers

I invite you to pause and reflect on a poignant piece of writing, a poem by Naomi Gwynne, a fourteen-year-old girl with autism. This poem, more than just words, is a window into the soul of a young student navigating the rigidities of our education system. Accompanied by a note from her mother, it sheds light on the often-unseen struggles children like Naomi face in public schools.

Naomi's mother's words set the stage for the poem, revealing a heart-wrenching journey. "It's now been a whole year since I removed my autistic daughter from school. The last twelve months have been intensive, exhausting, and heartbreaking as my daughter very slowly opened up about some of the traumatic events that happened while she attended school. As many children return to school, she reflects on what school *really* taught her. This is her truth, one that I am sure many will relate to."[68]

Naomi's poem, "What School Taught Me," is a candid and touching portrayal of her experiences in a traditional school setting. Through her eyes, we see a world where conformity is enforced and individuality is often stifled. Each line of her poem challenges us to reconsider our educational practices and policies:

What school taught me
You can only go in and out a building
If you're walking in a line
Lunch can only ever be eaten
When a bell goes to say it is time
Social time is wasted time
You can only learn in a class
You can only need the bathroom
If you have a toilet pass
Adults are always right
Kids' opinions do not matter
Work must be done in silence
You get punished if you chatter
You are not allowed to be different
Like robots all the same
You must wear what someone else decides
Even if it causes you pain
You can only read at the level they tell you
No choosing a favourite again
Hot sunny days you were stuck in a classroom
But in winter left out in the rain
Star of the week was just random

---

[68] Faithmummy, Facebook, September 5, 2023, https://www.facebook.com/Faithmummy1.

Regardless of how much you tried
Disappointment was never allowed
You were just told to be brave if you cried
Tests and grades all that mattered
Always compared to another
Wet paper towels solved everything
No need to be phoning your mother
Everyone's writing must be the same
With numbers all touching the line
No matter how much you were struggling
Teachers would say you were fine.
School taught me never to question
Never to just be me
Things are so much better now that I'm home
I'm happy, I'm learning, I'm free

By Naomi Gwynne, age fourteen
(https://www.facebook.com/Faithmummy1)

This poem is not just Naomi's story; it represents the experiences of many children who find themselves lost in the one-size-fits-all approach of our current education system. It's a call to action for educators and policymakers to rethink and reshape our schools into environments where every child can thrive, regardless of their neurological makeup or learning style.

As educators and policymakers, we must ask ourselves tough questions: Are we nurturing each child's unique talents and abilities? Are we acknowledging and accommodating the diverse ways children learn and express themselves? Naomi's message is clear – our educational system must evolve to be inclusive and supportive.

This reflection is not an indictment of our efforts but an invitation to grow and improve. Let's take inspiration from Naomi's courage and honesty to create learning spaces that celebrate diversity, foster individuality, and promote a true sense of freedom and joy in learning. It's time we ensure that every child feels understood, valued, and free to be themselves, just as Naomi now feels away from the confines of a traditional classroom.

CONCLUSION

I taught an estimated 6,600 pupils since I began my career as a qualified teacher, which equates to teaching around ten classes of thirty pupils each year. The estimated total number of students a teacher will likely have taught over an entire career is 13,000, assuming approximately forty years in the field. These substantial figures reflect the multitude of lives that we, as teachers, can shape and influence – a responsibility and opportunity far from insignificant.

I share these figures to highlight the profound impact a single teacher can have on society. Thus, teaching is not a profession to be taken lightly. The teaching profession deserves to be valued and respected in England, in the United States, and across many European countries. Fortunately, there are still places where teachers are held in esteem, comparable to doctors and other highly respected professionals. This is the case in regions like Finland, Denmark, Japan, China, Cuba, most African nations, Asia, and South America.

Public schooling is often hailed as one of the best institutions in the world, especially in modern Western countries. Its appeal is further heightened by its free and compulsory nature. However, there's a marked discrepancy between the idealised concept of public schooling and its actual implementation. A quote from the documentary *The Social Dilemma* comes to mind: "If you're not paying for the product, then you are the product." This documentary was, to put it mildly, eye-opening. Common sense suggests that if public schools were truly outstanding, or at least as commendable as governments claim, then wouldn't members of the government and affluent families enrol their children in them? In my view, it should be mandatory for all government officials, ranging from local members of Parliament to the Prime Minister or President, to send their offspring exclusively to public schools, thus leading by example. Were this the case, I'm convinced public schools would be allocated adequate funding and would adopt a curriculum more attuned to real-world challenges. Teachers would receive comprehensive training and fair compensation. Class sizes would decrease, averaging fewer than twenty students per educator. School cafeterias would offer food comparable to respectable restaurants. Bullying issues would be addressed more diligently; after all, no official would want their child to be bullied by their constituents' children.

There is something remarkable to notice about schools. Sending our offspring to an institution to be "educated" by strangers, among other strangers, forcing them to do things they are not always willing to do, besides not being willing to attend school in the first place, goes against our protective instincts. This has been so anchored in our minds – our habits – that we never even consider questioning it. Childhood is the most crucial period in a human being's life. Yet, children spend over three-quarters of their childhood with strangers who have no relationship with their family.

So, after reading all that, why am I still teaching? Why do I continue immersing myself in an education system that needs a radical overhaul? After completing my compulsory twelve years in a system I longed to leave, why did I opt for another six years of study to become a teacher, essentially "trapping" myself within the system I criticise? I am not masochistic by any means. Fortunately, I've grown and developed mainly outside formal education, drawing from my educational experiences as I saw fit. However, this is only feasible for some. Success in this endeavour often hinges on several factors, such as personality, personal interests, mental resilience, cultural background, and, of course, one's environment, including family and social circles.

My commitment to teaching extends beyond the walls of any institution or the framework of any curriculum. I persist because of the profound human connections I make daily, the spark in a student's eye when a concept finally "clicks," and the joy of witnessing a young individual blossom into a critical thinker. For every moment of frustration brought about by systemic issues, there are countless instances of genuine gratitude, be it a simple thank-you at the end of a lesson or an unexpected note of appreciation years later.

While the system might be somewhat flawed, the potential within young minds is boundless. They bring their dreams, aspirations, fears, and hopes to the classroom. It is an unparalleled privilege to share in their journey. In teaching, I have the unique opportunity to touch lives and leave a lasting impact. It's not about merely ensuring they remember the periodic table, solve algebraic equations, or conjugate French and Spanish verbs in the perfect tense; it is instilling in them the belief that they can conquer any challenge that comes their way.

Furthermore, every challenge the education system presents is an invitation to innovate. It drives me to adapt, seek new methods, and continuously learn and grow alongside my students. This dynamic nature of teaching ensures that no two days are alike, making it both challenging and stimulating. My critiques of the education system stem from a place of passion and a desire to improve it. This very passion compels me to stay, make a difference, and believe that the future of education, with collective effort, can be brighter than its past.

My father, who initially hoped I would become an engineer or architect, has expressed great pride in my choice to teach. I am grateful for his support, since my decision was firm, regardless. While I may not possess the formal qualifications of an engineer or architect, an educator can be seen as both the engineer and architect of humanity's future, with students as the raw materials of their transformative work.

Like an engineer, a teacher meticulously constructs pathways to knowledge, building bridges of understanding and erecting scaffolds of essential skills. Like an architect envisions and brings grand structures to life, a teacher imagines and nurtures a brighter, more enlightened society, guiding its development through education. Teachers are the master craftsmen of young minds, shaping them with the precision of skilled artisans. The classroom becomes their canvas, with each lesson adding to the construction of intellect, morality, and creativity.

As students enter the world, they embody the testament of the teacher's craft, showcasing the lasting impact of these architects and engineers of humanity.

Samples of People's Testimonies about Their Time at School

"I've learned, like, more than half of my knowledge of rocks from playing *Minecraft*." (Toby)

"I found that I learned more during the summer holidays, through my genuine interest in philosophy and history, than I did from any of my formal education in school." (Ross)

"During the school day, I was always brimming with creative ideas that I couldn't wait to explore at home. However, my enthusiasm waned the moment I remembered the pile of homework awaiting me. By the time I finished it, I was left with no joy or energy for the activities I was passionate about. I would just numb myself with games, having expended all my day's energy without doing anything truly fulfilling for myself. And when I say I had no joy left, I mean that in the gravest sense. After enduring four years of high school, the toll was too much, leading to medical issues. Eventually, I completed the remainder of my high school education from home. It was a revelation, and somewhat infuriating, to discover that what took eight hours at school could be accomplished in just one hour at home!" (Graham)

"A special teacher made literature come alive for me. He didn't just read to us; he performed each character, shared historical contexts, and encouraged us to see the stories as windows to different worlds. That's when I fell in love with reading." (Pierre)

"Math was just numbers to me until I met a teacher who showed us its beauty in music, nature, and art. Her passion made me understand that math is about understanding the world." (Lucy)

"I never understood the importance of financial literacy until I started my own business. Everything I know about budgeting, investing, and saving, I learned through experience, not in a classroom." (Rick)

"My love for coding began as a hobby. I watched online tutorials and tinkered with projects in my free time. It's amazing how much you can learn when you're driven by passion instead of a curriculum." (Regine)

BIBLIOGRAPHY

Abrantes, Roger. "Laughter is the Shortest Distance Between Two People." *Ethology Institute. Last updated April 23, 2014.* https://ethology.eu/laughter-is-the-shortest-distance-between-two-people/#:~:text=%E2%80%9CLaughter%20is%20the%20shortest%20distance,from%20other%20forms%20of%20life.

Akhtar, Zarina, and Shamsa Aziz. "The Effect of Peer and Parent Pressure on the Academic Achievement of University Students." *Language in India 11, no. 6 (June 2011).*

"Americans Want More Pressure on Students, the Chinese Want Less." *Pew Research Center. August 23, 2011.* https://www.pewresearch.org/global/2011/08/23/americans-want-more-pressure-on-students-the-chinese-want-less/.

Anna Freud Mentally Healthy Schools. "About." *Mentally Healthy Schools. April 2020.* https://mentallyhealthyschools.org.uk/about/.

Ayoub, Sarah. "When Young Children Battle Anxiety, Parents Don't Need to Feel Like Helpless Bystanders." *The Guardian. June 15, 2021.* https://www.theguardian.com/commentisfree/2021/jun/16/when-young-children-battle-anxiety-parents-dont-need-to-feel-like-helpless-bystanders.

Azoulay, Audrey. "244M Children Won't Start the New School Year." UNESCO. September 1, 2022. Last updated April 20, 2023. https://www.unesco.org/gem-report/en/articles/244m-children-wont-start-new-school-year.

Berne, Eric. Games People Play. New York: Grove Press, 1964.

Black, Paul, and Dylan Wiliam. "Inside the Black Box: Raising Standards through Classroom Assessment." Phi Delta Kappan 92.1, 2010: 81–90.

Black, Paul, and Dylan Wiliam. Inside the Black Box: Raising Standards Through Classroom Assessment. London: King's College London, School of Education, 1998.

Brock, Tom. "Roger Caillois and E-Sports: On the Problems of Treating Play as Work." ResearchGate. January 2017. https://journals.sagepub.com/doi/10.1177/1555412016686878.

Centre for the New Economy and Society. "The Global Education Crisis is Even Worse Than We Thought. Here's What Needs to Happen." World Economic Forum. January 16, 2022. https://www.weforum.org/agenda/2022/01/global-education-crisis-children-students-covid19/.

Chin, Annping. "Confucius, Chinese Philosopher." Britannica. Last updated February 16, 2024. https://www.britannica.com/biography/Confucius.

Dyson, Jack. "'Wake-up' Call for Schools as Weeks of Lessons Lost to Misbehaviour." Schoolsweek. June 8, 2023. https://schoolsweek.co.uk/wake-up-call-for-schools-as-weeks-of-lessons-lost-to-misbehaviour/.

Epistles Written. ""no matter how smart you are, you need a team of great people." - @ stevejobs." YouTube video. April 1, 2022. https://www.youtube.com/watch?v=ielsajw1j8k.

Faithmummy. Facebook. September 5, 2023. https://www.facebook.com/Faithmummy1.

Fazackerley, Anna. "Schools across England face unprecedented struggle to hire English teachers as recruitment crisis grows." The Guardian. June 17, 2023. Last updated April 20, 2023. https://www.theguardian.com/education/2023/jun/17/schools-across-england-face-unprecedented-struggle-to-hire-english-teachers-as-recruitment-crisis-grows.

Freud, Sigmund. *The Ego and the Id. 1923.* Reprint, London: Hogarth Press and the Institute of Psycho-Analysis, 1949.

Global Education Monitoring Report Summary, 2021/2: Non-State Actors in Education: Who Chooses? Who Loses? UNESCO. 2021/2. https://unesdoc.unesco.org/ark:/48223/pf0000380076.

Kearns, Laura-Lee. "High-stakes Standardized Testing and Marginalized Youth: An Examination of the Impact on Those Who Fail." *Canadian Journal of Education* 34, no. 2 (2011): 112–130.

Kilmer, Raymond W. III, "High School Stress and Cheating: Developing an Understanding of the Factors that Influence Stress and Cheating in High School Students" (2017). Education Doctoral. Paper 339. https://fisherpub.sjf.edu/education_etd/339

Kohn, Alfie. *The Case Against Standardized Testing: Raising the Scores, Ruining the Schools.* Portsmouth, NH: Heinemann, 2000.

Koretz, Daniel. *The Testing Charade: Pretending to Make Schools Better.* Chicago: University of Chicago Press, 2017.

La Fontaine, Jean de. "The Oak and the Reed." In *Fables of La Fontaine,* translated by Walter Thornbury. London: Cassell, Petter, and Galpin, 1868.

Larcher, Théophile. "Education: Do French Schools Deserve Their Harsh Reputation?" *The Connexion.* May 18, 2022. https://www.connexionfrance.com/article/Comment/Opinion/Education-do-French-schools-deserve-their-harsh-reputation.

Le Parisien. "Rentrée scolaire : il manque un professeur dans la moitié des collèges et lycées, selon le Snes-FSU." *Le Parisien.* September 11, 2023. Modified September 12, 2023. https://www.leparisien.fr/societe/rentree-scolaire-il-manque-un-professeur-dans-la-moitie-des-colleges-et-lycees-selon-le-snes-fsu-11-09-2023-CEZ5TNLHN5FB5PTCCXF6UPKWWI.php.

Lough, Catherine. "Childline Increases Counselling Sessions Over Exam Anxiety." *Independent.* May 14, 2022. https://www.independent.co.uk/news/uk/childline-children-gcses-alevels-nspcc-b2078866.html.

Merriam-Webster. "Inspiration." accessed April 19, 2024. https://
www.merriam-webster.com/dictionary/inspiration.

MJ23 His Airness Forever. "After Winning the Championship, Michael
Jordan Gave Credit to Teammates (1992.06.14)." YouTube video. June
17, 2022. https://www.youtube.com/watch?v=vT5vSrEy6VQ.

Muller, Jerry Z. The Tyranny of Metrics. Princeton,
NJ: Princeton University Press, 2018.

My Idol Elon. "Elon Musk's Incredible Speech on the Education
System | Eye Opening Video on Education." YouTube video.
May 21, 2021. https://youtu.be/YNQDp3v-VGE.

Niederle, Muriel., Vesterlund, Lise. Do Women Shy Away from
Competition? Do Men Compete Too Much?. United
States: National Bureau of Economic Research, 2005.

OECD. PISA 2022 Results (Volume I): The State of Learning and
Equity in Education (How did countries perform in PISA?). OECD
iLibrary. Last visited March 5, 2024. https://www.oecd-ilibrary.org/
sites/9149c2f5-en/index.html?itemId=/content/component/9149c2f5-en.

Organisation for Economic Co-operation and Development. "Education
at a Glance 2022: OECD Indicators." Accessed April 19,
2024. https://www.oecd-ilibrary.org/sites/9149c2f5-en/
index.html?itemId=/content/component/9149c2f5-en.

PISA 2022 Results. OECD. Accessed March 4, 2024. https://
www.oecd.org/publication/pisa-2022-results/.

"Pisa Chief: 'Mistrust of Teachers Holds England Back'." TES.
December 6, 2019. https://www.tes.com/magazine/archive/
pisa-chief-mistrust-teachers-holds-england-back.

Public Spending on Education as a Share of GDP. Our World in Data.
October 24, 2022. Last updated July 10, 2023. https://ourworldindata.
org/grapher/total-government-expenditure-on-education-gdp?tab
=chart&country=USA~GBR~ESP~FRA~NOR~ZAF~NGA~B

FA~SEN~QAT~IRN~SAU~ARG~BRA~MEX~IND~IDN~JP
N~THA~SGP~CHN~AUS~RUS~SVK~DEU~FIN~DNK

Ravitch, Diane. *The Troubled Crusade: American Education, 1945–1980.* New York: Basic Books, 1983.

Redding, Alexis Brooke. "Fighting Back Against Achievement Culture: Cheating as an Act of Rebellion in a High-Pressure Secondary School." *Ethics & Behavior* 27, no. 2 (2017): 155–172. DOI: 10.1080/10508422.2016.1145058.

Robinson, Ken, and Lou Aronica. "Chapter 2." In *Creative Schools: The Grassroots Revolution That's Transforming Education.* New York: Viking, 2015.

Robinson, Sir Ken. "Ken Robinson - What is Creativity?" YouTube video, 10:47. September 18, 2017. https://www.youtube.com/watch?v=X1c3M6upOXA.

SABC News. "Education is One of the Most Important Weapons: Nelson Mandela." YouTube video. December 11, 2013. https://youtu.be/h0w_PFEl1zs?si=FRcBalgmd2t0xvof&t=116.

Sahlberg, Pasi, and William Doyle. *Let the Children Play: How More Play Will Save Our Schools and Help Children Thrive.* New York: Oxford University Press, 2019.

School Workforce in England. Gov.uk. June 8, 2023. Last updated December 15, 2023. https://explore-education-statistics.service.gov.uk/find-statistics/school-workforce-in-england.

Shackle, Samira. "The Way Universities Are Run Is Making Us Ill." *The Guardian.* September 27, 2019. https://www.theguardian.com/society/2019/sep/27/anxiety-mental-breakdowns-depression-uk-students.

Singh, N. "Review of Diane Ravitch Book, 'The Death and Life of the Great American School System: How Testing and Choice are Undermining Education.'" *Poverty & Public Policy* 4, no. 2 (2012).

Sky Sports. "Ballon d'Or 2023 recap: Inter Miami and Argentina captain Lionel Messi wins men's Ballon d'Or for record eighth time." *Sky Sports.*

Accessed February 28, 2024. https://www.skysports.com/football/
live-blog/11095/12996706/ballon-dor-2023-recap-inter-miami-and-
argentina-captain-lionel-messi-wins-mens-ballon-dor-for-record-eighth-time.

Special Educational Needs in England. Gov.uk. June 22, 2023. Last
updated July 20, 2023. https://explore-education-statistics.service.
gov.uk/find-statistics/special-educational-needs-in-england.

TEDx Talks. "TEDxTucson George Land The Failure Of
Success." YouTube video, 16:33. February 16, 2011. https://
www.youtube.com/watch?v=ZfKMq-rYtnc.

U.S. News Staff. "Countries With Well-Developed Public Education
Systems, Ranked by Perception." U.S. News. September 25, 2020.
https://www.usnews.com/news/best-countries/slideshows/
countries-seen-to-have-well-developed-public-education-systems?slide=12.

UNESCO, UNICEF, and World Bank. "The State of the Global
Education Crisis: A Path to Recovery." World Economic
Forum. 2021. https://unesdoc.unesco.org/ark:/48223/
pf0000380128. https://doi.org/10.54675/JLUG7649.

Whitby, Greg. "Ken Robinson pt 3 (Ken Robinson at TED2010)." YouTube
video. April 28, 2014. https://youtu.be/J4p4xeXTTOM.

Whitman, Walt. Leaves of Grass. Electronic Classics Series.
Pennsylvania State University, 2007–2013.

WordToTheWise. "RESPECT YOURSELF - Powerful Life
Advice | Jordan Peterson." YouTube video. August 18, 2019.
https://www.youtube.com/watch?v=nT-tVPpXlzk.

Zhao, Yong. What Works May Hurt: Side Effects in Education.
New York: Teachers College Press, 2018.

Permission from Our World in Data website:

permission to use, distribute, and reproduce these in any medium, provided the source and authors are credited."

ACKNOWLEDGEMENTS

I am genuinely thankful to all the teachers who have significantly impacted who I am and how I have grown. Each one of them, in their own way, has helped shape me, even if it was not always apparent at the start. I give special thanks to Dominique Lebour, my German teacher, who became a close friend. I am also really grateful to Mr Jean-Pierre Luciani, my math teacher, who deeply inspired me; Mrs Paolini, who sparked my love for reading and writing; Mrs Rouanet and Mrs Lemoine, my English teachers, for their constant support as I dived into learning new languages; Mrs Lesplingard, for guiding me through history and geography and boosting my confidence; and Mr Simon Davies, for his continuous encouragement and support, and for being exemplar in fostering positive student-teacher relationships.

I also sincerely thank Martine Dorra for fuelling my love for reading with her generous gift of annual magazine subscriptions to J'aime lire *and* I love English. Moreover, to Olga, your loyal support has been vital in making this project happen.

This book would not exist without all the outstanding students I have had the privilege to teach and colleagues and friends like Hansy and Gonzales, whose friendship means the world to me. Special thanks to my sons, Franz and Tristan, who have made me a better dad and teacher by giving me new perspectives. I also want to thank Vanessa, Dan, Elizabeth (Batumi), Karen, Lux, Rebecca, Melissa, Hansy, Gonzales, Leanne, and all my tutor groups, especially 9th Edith.

Last but not least, thank you to all the students from the many schools who answered my questionnaires or shared their thoughts with me, and thank you to my parents and family for giving me such a strong foundation in life: Saintimène, Hollant, Laurent, Inocia, Jean, Dominique, Roseline, Fednel, Alix, Alex and Jean-Philippe.

Thank you, merci, gracias, and danke.

INDEX

www.ingramcontent.com/pod-product-compliance
Lightning Source LLC
Chambersburg PA
CBHW061558120626
46550CB00004B/1530